REMEMBERING DIONYSUS

Dionysus, god of dismemberment and sponsor of the lost or abandoned feminine, originates both Jungian psychology and literature in *Remembering Dionysus*. Characterized by spontaneity, fluid boundaries, sexuality, embodiment, wild nature, ecstasy and chaos, Dionysus is invoked in the writing of C. G. Jung and James Hillman as the dual necessity to adopt and dismiss literature for their archetypal vision of the psyche or soul. Susan Rowland describes an emerging paradigm for the twenty-first century enacting the myth of a god torn apart to be re-membered, and remembered as reborn in a great renewal of life.

Rowland demonstrates how persons, forms of knowing and even eras that dismiss Dionysus are torn apart, and explores how Jung was Dionysian in providing his most dismembered text, *The Red Book*. *Remembering Dionysus* pursues the rough god into the Sublime in the destruction of meaning in Jung and Jacques Lacan, to a re-membering of sublime feminine creativity that offers *zoe*, or rebirth participating in an archetype of instinctual life. This god demands to be honoured inside our knowing and being, just as he (re)joins us to wild nature.

This revealing book will be invigorating reading for Jungian analysts, psychotherapists, arts therapists and counsellors, as well as academics and students of analytical psychology, depth psychology, Jungian and post-Jungian studies, literary studies and ecological humanities.

Susan Rowland is Chair of MA Engaged Humanities and the Creative Life at Pacifica Graduate Institute, California, and was previously Professor of English and Jungian Studies at the University of Greenwich UK. She is author of *Jung: A Feminist Revision* (2002), *Jung as a Writer* (2005) and *The Ecocritical Psyche: Literature, Complexity Evolution and Jung* (2012). She teaches in Jung, gender and literary theory.

'Perhaps it is a staple of a living organic mythology that periodically it be remembered anew, complete with all the divinities that inhabit and inhibit it as the myth continues to flourish. Susan Rowland's fine lyrical study returns to recalibrate the value of two related schools of a psychology of soul by opening them to a conversation with the mytho-poetic imagination. Her own mythology is framed by the god Dionysus, both a force and a presence who dismembers, remembers and in so doing engenders new ways of imagining what we thought we knew. Her original work dares us to enter a cross-disciplinary discourse that awakens us to the familiar.'
— Dennis Patrick Slattery, Ph.D.; author of *Riting Myth, Mythic Writing* and *Creases in Culture: Essays Towards a Poetics of Depth*

'In this new work Susan Rowland has given us a true gem. One of the foremost contemporary scholars in Jungian studies, Rowland has produced another remarkably engaging, erudite volume that continues to take depth psychological approaches out of the consulting room and into a larger world. The intersection of literature and myth being woven here is also artfully integrated into the emerging holistic paradigm associated with complexity studies. Rowland creatively advances Jungian studies revealing the depths of its transdisciplinary possibilities through her exploration of archetypal themes manifesting as Dionysian.'
— Joe Cambray, Ph.D., Provost, Pacifica Graduate Institute; Past-President, IAAP

'That Jung was an intellectual in the tradition of Nietzsche, who dismembered his relation to the academy in order to create, in equally epigrammatic fashion, an intuitive critique of the very foundations of our understanding, not just of the texts by which we live, but of the way our lives have become texts, has been crucially grasped by Jung's most antischolastic follower, James Hillman. It is Susan Rowland, however, who makes good on the claim that this method of analysis has a future within the rigorous discipline of literary studies. One can only hope that she will be read with as open a mind as she displays in these well-wrought, lapidary chapters. Refocusing literary theory through a Dionysian rather than Apollonian lens, she identifies as her subject the vivifying experience of reading itself.'
— John Beebe, author of *Energies and Patterns in Psychological Type: The reservoir of consciousness* (Routledge, 2017)

'Susan Rowland is herself a paragon of interdisciplinary scholarship, who has brought Jungian depth psychology into critical, creative relationship with literary studies, gender studies, cultural studies, eco-criticism, and much more. In the present book she uses the myth of Dionysus, importantly culminating in the god's marriage to the mortal Ariadne, as a zone of energy and awareness from which to argue against disciplinary and epistemological hegemonies and the cultural dismemberment they perpetuate. Performing as well as comprehending psychological insights from Jung and Hillman, Rowland champions transdisciplinarity, vitality, and the multiplicity and open-endedness of knowledge and being.'
— Professor Roderick Main, University of Essex

'Susan Rowland's new study expands on a Dionysian concept as she defines it toward a transcendent discussion of genre, aligning it to the god, and finessing her theme that Jung was writing novels, the highest form for her, and epitomising the feminine. Establishing this and demonstrating it in her characteristic and brilliant close-up analyses of text, which is her forte, makes this a satisfying and enigmatic work.'
— Leslie Gardner PhD, co-founder of international literary agency Artellus, and founder member of IAJS, Fellow at the Centre Psychoanalytic Studies at the University of Essex, UK

REMEMBERING DIONYSUS

Revisioning psychology and literature in C. G. Jung and James Hillman

Susan Rowland

Routledge
Taylor & Francis Group

LONDON AND NEW YORK

First published 2017
by Routledge
2 Park Square, Milton Park, Abingdon, Oxon OX14 4RN

and by Routledge
711 Third Avenue, New York, NY 10017

Routledge is an imprint of the Taylor & Francis Group, an informa business

© 2017 Susan Rowland

British Library Cataloguing in Publication Data
A catalogue record for this book is available from the British Library

Library of Congress Cataloging-in-Publication Data
Names: Rowland, Susan, 1962– author.
Title: Remembering Dionysus : revisioning psychology and literature in
    C.G. Jung and James Hillman / Susan Rowland.
Description: Abingdon, Oxon ; New York, NY : Routledge, 2017. |
    Includes bibliographical references.
Identifiers: LCCN 2016007984 | ISBN 9780415855839 (hardback) |
    ISBN 9780415855846 (pbk.) | ISBN 9781315617992 (ebook)
Subjects: LCSH: Jung, C. G. (Carl Gustav), 1875–1961. | Hillman, James. |
    Dionysia. | Psychology and literature. | Psychoanalysis and literature.
Classification: LCC BF109.J8 R693 2017 | DDC 150.19/54—dc23
LC record available at https://lccn.loc.gov/2016007984

ISBN: 978-0-415-85583-9 (hbk)
ISBN: 978-0-415-85584-6 (pbk)
ISBN: 978-1-315-61799-2 (ebk)

Typeset in Bembo
by Apex CoVantage, LLC

CONTENTS

In memory of Edmund Cusick and Don Fredericksen, who knew how to dance with Dionysus.

ACKNOWLEDGEMENTS

While the errors in this book are entirely my own, no book such as *Remembering Dionysus* makes it to publication without tremendous support. Friends, students and colleagues at Pacifica Graduate Institute have been most generous and patient with my questions over earlier drafts. I thank Ginette Paris, Christine Downing, Keiron Le Grice, Glen Slater, Safron Rossi, Jennifer Selig, Cally Huttar, Pat Katsky, Cynthia Hale and Elizabeth Nelson, among others. Moreover, the welcome sabbatical granted by Pacifica enabled me to complete this book. I want also to particularly mention the talented students of the MA Engaged Humanities and the Creative Life, and the doctoral program in Jungian and Archetypal Studies, for inspiring me with their enthusiasm.

Friends and co-workers in the growing international arena of Jungian studies have been particularly important. Let me thank here especially: Leslie Gardner, Luke Hockley, Blake Burleson, Jerome and Susan Bernstein, Nancy Cater, Inez Martinez, Rinda West, Evangeline Rand, Alex Fidyk, Terence Dawson, Lori Pye, Jacqui Feather, Mathew Fike, Roger Brooke and many more. Andrew Samuels, who has done more than anyone to extend the published domain of Jungian studies, deserves especial thanks, alongside the wonderful and patient Routledge editors, Kate Hawes and Susannah Frearson.

Personal friends and my long suffering family have been important to this work. Thank you John and Cathy Rowland, Wendy Pank, Christine Saunders, Claire Dyson, Margaret Erskine, Ailsa Camm, Kathryn Le Grice and Evan Davis. Jungian analyst Julia Paton knows how much I owe her.

This book is dedicated to the memory of two remarkable and creative Jungians: poet Edmund Cusick and film scholar Don Fredericksen. Both danced with Dionysus in honouring their feminine.

My husband and editor, Joel Weishaus, is thanked in every moment of every day.

1

INTRODUCTION

Getting started with C. G. Jung, James Hillman and literature

Getting started with this book

This book proposes a relationship between psychology and literature in the work of two psychologists devoted to the visionary power of the imagination, C. G. Jung and his revisionary successor, James Hillman. Both thinkers belong in the tradition that sees the unknown and unknowable part of the psyche, commonly called the unconscious, as source of meaning, feeling and value. Both regard literature, and the arts overall, as authentic evidence of an intrinsically creative psyche, or soul. However, they also find literature problematic to their psychology, even as they adopt explicitly literary resources for writing it. The figure of that transgressive god, Dionysus, will prove indigenous to the psychology–literature conundrum.

> An essential part of the sacrificial act is dismemberment . . . the Dionysian mystery tradition.
>
> *(Jung 1968, CW13: para. 91)*

> In the majority of my cases, the resources of consciousness have been exhausted; the ordinary expression for this situation is: "I am stuck". . . the theme of many a fairytale and myth.
>
> *(Jung 1933: 70–1)*

At root of the problem of literature (here defined as imaginative writing in genres such as poetry, drama and the novel), and the writing of Jung and Hillman, known respectively as Jungian and archetypal psychology, is that of two mutually implicated yet different academic disciplines. Defined broadly as discrete fields of knowledge independently organized, disciplines validating scholarly endeavour proliferated in the later nineteenth and throughout the twentieth centuries. New in this era was psychology itself, in becoming detached from philosophy and theology. At much the same time there emerged a discipline devoted to the study of vernacular literature, which was grown from the previous focus in universities on writing in Latin and Greek.

In the English-speaking academic world the new degree in literary texts became known as 'English', although much later many adopted Literary Studies, or just Literature, to avoid some of the complications of this designation in a postcolonial era of world 'Englishes'. This book will use the latter two terms for the same reason. The notion that political colonialism might affect a particular construction of knowledge, a discipline, was most overtly debated in the later years of the twentieth century. However, much earlier colonial struggles were perceptible within universities and scholarly circles as the many new disciplines struggled for legitimacy, resources and prestige.

Calling the competition for status between disciplines colonial is more than a reference to the common spatial metaphor of knowledge, as 'fields'. Colonialism within and between disciplines rather points to the union of knowledge and power. Competitions for supremacy among the disciplines for being acknowledged as producing the best, most economically or spiritually valuable kinds of knowledge are, at the same time, struggles for cultural power.

For example, if materialist science is regarded as the superior knowledge of a particular society, then that not only determines how resources are shared out in the university, but it also shapes ideas about education and social policy. Ultimately, it supplies the vision of reality held by most citizens. Hence the argument that frames this book is that the contest and construction of disciplines such as psychology and literature in the nineteenth century is part of a greater series of changes in knowledge that deeply affects modern society today.

One attempt to explore this historical and social intimacy of disciplines and power has already been mentioned. Postcolonialism is an attempt to diagnose how far largely unconsidered assumptions about ethnicity, and the grandiose delusions of the most dominant nations, not only drove political strategies, but also the knowledge that underpinned them. Alongside the political approach, a further way to address the splintering of knowledge into disciplines was the idea of interdisciplinarity studies. Here more than one discipline is employed at the same time, with the aim of stitching together antithetical positions on what something like psychology or literature is supposed to be doing, and on what their fundamental assumptions is based.

A particular problem with the so-called interdisciplinarity approach is that stitching up the jagged edges of disciplines can too easily become a 'stitch up' in which one disciplinary vision or methodology simply colonizes another. Such a move, such as when a psychology uses literature as raw data, instead of material with capacities and histories of its own, actually replicates colonialism rather than resists it.

While I cannot pretend that this book will entirely avoid such a privileging of one discipline over another, it is the aim of *Remembering Dionysus* to generate a new approach to the multidisciplinary environment of writing with imagination, and to apply that new perspective to the work of Jung and Hillman. For I plan to combine a recent initiative known as 'transdisciplinarity', currently being offered mainly from a science perspective with the mythical insight of both these psychologists (Nicolescu 2005). Chapter 2 will consider the transdisciplinary in conjunction with Hillman's dissection of Jung's motif of the dismembered Dionysus; a god reborn from *parts*.

So *Remembering Dionysus* is devoted to investigating the literary in the writing of Jung and Hillman in the context of the disunited disciplines of their own respective psychology and literary studies. If the body of knowledge has been torn apart, how fares this ancient god in a twenty-first century all too familiar with a dismembering violence?

The rest of this chapter will outline how literature and psychology came to be different disciplinary approaches to the imagination as a way of knowing. But, first of all, I will introduce the work of Jung and Hillman for their building of a psychology dedicated to the innate creativity of the psyche.

Getting started with C. G. Jung

Given that the unconscious is the unknown, uncontrollable part of the psyche, Jung believed that it had a profound effect on what we know and how we know.

> Nobody drew the conclusion that if the subject of knowledge, the psyche, were in fact a veiled form of existence not immediately accessible to consciousness, then all our knowledge must be incomplete, and moreover to a degree that we cannot determine.
>
> *(Jung 1960, CW8: para. 358)*

Since we cannot know what our limited consciousness is missing, then what we claim to perceive about the universe can only be partial. Mystery is not only part of our being, it is also part of our knowing. Taking seriously such a proposition, Jung further argued that his psychology had to be seen as a hypothesis or model rather than a pretence to have found the ultimate and fixed truth (Jung 1960, CW8: para. 381). His ideas were a pragmatic way of working with mental properties, rather than the way to unquestionable knowledge. Crucially, imagination and creativity are prime tools for psychic investigation.   *archetypes*

One of Jung's most foundational hypotheses was that human beings possess, probably by inheritance, common psychic capacities for generating images. These capacities he called 'archetypes', and they could only be known by their manifestation as archetypal images. These images would also be influenced in content and form by an individual's history and culture. Images here mean any psychic inscription in consciousness such as dreams, emotions, exciting unbidden thoughts, bodily sensations, etc. Archetypal images are the matter of innate psychic creativity. They are how the psyche makes experience out of archetypal shaping energy meeting the world.

All humans possess the same archetypes as inner creative drives. Jung called this common inheritance the 'collective unconscious'. Within the person, the archetypes of the collective unconscious possess a goal-oriented or teleological impulse towards wholeness and meaning. This indicates that the psyche is in a constant creative process of seeking balance through ever greater connections between archetypal generators and a person's actual archetypal image-made life.

Jung named as 'individuation' this continual weaving, severing and relating between the conscious part of the mind, or ego, and the unconscious realm of archetypes. Jungian psychotherapy is supposed to facilitate individuation by liberating the self-healing teleological direction of the psyche towards ever greater meaning, feeling and value. He was ambivalent about whether individuation required the assistance of psychotherapy, while suggesting that modern conditions rendered the practice invaluable.

What does characterize individuation for everyone, and by extension culture itself, are common themes of resistance, 'stuckness', in conflict, love and sexuality, meaning and aging. The 'shadow' was what Jung called those negative forces that trap the blithe ego, including what we deny in ourselves on moral or hypocritical grounds. To counter 'stuckness', individuation operates by means of compensation. The unconscious manifests what the ego is strenuously denying. Hence, the shadow can be extreme evil or extreme good. It can perversely implant divine faith in the soul of the atheist, or the terror of meaningless annihilation in a person full of life's joys. The shadow is 'other' to who we think we are. It typically forms a stark version of what Jung liked to see as the psyche's tendency to work by opposites.

Yet another version of opposites is that of gender. On the one hand, Jung took an essentialist view of gender by being sure that a male body denoted a masculine ego, and vice versa. On the other hand, such essentialism is also entirely untenable in Jungian psychology. For individuation means that the collective unconscious dimension of archetypes is more *essential* to being than the ego's culture-coloured preferences. And the psyche individuates by integrating what is 'other' to the ego. Often what is other is the other gender.

Archetypes are androgynous, equally able to manifest feminine, masculine, and even transgender forms. They are not limited to a society's stereotypical notions of gender propriety because they are not limited at all. As archetypal images, archetypes are immanent in being contingent, historically and bodily influenced, and never absolutely defined, because of the core mystery of the psyche. Archetypes (and through them, archetypal images) have a transcendent pole of limitless creative possibility. They may also have existence beyond the human psyche, as we will see later.

Meanwhile, Jung liked to try to stabilize his notion of gender by offering an unconscious feminine archetype in a man that he called the 'anima', and a complimentary masculine figure in a woman he named the 'animus'. Yet individuation means that these opposites are not stable; they must be integrated. For Jung, fidelity to his organic and creative idea of the psyche means that gender is fluid, partially culturally constructed, and not restricted to heterosexual presuppositions. Regardless of Jung's personal preference, many genders and various sexualities are possible in his intrinsically creative psyche.

Another archetypal figuration important to Jung's work he named the Self, which he tended to describe as the goal of individuation. This Self is far from the ego-dominated 'separate' identity assumed by the word 'self' in English. Rather, the Self has a dual sense of being the archetype of organization within the psyche, and the potential, expansive totality of it. The Self is the mythical centre, or heart of being provided by the dynamic, even divine archetypes. Archetypes are divine to Jung because they are limitlessly creative. They create *us;* they take the lead in making meaning and being out of the awkward material of conscious embodiment.

[margin note: Self is also "person" – not a. Self is also "person" – not a]

The Self suggests that wholeness and oneness of being can be made or found when the contingent and cultural ego becomes a satellite to this unknown divinity. It is not surprising that Jung in a Christian or post-Christian society saw the Self as an image of God, or even suggested that it was the actuality of God within humans. The Self is where monotheism, here the belief in one God making a world separate from himself, finds a home in Jung's psychology.   *[margin note: God - image]*

One result of this implicit adherence to monotheism in the importance of the Self, whether as ordering archetype or wholeness as the goal of being, is a foundational dualism in his work. Jung is here heir to a long tradition of dividing up experience into dual, or often opposite, qualities. Older than Ancient Greek philosophy, dualism intensified in the emphasis on rational faculties in Western modernity. So, just as we habitually divide time into night and day, we distinguish 'good' by defining it in relation to 'evil', and experience into 'inside-psyche' versus 'outside-world'. Psyche is considered a property of 'inside', although Jung was among other theorists of the unconscious to notice that it could be projected unwittingly, without conscious knowing, onto things or other people 'outside'.

Nevertheless, dualism is far from the inevitable response to human attempts to know the cosmos. Mythical alternatives to dualism will be considered in Chapter 2. Here it is worth noting that in two key and related areas, Jung moved to a more holistic position of seeing psyche, body, matter, spirit and cosmos as vitally interconnected. These areas were alchemy and synchronicity.   *[margin note: beyond dualism]*

Alchemy is more than its popular reputation as the practice of transforming cheap lead into valuable gold. It is believed to originate in prehistoric attempts to quickly 'ripen' metals found in the womb of Mother Earth, but by the time of the European Renaissance it was a non-dualistic practice seeking to unite the emerging science of chemistry with religious, artistic and philosophical realms. Alchemists laboured in an interactive field that conjoined body, spirit and matter. The gold they sought was both material and divine. Everything united in the symbol that was produced in the reading and writing of their enigmatic texts *and* in mystical laboratory rituals.

To Jung, his discovery of Renaissance alchemy books was a key moment in finding historical validation for his psychology. Initially, he decided that the alchemists were so intimately and somatically involved with their experiments because they had unknowingly projected their individuating psyches onto the chemicals. Changes within (in the psyche) were being conducted by facilitating changes without (in the laboratory). However, Jung later came to credit something closer to alchemy's original holistic vision, with his development of the theory of synchronicity.

Synchronicity is another approach to those so-called coincidences when an apparently psychic event is linked to a material one in a meaningful way. There is no rational, material causal explanation to such events. For example, a dream may accurately predict an event, or show something happening at a distance too great for the ordinary senses of the dreamer to perceive. To Jung this indicated an additional factor to conventional scientific ideas of cause and effect. He called such phenomena oriented towards meaning 'synchronicity', in order to show that relations of space and time were involved. A particularly suggestive aspect of his examination of synchronicity was to see it as a kind of creativity between psyche and matter, or, *acts of creation in time* (Jung 1960, CW8: para. 965).

In the late volume of his *Collected Works* on alchemy, *Mysterium Conjunctionis*, Jung speculated that synchronicity referred to what the alchemists sensed in the vision of matter, spirit and psyche as inextricably co-creating (Jung 1970, CW14: paras. 759–70). For synchronicity, distinctions of inside and outside no longer apply. Consciousness itself is caught up in a web of connections, as the deep psyche has a 'psychoid' quality. By this Jung meant both a hypothetical point where psyche and matter meet, and the mind/body connection, where archetypes meet soma as bodily instincts enter psychic realization. The psychoid unconscious makes possible a notion of alchemy largely as the alchemists envisaged it: generating an interactive field in which archetypes are organizing energies that span soul, body and world (ibid.: 787–8).

Another way of exploring the potential of Jungian archetypes is condensed in Jung's memorable line: 'the Gods have become diseases' (Jung 1967, CW13: para. 54). Again, a historical viewpoint gives depth to Jung's naming of archetypes as those overwhelming psychic powers that in one age might be called Aphrodite or Saturn, and in another, irresistible passion or a crippling depression. Archetypes are gods, in that they do not die because the archetypal unconscious is *collective*; it is reborn, or re-animated in every human (and in a synchronicity pervading the cosmos). They are gods and goddesses in that they *create* us. Moreover, they create *through* us, using individual human existence to incarnate their different qualities of being in the world.

Hence, archetypes are story-generating, deathless, and endlessly creating via their images. They are gods seeking to live out their particular genre of stories, known, of course, as myths. In Jungian psychology, myth has a specific function as the narrative form of the archetype, or a god prominent at any particular moment of individuation. Put another way, myths fashion relations between consciousness and the archetypal collective unconscious. Myths are not what the ego chooses, but rather how the individuating psyche generates a story of being in a dialogue between the ego of consciousness and the greater divine powers of archetypes. For the individual person, myths are the stories of our fate.

Lastly, in introducing Jung is his undervalued definition of the symbol, which will become very important to the matter of this book. Later chapters will argue that Jungian symbols are Dionysian fragments with the potential to re-embody psyche and knowledge. In essence, symbols are images or psychic expressions that lead to psychic depths and mysteries. Jung often discussed symbols in words that revealed them as conveying a non-rational dimension of psychic reality. For symbols are images that point to something not yet fully known, or not knowable in any other way (Jung 1921, CW6: para. 819).

Jung called symbols 'living' when they manifest something not accessible to consciousness *except* by means of this pregnant expression (ibid.: 816). Symbols are also remarkably pervasive.

> Since every scientific theory contains an hypothesis, and is therefore an anticipatory description of something still essentially unknown, it is a symbol. Furthermore every psychological expression is a symbol if we assume that it states or signifies something more and other than itself which eludes our present knowledge.
>
> *(ibid.: 817)*

Here, Jung suggests that science is largely, or at least largely directed to, symbolic writing. Furthermore, psychology, by association a science, is also symbolic. Crucial to this multidisciplinary treatment of symbols is Jung's recognition that they are fragile in the face of conscious attitude. The same image in words or in a dream item can be considered symbolically as an attempt to express the relatively unknown, or it could be regarded as a mere vehicle of a straightforward, known and conscious meaning. A rose in a poem can be a symbol of divine and sensual ecstasy, or it can be what Jung termed a 'sign', an image without a symbol's mystery, perhaps showing the lack of imagination in a poet using a cliché (Jung 1966, CW15: 105).

When discussing symbols at length, Jung is explicit that a symbol for its very *life* depends upon the attitude of the observer (Jung 1921, CW6: Para. 818). However, when discussing symbols in the context of literature, his sense of disciplinary boundaries takes symbols in a new direction as we will see in the next section.

Getting started with Jung and literature

Two essays outline Jung's attitude to literature and extend to art in general, as he remarks in 'On the Relation of Analytical Psychology to Poetry', and maintains in 'Psychology and Literature' (Jung 1966, CW15: paras. 97, 133). In the earlier piece he makes a fundamental statement about disciplines and why there cannot be one superior way of knowing and being.

> The fact that artistic, scientific and religious propensities still slumber peacefully together in the small child . . . all of this does nothing to prove the existence of a unifying principle which alone would justify a reduction of one to the other.
>
> *(ibid.: para. 99)*

Jung says here that the psyche has no single root cause, no 'unifying principle' that would bestow upon psychology the role of the most foundational explanation of human beings. If psychology discovered a unifying principle then it could be used to reduce artistic production to the fulfilment of psychic drives. Jung explicitly denies any such possibility for his psychology. Art can never be wholly explained, or explained away, by psychology. Rather, Jung insists, aesthetics, or the investigation of artistic beauty, will have a role quite apart from anything that psychology might contribute (Jung 1966, CW15: para. 97).

Of course, the psyche itself is the maker and consumer of art and literature. For that reason, the psyche's sufferings or pathology may be deeply involved in making art (Jung 1966, CW15: para. 100). Yet to claim that art can be reduced to infantile sexual repression, for instance, is false to what art is (ibid.: para. 103). Here Jung is implying an ontological (being and reality) difference between psychology and literature: that the latter has meaning and existence beyond that bestowed by the psychic peculiarities of its author. A work such as Plato's *Republic* has a claim upon the world quite apart from its ability to supply evidence of its author's mental condition: 'a work of art is not a disease' (ibid.: para. 107). It is not 'transmitted or derived' as if it were a straightforward cause or result of the human psyche (ibid.: para. 108). Art requires creativity or the making of something new in its organization (ibid.: para. 108).

Creativity in this essay is described as 'a force of nature' (Jung 1966, CW15: para. 115). It is a power that Jung refuses to speculate upon, by calling creativity a secret of nature (ibid.: para. 120). Yet this mysterious ability to bring the 'new' into being is sometimes subdued to an artist's conscious will, and sometimes is not so controllable (ibid.: para. 109). Some art stems from careful crafting by the artist, so that creation is identical to deliberate design (ibid.: para. 109). On the other hand, for some works, a mysterious natural creativity completely overwhelms any ego intentions. Here the work of art is alien, i.e., largely autonomous of conscious will (ibid.: para. 110).

In this essay on poetry, Jung persists with a plant metaphor for the nature of those artworks arising apart from the consciousness of the artist (Jung 1966, CW15: paras. 108–120). Such an approach emphasizes both the independence of the art from the artist, and hence his personal psychology is barely relevant, and also that the meaning of this ontologically separate entity is far from straightforward. Insofar as art originates from nature's mystery of creativity, it cannot be corralled or tamed by an ego's speculations in its own interests. Indeed, here Jung makes another foundational statement about knowing, being and rationality.

We have to break down life and events, which are self-contained processes, into meanings, images, concepts, well knowing that in doing so we are getting further away from the living mystery . . . But for the purposes of cognitive understanding we must detach ourselves from the creative process and look at it from the outside . . . In this way we meet the demands of science.
(ibid.: para. 121)

Science is here Jung's psychology that demands that the living mystery of the psyche be *broken down* in order to secure suitable meanings, images and concepts, in providing ideas that will prove universally applicable. After all, Jung does not find a unifying principle in the psyche that would enable him to assert conceptual unifying principles as epistemologically complete, or forms of knowing that cannot be undermined by anything more fundamental. Rather, the psyche has to be torn apart to make it reasonable. I will take up this sense of Dionysus dismembered in the following chapter. For now, it is important to emphasize that art has its own purchase on this living mystery, which only emphasizes that it cannot be reductively defined by Jung's psychology.

Art has its own being and may, because of originating in the living mystery, resist conscious meaning (para. 121). On the other hand, Jung incarnates the mystery in art in symbols, and then suggests that less aesthetically successful literary works will have more of them (Jung 1966, CW15: para. 119). Art lacking symbols is more able to offer a sense of completed purpose that is aesthetically satisfying (ibid.: para. 119). As we remember, symbols denote a meaning that cannot be represented in any other way, while being incomplete to conscious rationality. Jung here overtly contrasts symbols with signs, which are uncomplicated images indicating the causal effect of symptoms. Symbols, in distinction, incorporate nature's creativity.

Late in his poetry essay, Jung offers a description of artistic creativity starting in its unconscious generating of an archetypal image, which is then worked into the matter of art (Jung 1966, CW15: para. 130). At this point, the *collective* nature of unconscious archetypes also has a collective social function. Art that draws upon collective depths educates society by supplying that which it lacks (ibid.: para. 130). Here the art that does summon symbols into being is of the 'backstreets and alleys', in that it brings to the foreground what has been forgotten, ignored, repressed or undiscovered in the world (ibid.: para. 131).

To Jung, who prefers a self-balancing notion of the psyche, such a dynamic social role for art represents a similar mechanism in the collective culture (Jung 1966, CW15: para. 131). Much of the basic approaches of his essay occur again in the later chapter 'Psychology and Literature'. Prominent among these are the notions that psychology and art are not to be falsely used to explain each other, the development of the distinction between signs and symbols into two categories of literature, the limitation of the personal in art, and that some art arises from compensatory drives in the culture. For the latter, collective art, society behaves like an individual psyche (ibid.: para. 153).

Of particular interest to this book is the latter essay's greater insistence on the feminine quality of the creative process and the language used to explore the visionary, or more symbolic literary works. However, first noticeable is Jung's need to propel himself outside a discipline which has become a 'thickly walled specialist fortress' (p. 85). A scholarly discipline could either be a potential prison or secure defensive apparatus. Such a position of disciplinary anxiety is challenged when it seems that psychology and aesthetics need each other's help, rather than negating each other's approach (Jung 1966, CW15: para. 135).

Jung demonstrates this intriguing multidisciplinary lens by showing that, while the literary critic may be astounded by the subtle psychology of some sophisticated novels, the psychologist ought rather to prefer something more naïve, less consciously textured. Here we get a division of literature into two categories: 'psychological', denoting where the author has deliberately carved a convincing sense of human complexity, and 'visionary', where the collective unconscious has pushed aside the hapless author's ego (ibid.: para. 139).

> Sublime, pregnant with meaning yet chilling the blood . . . timeless depths: glamorous, daemonic, and grotesque, it bursts asunder our human standards of value and aesthetic form, a terrifying tangle of eternal chaos.
>
> *(ibid.: para. 141)*

The tone here is very different from the poetry essay, in which symbols emerged to surprise writers and regulate society. Here, visionary literature in the symbolic mode seems little concerned with balance or restoration, or supplying the deep roots of a culture with what it most lacks. Rather, the visionary is a far more monstrous pregnancy, capable of dismembering the values and artistic form in some Dionysian frenzy (see Chapter 6 for more on the dismembering of meaning). Notable here is the sense of the eruption of the inhuman, perhaps emphasized by the essay's more explicit endorsement of myth as the true language of visionary art (Jung 1966, CW15: para. 151). Dragons become runaway trains, eagles become divine Zeus, aircraft and the Earth Mother, 'a stout lady selling vegetables' (ibid.: para. 152).

In the latter myth is a trace of the feminine quality Jung ascribes to creativity, with not only repeated references to pregnancy but also to art stemming from the domain of 'the Mothers' (ibid.: para. 153). I will suggest in Chapter 2 of this book a connection between the vegetation god, Dionysus, and visions of an Earth Mother. Now it is worth noticing how Dionysian visionary art dismembers psychic and social integrity.

Ultimately, visionary works are to the collective what a dream is to the individual (Jung 1966, CW15: para. 161). A dream, insists Jung, is not to be explained, nor explained away. Its motifs are ambiguous (ibid.: para. 161). Jung ends 'Psychology and Literature' equally ambiguously, poised between the calming notion of cultural compensation in symbolic art and the terrifying vision that the same works are the channel for the abyss that threatens to overwhelm our consciousness (ibid.: para. 141).

Yet visionary art does have the power to make or create the artist's being, just as daemonic *Faust* remade its author, Goethe (ibid.: para. 159). So could art in its compensatory form have a similar creative function in the sinews of a whole society? 'Psychology and Literature' is not explicit about such a possibility, nor does it clarify how historical changes might shift a work from one category to another. A work may be psychological in one era and visionary in another, or vice versa. As such, as I have argued before, 'psychological' and 'visionary' could be used as contrasting ways of reading, rather than as absolute and unchanging categories (Rowland 2010).

To read in a psychological way means to pay attention to the conscious artistry and to the debate between collective consciousness and individual expression in the work. Reading in the visionary mode is to open up to the work's Dionysian powers to rend apart and re-member the psyche and its collective environs. Such an embrace of a particular divine perspective is the perfect vantage point to begin with Jung's revisioning successor, James Hillman.

Getting started with James Hillman

Archetypal theorist Glen Slater stresses three aspects of James Hillman's 'Archetypal Psychology', in comparison to that of its 'first immediate father', C. G. Jung (Hillman 2004: 14; Slater 2012). These three approaches are Hillman's development of a perspectival emphasis, or polytheism, moving from individuation to 'soul-making', and the use of 'archetypal' for images. Concerning the latter, Hillman refused to speculate about whether images relate to some prior entity called an archetype. Images are archetypal; the unrepresentable archetype as such is not needed.

First of all, Slater points out that Hillman's distinctive archetypal psychology grew out of conversations he had with other Jungian analysts in Zurich during the 1960s and 1970s, principally Patricia Berry and Rafael Lopez-Pedraza. By 1985, Andrew Samuels, in his seminal book, *Jung and the Post-Jungians*, was able to identify three post-Jungian schools of significant distinctness. Archetypal psychology was one of them, alongside the Classical, or close-to-Jung analysts of Zurich, and the neo-Freudian Developmental School, based in London (Samuels 1985).

Significantly, Hillman's work sought to deepen some aspects of Jung's intellectual context and downplay others. So Hillman prioritized Jung's ambivalent relation to the humanities (of which more below), and eschewed a rhetoric of science that might be seen as marginalizing the foundational importance that both men gave to the imagination. Hillman chose to emphasize a heritage of Ancient Greek philosophy deriving from Heraclitus and its Neoplatonic heirs in the Renaissance. Above all, Hillman's archetypal psychology pivots away from Jung's attempt to reconfigure Christian and monotheistic structures to a polytheism that he based on the Greek gods and goddesses.

Such a psychology is *perspectival* in that it refuses a central or fixed epistemological position from which to know. Epistemology refers to the ways in which we know and the ways we justify that knowing. To Hillman, Jung's psyche of archetypes and archetypal images is still biased towards an essentially Christian epistemology because of the central role of the monotheistically functioning Self. Moreover, he saw the prime attention paid to the ego in individuation as a dangerous legacy of a hero myth, meaning that it is a vestige of a time when heroic warrior egos were necessary for survival. In a Nuclear Age, the building of a psyche predicated upon winning battles at any cost can be disastrous.

Polytheistic psychology means that archetypal forces in the psyche are best termed as multiple goddesses and gods, because they 'see' the world in many diverse styles. Hillman's myriad archetypes are divine because they create who we are, and also destroy who we are. The gods are not devoted to human success, or to the narrow ambitions of a single human life. Nor can they be corralled, tamed, or tempted to adapt comfortably to our egos.

Rather, the goddesses and gods are immortal (existing in all human psyches) and demand *their being* through us. They bestow types of consciousness, according to who they are: Aphroditic, Hermetic, Apollonian, Dionysian, etc. So our knowing and being are rightly the result of competing, loving, quarrelling gods; there is no neutral or extraneous vision.

These gods are the structuring factors of the human imagination. We know them by the mythical patterns they provide through human products and institutions. It follows that archetypal psychology erodes the distinction between inside and outside in psychology because the gods have no such regard for this human framework. The psyche is everywhere in what Hillman termed, after Jung, the *ONLY INSOFAR?* *anima mundi*, or soul of the world. The world is ensouled because divine beings reach out to its matter and animate it. Or, as Hillman says of *anima mundi*, it is 'that particular soul-spark, that seminal image, which offers itself through each thing in its visible form' (Hillman 1992: 101).

As a result, Hillman shifts from the ego–self centrality of Jungian 'individuation' to what he calls 'soul-making', preferring the term 'soul' to 'psyche'. Whereas individuation is directed towards a goal of ever greater union with a monotheistic self, soul-making has no such expectation of linear progression towards a desired endpoint of wholeness. Rather, soul-making welcomes the 'falling apart', the dismemberment that is the sign of a god or goddess entering into being and knowing.

Indeed, in a major work examined in Chapter 7 of this book, *Re-Visioning Psychology* (1975), Hillman argued for four pillars of archetypal psychology as: Personifying, Pathologizing or Falling Apart, Psychologizing or Seeing Through, and Dehumanizing. 'Soul-making', he wrote, requires life-long attention to the overwhelming and dehumanizing creative and destructive power of the gods. It does not bolster the heroic ego, nor necessarily make us whole.

Finally, Slater shows that it is possible to understand the profound difference between Jung and Hillman in the shifting ground between archetypes and the archetypal. Both psychologists adhere to the archetypal as fundamental to being and knowing, or as Slater states, the 'core insight that archetypes structure experience from the ground up' (Slater 2012: 31). Indeed, archetypes (for Jung), or goddesses and gods (for Hillman), is all the ground we have to stand on in the process of making meaning.

However, for Jung, his psychology was potentially (if not actually) reconcilable with medical and scientific modes of knowing, because archetypes were posited as inborn and inherited. They are *there* in the human creature. By being energized in daily life, archetypes create with its matter the archetypal images that are part transcendent structuring (archetype) and part immanent being (the historical matter gained by embodiment).

For Jung, archetypes produce archetypal images that form our conscious experience and are recorded in our cultural products. For Hillman, being true to the gods means seeing the soul (his preferred word) as *archetypal*, neither requiring nor restricted by any form of prior being that could possibly threaten the polytheistic un-harmony. Jung's preference for medical, scientific or biological dimensions to his psychology is far too dominated by the heritage of Judeo-Christian monotheism.

One legacy of Christianity is the emphasis on dualism, which in scientific and medical modes enacts a separation of matter and psyche, as the human mind is seen as inherently separate from the world. Devoted to detonating dualism as fundamental structuring in favour of polytheism and *anima mundi*, Hillman's soul is perspectival and archetypal. Archetypal psychology does not regard soul as emanating from a bodily incarnation of archetypes, which for Jung deal with the dualist mind–body split by having poles of body and instinct in a continuum with spirit.

Hillman's polytheistic, soul-making archetypal psychology therefore differs from that of Jung in its epistemology, or way of creating knowledge. The consequence of the relationship between psychology and literature from an archetypal as opposed to a Jungian, approach is intriguing. Thus, this book will look at Hillman on literature through an exploration of his great work, *Re-Visioning Psychology*. For now, we need to explore another divide in the Dionysian and fragmented body of academia: how did the disciplines of literature and psychology become so estranged?

Historical disciplinary framing (1) literature

Psychology and literature as academic disciplines emerged from social, educational and cultural revolutions in the nineteenth century. Indeed, prior to the upheavals of Civil War in America and the expansion of education especially in the United States and Britain, power over knowing in Western universities polarized between the various natural sciences and philology, the study of language in written forms. Philology then combined its successor disciplines of literature, history and linguistics, in focusing on the reliability of historical sources, language variations and their interpretation.

In social terms, the educational role of preparing a male elite for political and cultural power was channelled into the long-lived discipline of Classics, a philological study of surviving Greek and Roman texts studied only in their original Greek and Latin. Students absorbed the 'values' of their civilization by tracing their founding origins in a specific ancient world. Classics secured for gentlemen their society's transmission of taste, aesthetics and cultural values, while the more vocationally oriented degrees in Theology were deemed to preserve ethical and spiritual values.

This situation had to change. The democratic and technological challenges of the second half of the nineteenth century could not be met by such an elitist curriculum. After the Civil War, America saw the rise of a 'field coverage' model in higher learning which soon produced specialist departments in universities. These were perfectly able to defend their field and fight for intellectual territory (Graff 2007: viii).

During the later nineteenth century, a progressive movement developed that demanded education be extended beyond the upper classes, and that learning should be oriented to what was socially useful. Within this drive there was considerable ambiguity about whether the aim was social change or preservation of the status quo. Typically, agreement was possible that studying dead languages was frivolity, compared to the utility of the sciences (Wilson 2002: 65).

An immediate result of the influence of the progressives was the rejection of philology's stress on historical documents, in favour of adopting the empirical methods of the natural sciences for the same intellectual fields. The Social Sciences were born of this triumph of empiricism, the notion that all knowledge is derived from actual experience, and positivism, the standpoint that reality is intrinsically independent of consciousness (Saban 2014: 35). If reality is ontologically separate from the psyche, 'out there', rather than caught up with our perceptions, then it can be studied objectively as quite apart from human desires, feelings and motivations, whether known or unknown.

As an example of the new epistemological and cultural capital of the Social Sciences, in the 1930s there were efforts at converting history to quantitative methods (Wilson 2002: 75). Literature, a discipline devoted to imaginative works in the vernacular, has a complex relationship to the rise of progressive Social Sciences. On the one hand, it proclaimed a progressive emphasis in the curriculum of the communication of human experience, rather than abstract ideas deemed less socially useful. On the other hand, it was devised as a discipline to replace Classics as the vehicle for moulding aesthetic taste, promulgating great 'truths' and communicating imaginative realities (ibid.: 67).

The triumph over Classics was to be short lived. Literature or English departments immediately began to lose ground to the scientific-oriented Social Sciences. Learning needed to show that it connected to something real in positivistic terms and, as a result, could be offered as pragmatic in a maturing industrial society. No wonder that eminent literary critic John Crowe Ransom felt compelled to proclaim, in *The World's Body* (1938), that the arts *are* real and reveal as much 'fidelity to the phenomenal world as history has' (Ransom 132 quoted in Wilson 2002: 76).

While Britain had different emphases in the call for a socially useful higher education, it was similarly faced with opening universities to an expanded population of middle-class men, and that new creature on campuses, women. There was more than one starchy old school professor who thought that literature in English was a suitable compromise for such innately inferior students. As elsewhere, English was handed the torch previously carried by Classics of saving the nation in a time of religion's declining influence. In fact, George Gordon, an early Professor of English Literature, insisted that with the decline of the Church's moral authority, only the study of vernacular literature could delight, instruct, save souls and mend society (Wilson 2002: 76).

With such a charge, combined with the encroachments of empirical Social Sciences, perhaps it was inevitable that a *theory* of literature emerged to justify the study of literature as criticism and imagination, rather than the tradition of philological and historical attention to authenticating texts. For history had split off, and was flirting with, empiricism via quantitative methods, while language studies were evolving into modern linguistics. Given that English had taken on the socially coded justification as the guardian of aesthetics and values, it badly needed an epistemology to fend off charges that it lacked the properties of positivism and empiricism. Literature badly needed to find a field of study, and a way for criticism, that empowers the notion that it was open to a more concrete grasp of reality.

To answer such anxieties, English generated modern *literary* theory that would continue to seek, to this day, an ontology and epistemology, a way of being and knowing, for Literature. Its early most influential manifestation is known as New Criticism, which, this book will argue, possesses an unconscious relationship to Jungian psychology. Before looking at this no longer new critical theory, I want to turn to the fate of psychology as it broke free from nineteenth-century philosophy to find itself struggling with the demands of the nascent Social Sciences.

Jungian psychology and its framing as a (social) science

Jung and the Question of Science (2014) edited by Raya A. Jones, brings together Jungian scholars to explore the issues around Jung's repeated use of the word 'science' to describe his approach to the psyche. Jones points out that historical and linguistic pressures shape contemporary understanding of Jung's adherence to the term. Efforts to carve out a 'field' for the new psychology in the nineteenth century were themselves affected by philosophy and, less immediately, theology, as precursors. Wilhelm Wundt founded the first laboratory for psychology in Leipzig in 1879, at a time when spiritualism and the paranormal threatened to usurp the ground of the new discipline (Jones 2014a: 53).

Moreover, Jones argues that the philosophical legacy of empiricism from British philosophers of earlier centuries subtly influences the status of the natural sciences as paramount forms of knowing (Jones 2014a: 50). Another crucial presence in early psychology, philosopher William James, brother of the novelist Henry James, unequivocally stated that associating the new field with natural sciences could not bestow stability and ontological security. For, if psychology was to proceed scientifically, by experiments, its ability to track the myriad facets of a mobile psyche offered real difficulties in providing knowledge.

> When, then, we talk of 'psychology as a natural science' we must not assume that means a sort of psychology that stands at last on solid ground. It means just the reverse; it means a psychology particularly fragile and into which the waters of metaphysical criticism leak at every joint . . . [We have] not a single law in the sense that physics shows us laws . . . This is no science, it is only the hope of science.
>
> (*James 1983 [1892]: 468*)

Perhaps then, Jung's affinity for the word science is more rhetorical than onto-logical? Perhaps too he saw that the psyche of modernity split between objective and subjective knowing might be resolved through a psychology that insisted on the psyche's propensity for imagination, dream and depth?

Both Joe Cambray and Roderick Main have argued that one aim of Jung's entire project is to produce a science of wholeness that can span the spectrum of human knowing, including material science and religion (Cambray 2014; Main 2004). It is the proposal of this book that not only is the Jungian project devoted to reconciling forms of knowing typically defined as masculine or feminine, but that it also offers us in the twenty-first century a chance for enlivening our scholarship by re-aligning the disciplines through re-membering the dismembered body of Dionysus. This argument will be developed in Chapter 2.

Meanwhile, it is worth considering further Jung's worldview in his use of sci-ence to describe his psychology. As Mark Saban, in *Jung and the Question of Science*, shows, Jung certainly did not sympathize with the materialism and positivism of the science of his age. He did not agree with this science's underlying assumption of matter stripped from spirit and knowing as possible without considering the role of the knowing psyche (Saban 2014: 35). Also important in Saban's research is that the German word translated into English as 'science' encompasses disciplines such as history, anthropology and mythology, which are foreign to the British empiricist flavour of the term.

Furthermore, he demonstrates that Jung's insistence on the ineradicable personal equation in knowing belongs to a rich tradition of largely German Romanticism which includes Goethe (Saban 2014: 42). Knowing cannot be regarded as split off from being in a psychological as well as cultural and embodied sense. Jung's so-called science is not going to be about the investigation of phenomena regarded as intrinsically separate from the human psyche.

What Jung does insist on, scientifically, Saban says, is that preconceptions, principles or 'theories' should not pre-structure and hence predetermine psycho-logical knowing. Here Jung is a phenomenological empiricist, in that he tries to grasp what the psyche produces and does so quite apart from preconceived ideas, including his own (Saban 2014: 41–3). As Jung put it:

> A psychology that wants to be scientific can no longer afford to base itself on so-called philosophical premises such as materialism or rationalism. . . . [I]t can only proceed phenomenologically and abandon preconceived opinions.
> *(Jung 1949, CW18: para. 1249)*

To the extent that psychology is frequently placed as a Social Science, part of Jung's argument is won in the sense that historical and cultural factors in the psyche are acknowledged in the discipline. On one hand, it is not merely a mat-ter of deducing universal laws as was presumed appropriate for the natural sci-ences. On the other hand, Leslie Gardner, in 'Speculations on Jung's Dream of Science', notes how Jung's own writing invites further knowing, thereby pushing his work towards the humanities, with their emphasis on qualitative, not quantitative modes of research. It also takes Jung into science as rhetoric, and, I would suggest, literature.

To back up: quantitative research uses statistics or mathematics to gauge results according to frequency. Something is deemed scientifically true by means of quantitative methods if it happens most of the time; anomalies are screened out. By contrast, qualitative approaches consider aspects of knowing not amenable to the study of large groups, such as the intricacies of human behaviour. A qualitative researcher may employ such personal approaches as individual in-depth interviews in which trust between interviewer and subject is key to obtaining data. She might also use imaginative and artistic modes to re-present her findings, because only such language can enact intimate and evocative conclusions.

While today the social sciences endorse both research paradigms, its individual disciplines do not agree on their validity. In this perspective, Jung was a phenomenological empiricist in the qualitative mode, not surprising given his assessment of the importance of the unconscious. Incorporating into knowing the effects of the unknown psyche is most conducive to a qualitative approach, if it allows the parts of the psyche independent of the ego to manifest. What Gardner also points out is that Jung's writing is a device to open the reader to *more* apprehension of the world.

> The rhetorical or poetical faculty of science is its capacity to notice those anomalies – those 'puzzles' of science – and to frame them in a way that simultaneously initiates fruitful inquiry.
>
> *(Gardner 2014: 79)*

Science proceeds by noticing when things do not fit. A hypothesis does not work for all occasions. Scientific writing is rhetoric, an art of persuasion, in noticing and causing others to notice what is not fully congruent with current hypotheses. Jung was entirely this kind of rhetorical writer of science.

> The empirical reality summed up under the concept of the anima forms an extremely dramatic content of the unconscious. It is possible to describe this content in rational, scientific language, but in this way one entirely fails to express its living character. Therefore, in describing the living processes of the psyche, I deliberately and consciously give preference to a dramatic, mythological way of thinking and speaking, because this is not only more expressive but also more exact than an abstract scientific terminology, which is wont to toy with the notion that its theoretic formulations may one fine day be resolved into algebraic equations.
>
> *(Jung 1951, CW 9ii: para. 25)*

Jung uses dramatic and mythological expressions because they are more *exact* than scientific concepts. These have to claim a universal validity, and so miss the particularity of the living mystery of the psyche's being and knowing. While Jung wanted the kind of qualitative science that embraced actual psychic phenomena in all its particularity *first*, before the imposition of a philosophical or metaphysical theory of reality, he arguably produces a social science that also has roots in the humanities and their arts. Given such epistemological struggles and their larger context of the contested ground of natural and social sciences, it is time to return to how Literature, or English, tried to shore up its insecure beginnings as an avatar of Classics.

Literary studies getting started: The New Criticism

Perhaps not surprisingly, New Criticism begins in America and Britain with a partial endorsement of positivism and empiricism in objectivity, and a vigorous attempt to carve out an independent ontology, or being, for literature. The result, as demanded by its exponents, was to entirely sever this newly autonomous entity called Literature from its heritage as 'fine writing' in whatever domain. No longer would valued writing of the law, religion, history or even science count as Literature for disciplinary purposes. Prior to nineteenth-century disciplinary reconfigurations, philology took care of scrutinizing texts (of a far wider variety than just the imaginative or fictional) for authenticity, while stalwart Classics took care of the values of taste and civilization for its future rules. While the New Critics did not entirely invent the category of Literature, they certainly insisted on its difference from other kinds of writing and, for the wider university constituency of the twentieth century, insisted that it was the destiny of imaginative fiction to preserve humane values.

Above all, English was to be a wholly separate discipline, dismembered from historicizing philology and outmoded Classics. And yet what made English into a subject that *must* exist apart from disciplines such as History is its absorption via New Criticism into positivism. The New Critics emphasized that a literary work has its being entirely separate from consciousness, whether that of the author or the reader. The author has no say in the critical meaning of literature, nor should anything personal from the critic be a factor.

To substantiate this position of rigorous objectivity, W. K. Wimsatt and Cleanth Brooks initiated the influential 'intentional fallacy' and 'affective fallacy' to utterly forbid contamination by the psyche of the literary qualities of a text (Wimsatt & Beardsley 1954). To consider what the author may have intended is to be as false to literature as it is to consider the reader's own affect or feelings. Chapter 5 will consider these notions for their affinity with Jung's theory of active imagination.

Even more in line with the scientific paradigm of positivist empiricism is I. A. Richards' claim to divide writing into science, as statement of facts, opposed by poetry, as a pseudo statement to be properly examined with rigorous objectivity (Richards & Ogden 1923/1989). Both descriptions of language assume an ontology, or being in words, that exists as separate from the mind. Literature becomes a distinct body requiring professional academic attention. It also becomes immune from quantitative research methods, by being granted guardianship of aesthetic values. That these values are incarnated in words on the page, and not in the psyche, writing or reading them secures English from being contaminated by the social sciences new recruit –psychology.

As Wilson puts it:

> [In its] insistence on the specificity of literary language, New Criticism pro-vided strong institutional protection against the social sciences, ensuring the need for at least a minimum of specialists competent in the aesthetic realm. The implicit ontology in professional discourse – the idea that the existence of a profession of literary study requires the definite object, "literature" – dates from the rise of New Criticism.
>
> *(Wilson 2002: 77)*

A new discipline, however in debt to scientific positivism and the elite educating role of the Classics, needs a new methodology to enact its unique perspective on being and knowing. Named by Richards as 'practical criticism', and later known as 'close reading', this newly minted hermeneutics stressed the most careful scrutiny of words on the page, while stripping out any possible context that might daringly claim to be a co-text capable of affecting interpretation.

Forbidden contexts include, of course, emotions, feelings, personal associations, anything known of the author or time of writing, and word etymologies. The poem, play, novel, etc., is an organic, autonomous entity (Eagleton 1983: 29). It is capable of a wholeness and balance not to be disturbed by human inadequacy, historical contingency or cultural differences.

On the one hand, nothing can be more dismissive of psychology than New Criticism's ideology of empirical objectivity: the words of *this* text are empirical data wholly severed from contaminating consciousness. On the other hand, Jung may have found something not entirely alien in this notion of something supremely of the imagination becoming some-thing, a Being possessing objectivity.

In later chapters I will explore the uncanny dance, oblivious to Jung and the New Critics themselves that brings Jungian Depth Psychology, New Criticism and later developments in close reading, into the same orbit. For now, I want to end with Jung's work as a counter-tendency to the splitting of learning into ever more scholarly disciplines.

Jung in/as science and literature

In insisting on unconsciousness as integral to knowing, Jung did not eschew objectivity and science, as has been already shown. As Joe Cambray puts it, refer-ring to Jung's *The Red Book* (2009), and explored later in *Remembering Dionysus*:

> My suggestion is that in *The Red Book* Jung is in fact attempting to engage his own psychological nature in a manner consistent with the way the

> German Romantic scientists sought to engage objective reality with their subjective responses.
>
> *(Cambray 2014: 22)*

Definitely not a positivist, Jung's work refuses the reductionism within positivism's ideal of absolute objectivity. Positivism is reductive because it has to omit any so-called irrelevancies of an experimenter's subjectivity, or historical conditions (Saban 2014: 35). Hence, Jung's rhetoric of the objective psyche is not an ontological separate realm (ibid.: 41). Rather, it is an attempt to formulate a dialogical notion of apprehension through a relationship of subjective or ego-associated impulses with objective or non-ego associated powers.

Jung's way of knowing is primarily through the image, or the manifestation of psyche sufficient to suggest possible meaning. When the image manifests as symbol it stands for being beyond the full possibility of conscious knowing or expressing. Here we are back to Jung's writing as rhetorical science, a rhetoric that *is* science, in opening up the possibility of more knowing via its symbolic (Jung would say also mythical) mode.

Given the symbol as materialized imagination, such an entity is inevitably literary and creative. Moreover, Jung explicitly recognizes that hermeneutics, the art of interpreting texts, may be a science in the looser, older, European sense, but it is also a science by provoking exploration and discovery. Such work unites individual subjectivity with objective collectivity, whether the collective is of the unknown psyche or of human disciplinary knowledge.

> The essential character of hermeneutics, a science which was widely practiced in former times, consists in making successive additions of other analogies to the analogy given in the symbol: in the first place of subjective analogies found by the analyst in the course or erudite research . . . in which certain 'lines' of psychological development stand out as possibilities that are at once individual and collective. There is no science on earth by which these lines could be proved 'right'. Their validity is proved by their intense value for life.
>
> *(Jung 1916, CW7: par. 495, quoted by Dawson 2014: 168)*

In espousing 'intense value for life', Jung is talking the language of New Criticism's moulding of a distinct category of Literature in order to secure values that, for them, would be lost in such psychological connectivity. One purpose of this book is to show that Jungian psychology can contribute to a revised close reading that offers more life than its legacy in literary studies currently suggests. And the god of the disease of the too absolute division in academia to serve our need for more life in our learning is the god of dismemberment (for Jung), Dionysus. His role as the gendering and potential healing of the academy will be the subject of the next chapter.

2

THE FEMININE, DIONYSUS AND TRANSDISCIPLINARITY

Introduction: Jung's turn to the feminine (and the novel)

C. G. Jung was no feminist. Yet despite his lack of interest in equality for women and social reform of gender, I suggest that his entire project was devoted to restoring the lost and repressed feminine to the collective psyche of Western modernity. For what haunts the heritage of dualism, the notion of a fundamental 'twoness' or binary quality to meaning and being, is the dominance of one partner and the subordination of the other.

Particularly emphasized in monotheism or systems of belief stressing one divine creator, is how what is other to divine potency is *other* in the sense of inferior; the created, not the creator. Such a structure is patriarchal when it sets up a Father God as its one deity. Fathering becomes the prime distinction of human status linked to consciousness as separate from mindless matter. Mapped onto such dualist treatments of gender, the feminine not only is regarded as marginal, but also comes to denote all that is other to the paternal God's masculine creative spirit. This feminine is construed as matter, body, unreason, unconsciousness, negativity and sexuality.

Jung's project is psychological wholeness rather than ultimate perfection, the latter goal only achievable by casting out the other. To him, Western modernity is characterized by privileging rationality as the gift of a God transcendent of body, matter and nature. Such repression makes modern consciousness dangerously fissile. What modernity has rejected must be recuperated. The feminine must return *as feminine* as well as nature, body, matter, etc., to psychological being and knowing.

One way the feminine returns within Jung's psychology is in his writing. Here rationality as the supremely valuable form of consciousness, monotheistically enacted as oneness intact, has to make room for an acceptance of other ways of knowing. So psychology might as well stop pretending to merely describe the psyche and start embodying it. In the following quotation, Jung abandons rational discourse for feminine and Dionysian writing. He tells a story.

> We kept bantams, and bantam cocks are renowned for their singular quarrelsomeness and malice. One of these exceeded all others in savagery, and my mother commissioned the cook to dispatch the malefactor for the Sunday roast. I happened to come in just as she was bringing back the decapitated cock and saying to my mother: 'He died like a Christian, although he was so wicked. He cried out, "Forgive me, forgive me!" before I cut off his head, so now he'll go to heaven.' My mother answered indignantly: 'What nonsense! Only human beings go to heaven.' The cook retorted in astonishment: 'But of course there's a chicken heaven for chickens just as there's a human heaven for humans.' 'But only people have an immortal soul and a religion,' said my mother, equally astonished. 'No, that's not so,' replied the cook. 'Animals have souls too, and they all have their special heaven, dogs, cats, and horses, because when the Saviour of men came down to earth, the chicken savior also came to the chickens, and that's why they must repent of their sins before they die if they want to go to heaven.'
>
> *(Jung 1944a, CW12: para. 494)*

Jung's mother and their cook debate the nature of nature in relation to Christian salvation and a troublesome chicken. On the one hand, a conventional feminine pervades this amusing anecdote in the participants and the setting with a gendered domesticity between mother and cook. On another level, the story is feminine for expressing what has been rejected by rationality and its dominant religious formation, that animals have souls and saviours, that nature is also divine. Furthermore, I suggest that *the writing here is feminine* for its participation in a genre with extensive feminine and perhaps *animistic* properties: the novel. One of the best authors to explore what is intrinsically feminine about the novel is the renowned Ursula K. Le Guin.

Ursula Le Guin: Literature for Jungian psychology

In 'The Carrier Bag Theory of Fiction', Ursula K. Le Guin offers what amounts to an archetypal theory of Western culture (Le Guin 1986). Significantly, it is one distinguished by a primal division of gender. This bifurcation occurs not in sexual or somatic structures, but rather from formal distinctions arising from a division between labour as productive or reproductive. While prehistoric hunters had exciting adventures by shooting spears at nimble prey, the gatherers, who in addition to this task were also caring for children, were forced to multitask.

For these thousands of years, the only surviving clue to human ingenuity is the carved flint arrowhead or spear point. Its shape seems organically linked to our early literature of heroes wielding weapons. After all, the best stories will surely come from those adventurous hunters, not the wanderers amongst the berries. The spear point hunters suggest the primacy of the epic, a genre characterized by masculine warriors with phallic projectiles. Such archetypal legends set up a legacy of linear stories centred around a hero who is linked to phallic potency.

Epic's high status survives into modernity, where its heroic quest for supremacy over the Other (be that other a monster, an opposing city, nature, or the other gender), in its binary logic, provides a *forming* influence on modern science and its technology. Scientific endeavour becomes obsessed by engineering arrow-like missiles as weapons of mass destruction. So far so patriarchal. The historical imagination of Western cultural heritage privileges the lasting quality of flint arrow heads as indicative of where we come from. But what if the spear point is not the first cultural object?

> A leaf a gourd a shell a net a bag a sling a sack a bottle a pot a box a container. A holder. A recipient.
>
> *(Le Guin 1986: 150)*

If we consider early human development as fostered by the first 'thing' groups of humans used *creatively* to enable their communal lives, then the first cultural object would more likely be something used to drink from, cook with, or to carry water or food. The first cultural artefact was probably the proto-carrier bag! In this sense, the container is at least as equally significant as the arrowhead as a founding structure of human creativity.

Here Le Guin proposes another crucial descendant of the primal gourd in the art form that has come to be known as the novel. The novel is art devoted to stories of *the thriving of a group* in distinction to the epic's focus on a single testosterone-fuelled hero who triumphs in battle. Novels *contain* heterogeneous elements forced into a relationship. Moreover, I suggest that the novel is Dionysian, as the god of the dismembered and re-membered psyche. For the novel genre consists of a tension between its many characters who love, grow, mate and disagree. Novels weave different modes of consciousness together, and suffer their capacity to break apart.

Recognizing the probability of the novel as an additional archetype of culture and consciousness enables Le Guin to challenge the masculine epic form as inevitable and dominant. This is not to suggest that these are the only two archetypal and gendered artistic forms, nor to imply that C. G. Jung identified them in this way. Rather, I argue that Jung's form of novelistic writing is performative (another Dionysian link), and a contribution to his project of restoring to modernity all that patriarchy has dismissed as feminine.

Jung writes to foster the presence of other voices *within* his psyche-logos, or psychology. Put another way, what Jung identifies as a principle of consciousness in distinction to rational, discriminating Logos, his feeling connecting Eros, also lives in his *Collected Works*. The Christian chicken is as much part of Jungian psychology as any concept identified in Chapter 1.

Of the possibilities that follow from Jung as the 'novelist' of psychology, this book will trace those that draw on, and also draw away from, disciplinary liminality with literature. Chapter 2 will concentrate on how Jung's feminine qualities in writing facilitate what is coming to be called 'transdisciplinarity'. Such a move is designed to make a home for other goddesses and gods within a Western psyche suffering from an excess of one type of divine inhabitant.

By opening psychology to other creators of consciousness, Jung's work possesses a particular historical epistemological narrative that I will show to embody the myth of Dionysus and Ariadne. These divinities become sponsors of the feminine beyond essentialist conceptions of it (gender as innate to male or female bodies).

I am proposing that Jung's entire *Collected Works* amounts to an attempt to rebalance the gendered psyche of modernity in a way that can be further illuminated by first a structuralist, and then a transdisciplinary, paradigm. These moves are mythically described by James Hillman on Jung as Dionysian. (Although Hillman misses the crucial role of Ariadne, as we will see). Writing as Dionysian, as Jung does, may offer the twenty-first century a remarkable transdisciplinary potential for psychic renewal via knowledge, or epistemology itself. Hillman enters this equation by inscribing the necessary archetypal map.

We begin structurally by considering how Jung's turn to the feminine can be understood through yet another binary, in the mutually constituting myths of Earth Mother and Sky Father.

Jung's turn to the feminine as recovering Earth Mother for Sky Father

To summarize, three principal developments in Jung's overall project characterize Jung's attempt to re-orient consciousness to encompass the non-essentialist feminine. They are his adoption of Eros and Logos as gendered styles of consciousness, the role of the ambivalent figure of the trickster, and his paradigm-shifting notion of synchronicity. All three resonate with his own psyche's resistance to a portrayal of female equality. Jung summons a powerful feminine, the 'mater' of the Goddess, in order to secure masculine wholeness, not to change the existing social order. And yet, his innate conservatism is marked by truly revolutionary implications.

First of all, Eros and Logos appear within Jung's preference for an essentialist gender, in which males are born to achieve an unproblematic masculinity, and females 'ought' to cultivate the feminine. So, by inborn qualities, a male's consciousness will align with the discriminatory and disembodied spirit of Logos. Conversely, a woman's natural feeling of relatedness give to her ego its Eros (Jung 1951, CW9ii: para. 29). In addition, each gender, according to Jung, has access to the opposite quality in the unconscious.

Nevertheless, Jungian individuation counters such essentialism. By becoming more individual, more whole, by an ever growing involvement with the unconscious, it is inevitable that Eros, associated with a male's unconscious anima, be integrated and accessible to the ego. So too a woman's animus will conjure a living Logos in her psyche, even if Jung was at times sceptical of its success (Jung 1951, CW9ii: para. 29).

Moreover, there are far-reaching implications in the infusion of Eros and Logos into the other, as other gender. These capacities, as inhabitants of the human psyche that *require* mutual negotiation, evoke a structuralist myth of consciousness proposed by Jungian scholars Ann Baring and Jules Cashford in *The Myth of the Goddess* (1991). This magnificent work describes the building of the modern Western psyche as fatally flawed, due to the unequal relationship of monotheism's dominant spiritual Sky Father to his predecessor, an animistic embodied Earth Mother.

The theory of an Earth Mother goddess is a hypothesis that prior to the arrival of the three great monotheisms of Judaism, Christianity and Islam, religious practice regarded the Earth as alive, sacred, generative and the source of all being. This Earth *Mother* was not a woman as opposed to a man, because she existed prior to gender division. She gave birth to women and men, animals, rocks and plants equally. In her, matter and spirit are one being. Most often she was figured through animistic cultures which saw nature as animated, full of diverse and articulate spirits.

Monotheism forcibly marginalized animism and installed a dominant dualism because its Sky Father god created nature as separate from himself; so non–divine, non–embodied, matter is without spirit. Separation and disembodiment characterizes Sky Father religion in structuring a dualism between God and nature/matter. These divisions were mapped into human culture as hierarchical splitting between spirit or mind, and body, human as intrinsically severed from nature, men as superior in intellect and more naturally spiritual than women.

Here Jung's Eros and Logos consciousness can be seen as a stark attempt to re-orient the creation myths of the Western psyche. Of course Earth Mother never entirely disappeared. Repressed for centuries, she re-emerged in such arts as the animated matter of painting and sculpture, as well as the multiple in-spirited characters of the non-hero–driven novel, as Le Guin reminds us. Hence, Jung's instinct for the price paid in modernity's repression of what has been deemed feminine. He brings her back as the Eros that is necessary to the survival of the modern psyche.

Earth Mother also lived on, I suggest, in the myth of the trickster, and as such found another home in Jungian psychology.

> Even [the trickster's] sex is optional despite its phallic qualities: he can turn himself into a woman and bear children . . . This is a reference to his original nature as a Creator, for the world is made from the body of a god.
>
> *(Jung 1954/1959, CW9i: para. 472)*

Capable of either gender or multiple variations of gender, the trickster is the embodied, amoral, protean psyche itself. In the trickster's infinite variety we see the seedbed of an animistic vision of matter as sacred. Trickster is all feeling and no logical or rational separation from what *matters*. In this way, he demonstrates the core principle of *The Myth of the Goddess*: the need for various types of consciousness without one taking priority over the other.

Later in his career, Jung found the goddess again in his notion of synchronicity as meaningful coincidence between matter and psyche. Such an immanent arising of meaning *within* this world is creation no longer exclusive to the narrative of Genesis when God severs himself from his creatures and his planet. Union with the Creator can come only with death, or an eschatological end of time, as distinguished by divine separation. By contrast, synchronicity is described by Jung as '*acts of creation in time*' (Jung 1960, CW8: para. 965).

Synchronicity occurs when the psyche and material reality come together in a way that reveals meaning rather than a causal connection. It is a vision of reality from within Jung's depiction of the psychic quality of Eros, the feminine function of relationship, as opposed to (inevitably) the masculine Logos principle of conscious discrimination.

So nature is to be investigated because and *by means of* the human psyche that is part of it. True knowledge is that which is inclusive of the psyche.

> For [experimental science] there is created in the laboratory a situation which is artificially restricted to the question and which compels Nature to give an unequivocal answer. The workings of Nature in her unrestricted wholeness are completely excluded . . . . [W]e need a method of enquiry which . . . leaves Nature to answer out of her fullness.
>
> *(Jung 1960, CW8: para. 864)*

Perhaps here is Jung's Earth Mother most completely because she is Nature as wholly creative, divine. This is the animistic universe in which dreams inform of momentous events otherwise unknowable, feeling and somatic archetypal images prove prophetic beyond the rational understanding of a mechanistic or causal approach to reality.

Synchronicity forced Jung to reassess the fundamental Logos orientation of modernity that separated psyche from non-human nature. He began to see modernity's repression of a feminine other as dismembering human wholeness. By contrast, synchronicity suggests an animistic universe in which archetypes extend beyond the human psyche to its union with matter in the psychoid. In so doing, Jung's entire project fulfils what James Hillman described as his treatment of Dionysus. Perhaps Jung's 'novel' psychology may itself be animated by the ecstatic god?

Dionysus and his stories

Born of a mortal, Semele, and the god Zeus, Dionysus is god of wine and wine-making, fertility, ecstasy and madness. Tricked by a jealous Hera into asking to see the true nature of her lover, Semele is blasted by the revelation of Zeus's super-natural radiance. Rescuing the unborn child, Zeus stitches him into his thigh, from which he is subsequently born. Emanating from the thigh of the greatest god gives Dionysus a significantly different, more phallic orientation, than wily Athena, who was born from Zeus' head.

And yet, baby Dionysus is still not safe from Hera's jealousy. She incites the Titans to tear him to pieces. It is Rhea, Titaness daughter of Earth goddess, Gaia, and Sky god, Uranus, who re-member the dis-membered divine child. Later, Dionysus will in turn inspire dismemberment. When Pentheus, King of Thebes refuses to worship the new god – because he disbelieves Semele's tales of a divine lover – Dionysus sends the king into madness and exile in the woods. There Pentheus spies upon the maenads, women followers of Dionysus, in their raging possession by the god. Mistaking the crazy King for an animal, they tear him to pieces. Those who do not acknowledge Dionysus are dismembered by what he inspires.

Two happier tales centre again on Dionysus and the feminine. Remembering his dead mother, he literally re-members her, and becomes the only god to bring a mortal back from the Underworld, so increasing his association with death and rebirth. Moreover, Dionysus's death and rebirth is the harsh pruning of the vine required to make it bear good fruit the following year. Additionally, yet another bereft woman is rescued by him.

Cretan Ariadne aided mortal hero Theseus to defeat her half-brother, the Minotaur, in the labyrinth. Despite such devotion, Theseus abandons Ariadne on the island of Naxos. Dionysus rescues and marries the distraught woman, who is elevated to the stars. Ariadne's heavenly fate increases the speculation that she may be a figure derived from a Cretan goddess. Either way, the marriage of Dionysus and Ariadne seems to have been unusually stable for an Olympian family.

Unlike any other god, Dionysus was honoured in the wilderness, not in a temple. He is instinctual nature perilously close to undifferentiated force. He is wild, even maddened sexuality, and the drives that erode the boundaries between human and animal, human and god. His own origin and habits betray a dangerous carelessness about boundaries and safeguards between different orders of being. Arguably, he represents a version of Earth Mother in her undifferentiated aspect, before fixed distinctions between masculine and feminine, animal and god, even life and death.

Dionysus is Earth Mother beginning to individuate. He is animistic nature and human nature starting to evolve a masculine spirit of sexuality and divinity in the body. In turn, Dionysian-limited differentiation will be met by feminine incarnations of more evolved characteristics of Earth Mother, such as Artemis, Aphrodite and even Athena. Artemis is wild nature personified as the instinctual feminine, Aphrodite enacts the sexuality of humans and non-humans as sacred without the dangerous frenzies of Dionysus. And shrewd Athena possesses the trickster qualities of Earth Mother, as well as aspects of Sky Father's rationality.

After all, Earth Mother is a structuralist idea, a mythic paradigm, rather than an actual goddess or god from a specific mythology. The Greek divinities themselves span, often within their being, aspects of both Earth Mother and Sky Father. A dualist structural and hypothetical lens gives way to a more unstable and exciting polytheism. Of course, in psychological terms, Earth Mother is the pre-Oedipal Mother, that amorphous pre-conscious being who may fragment into, or beget, as archetypes, the myriad goddesses and gods.

It is time to consider Jung's own treatment of Dionysus as found in the individuating psyche.

Hillman on Jung and Dionysus

In 'Dionysus in Jung's Writings', archetypal psychologist James Hillman points out that C. G. Jung stresses 'dismemberment' as his key narrative in the many stories of Dionysus (Hillman 1972/2007). In Jung's version of the tearing apart of the divine being, Hillman sees a possibility of psychic rejuvenation in the corporeal dismembering of an aging god. He calls Christian modernity too Apollonian, seeing in Apollo the emphases of Sky Father dualism taken to excess.

So, in Hillman's polytheistic approach to the psyche, an era dominated by one god defined by distance and disembodiment is to be followed by dismemberment and multiple stories of being. In Chapter 7, I shall explore Hillman's polytheism in relation to psychology and literature. For now, I will entertain the possibility that Jung's dismembering of Dionysus has potentials not considered by Hillman. These include re-membering Ariadne in a revisioned disciplining of knowing.

According to Hillman, Jung sees a two-stage dismembering process: first comes a separation into opposites, such as the very notion of the Apollonian and Dionysian itself. This division satisfies Jung, the lover of polarities, who is reluctant to truly integrate the feminine. Yet Jung, the rebalancing psychologist of the modern Western psyche, needs Earth Mother animism, and one crucial in-forming invites embodied, ecstatic Dionysus. Therefore, in the second stage of Dionysian dismemberment, the god is scattered into pieces.

At this point, it is important to recall the larger picture of dualism, revisioned by Baring and Cashford as Earth Mother and Sky Father. I have used these hypothetical myth-systems in order to explore Jung's explicit and implicit countering of Christian-dominated modernity's preference for rationality based on repression of the other. In this structuralist analysis, specific Greek gods show preferences for either Earth Mother or Sky Father, as might be expected from the position from which they characterize the human psyche. Trickster Hermes and ecstatic Dionysus embrace Earth Mother far more than the cooler ordering of Sky Father preferred by Apollo.

Returning to Hillman on Jung's Dionysus shows a dualistic opposition transfigured into multiplicity. The god is dismembered, seeding the divine in matter. To both Jung and Hillman inspired matter is archetypal, the multiplicity of psychic archetypes.

> Dionysus is the abyss of impassioned dissolution, where all human distinctions are merged in the animal divinity of the primordial psyche – a blissful and terrible experience.
>
> *(Jung 1944b, CW12: para. 118)*

Dionysus arises in an age too dominated by the sun god Apollo's rationality. Instead of a distant divinity that has lost contact with the human psyche, a god of frenzy is torn apart to re-member the divine in nature. Dismembered Dionysus is animistic Earth Mother as archetype. Jung's Christian chicken is Dionysian! He may have been colonized for modernity by Christian missionaries, but his articulate argument for salvation is the voice of Dionysian nature.

Additionally, here the feminine novel genre can now be considered as a primal containing animism of Earth Mother emerging within her somewhat more differentiated son. Characters come into conflict, tearing each other apart, before the containing form can be structured anew, or with a new Dionysian drive for instinctual life. Again, Dionysus is more Earth Mother than Sky Father, in his primal, instinctual drive of nature. But fortunately his dismembering processes allows for some Sky Father separation to mitigate the overwhelming embrace of the animistic Earth Mother. The novel, Dionysian in essence, weaves animistic plurality as Earth Mother feminine into modernity. It is a non-essentialist feminine, because 'she' is prior to gender differentiation.

And there is more. For Hillman goes on to suggest that this second stage of Dionysian dismemberment provides a different type of consciousness. We enter a new cosmos with the dispersed fragments of the body of the god (Hillman 1972/2007: 26). Distance from the divine is replaced, re-placed, by interiority and animistic multiplicity within the domain of the god.

> The movement between the first and second view of dismemberment compares with crossing a psychic border between seeing the god from outside or from within his cosmos.
>
> *(ibid.: 1972/2007: 26)*

Matti's UNS

We are back in Jung's realm of synchronicity, of '*acts of creation in time*', or *Eros knowing*, connected, feeling, relational, embodied (Jung 1960, CW8: para. 965). Second-stage Dionysian dismemberment is the synchronous universe, an Eros, trickster and feminine mode of knowing and being. Symptomatically, Hillman notes that *zoe*, the life force of the body in Eros, is awakened by this process of divine dismemberment (Hillman 1975: 29). This new consciousness, or *zoe*, is an intimation of wholeness that does not erode differences. New enlivening *zoe* is animistic in a particular awareness of its own *partial* consciousness, i.e., aware of itself as *parts*.

HOLONS

> Rather the crucial experience would be the awareness of the parts *as parts* distinct from each other, dismembered, each with its own light, a state in which the body becomes conscious of itself as a composite of differences. The scintillae and fishes eyes of which Jung speaks . . . may be experienced as embedded in physical expressions. The distribution of Dionysus through matter may be compared with the distribution of consciousness through members, organs, and zones.
>
> *(Hillman 1972/2007: 28)*

Earth Mother consciousness returns in Jung's work as dismembered Dionysus, the fragmented divine body seeding the universe with its archetypes. But this is not all. Dionysus does not comprehend all that is Earth Mother, since the Greek pantheon itself is intrinsically polytheistic; meaning that one god alone makes no sense, is nonsense. It is no accident that these gods are mutually involved, incestuous, quarrelsome and unable to leave humans alone. They *must* be mated or related.

Archetypalist Karl Kerenyi puts it this way:

> Just as Dionysos [sic] is the archetypal reality of *zoe*, so Ariadne is the archetypal reality of the bestowal of soul, of what makes a living creature an individual.
>
> *(Kerenyi 1976: 124)*

He describes *zoe* as instinctual life experienced without limits (ibid.: xxxvi). Hillman's *zoe* consciousness may be of a differentiated divine scattered throughout the cosmos as parts, but it nevertheless lacks creaturely soul, the grounding in a lived human life. To Kerenyi, Ariadne wedding Dionysus is the marriage of instinctual differentiated life force with soul focus and compassion. Ariadne ensouls *zoe*, gives it humanity.

The union of Dionysus and Ariadne is a rare successful conjoining of human and divine. Becoming immortal herself, Ariadne ascends to the stars with her husband, the god. Just as Psyche's wedding to the god of desire, Eros, signifies the union of soul and love, so does Ariadne's marriage provide a soul-full tempering of Dionysus dismembered as *zoe*. Ariadne, or the feminine, makes Dionysian limitlessness creaturely, bearable, experienceable. Ultimately, I will propose that the marriage of Ariadne and Dionysus makes the rejuvenation by *zoe* knowable.

Symbols as Ariadne marriage to Dionysus

> Whether a thing is a symbol or not depends chiefly on the attitude of the observing consciousness; for instance, on whether it regards a given fact not merely as such but also as an expression for something unknown.
>
> *(Jung 1921, CW6: 818)*

I suggest that Dionysian dismemberment as Jung and Hillman together see it is a fundamental condition of fragmented modern consciousness. Not only does it characterize the fragile modern Western ego, but it also pervades knowledge itself through its splintering into academic disciplines. However, the psychology of both Jung and Hillman provides the opportunity of *zoe* as rejuvenated consciousness, by remembering the Dionysian body *as parts*. Such remembering occurs individually in individuation, and could also happen collectively in academia by re-modelling disciplines as *parts* of a never entirely knowable (and so divine) body.

Might it be possible for academic knowing to be at the forefront of a changing paradigm of consciousness, by re-membering its disciplinary splintering in the context of an unlimited *zoe*'s lust for instinctual life? Could the urge to know be infused with the desire to be alive? This book, *Remembering Dionysus*, aims to facilitate such an ambitious project, in its examination of psychology and literature, not as separate fields, but as discrete (and mutually implied) members or parts of a larger body.

Three additions to this mythical perspective on knowing could contribute to re-membering disciplines as parts. All three are arguably ways to invite the feminine into a partnership with masculine knowing, which has been structured as transcen-dent of body and nature. They are the role of symbols in wedding an immanent and transcendent being, Ariadne as symbol of feminine ensoulment of *zoe*, and, thirdly, transdisciplinarity, which will be considered in a later section of this chapter.

First of all, on the symbol: Jung saw its most defining quality as its capacity to express something unknown. Indeed, symbols offer what Hillman, on Jung's treatment of Dionysus, calls *zoe*, in their rebirthing of consciousness.

> A symbol really lives only when it is the best and highest expression for something divined but not yet known to the observer. It then compels his unconscious participation and has a life-giving and life-enhancing effect.
>
> *(Jung 1921, CW6: 819)*

Jung's reference here to the 'best and highest' is a clue to the symbol's ability to unite transcendence and immanence. For a symbol's route to the unknown invokes the archetypal qualities of psyche, those capacities possess roots in the instinctual body, while also extending to the realm of spirit. Disciplinary concepts are symbols when they do *not* forget their connection to the 'living mystery' (see Chapter 1), which Jung says is too often left out of knowing:

> We have to break down life and events, which are self-contained processes, into meanings, images, concepts, well knowing that in doing so we are get-ting further away from the living mystery.
>
> *(Jung 1966, CW15: para. 121)*

Dionysus is the mythical embodiment of such 'living mystery' (ibid.: para. 121). Yet, if knowledge can break down life and events into parts that retain awareness of the living mystery, then that knowledge, written in symbols is Dionysian dis-memberment founding *zoe*, or a consciousness rejuvenated by intuition through knowledge of a limitless instinctual life.

At this point we recognize that knowledge in *zoe* will be written in symbols. Put another way, treating all our disciplines as the articulation of symbols is put-ting them back in touch with the living mystery of the dismembered god. Jungian and archetypal psychology can do this. Another such vision will be through the apparently unrelated development of transdisciplinarity.

> Since every scientific theory contains an hypothesis . . . it is a symbol.
>
> *(Jung 1921, CW6: para. 817)*

On the other hand, Dionysus is a dangerous god to approach too closely, or to offend. Limitless instinctual life as consciousness sounds like a prelude to a maenad condition of inhuman frenzy. *Zoe* must be ensouled, so that Dionysus enters the human world through compassionate love, rather than mindless sacrifice or sacrifice of the mind. Here Ariadne returns as the mistreated, undervalued and abandoned feminine of our age. Stranded far from home, she has been divorced from her divine earthly roots and denied the hero's embrace and queenly status. She is lost, and she has been lost to us.

Perhaps only a god can rescue her. A god such as Dionysus, the wild masculinity of Earth Mother's divine nature, since the heroic ego (Theseus), has lost his feminine side. If Theseus sailed away, maybe it is left to the over-rationalized academy his descendants founded to re-story the wilder masculine in *zoe*. Thereby, we let our disciplined psyche wed Dionysus through Ariadne as soul. For then, knowledge itself becomes *zoe*, in touch with the infinite and poised to rejuvenate modern consciousness. It would also, I suggest, be a knowledge deeply woven into non-human nature, and so ready to work *with* it, rather than upon it.

How does that divine marriage in knowing occur? It happens by means of symbols. Here I suggest that the shift to *zoe* in disciplinary knowing demands that disciplines be re-imaged, re-imagined as symbols, in symbolic language that enlivens the psyche. Disciplines enacted in symbols are fragments of the living mystery, or ecstatic god, made soul-full by psyche as Ariadne.

The knowing psyche becomes Ariadne's, whose embrace of symbolic being is the passion of Dionysus. This union bestows *zoe*. Limitless instinctual life is made human, bearable and enlivening by the work of symbols conjoining transcendent divinity to immanent being.

It is time to look at how transdisciplinary practice also plots, is a plot or narrative, to re-story being through knowing.

Transdisciplinarity and Dionysus

The term 'transdisciplinarity' was coined in 1970, by Jean Piaget to denote a total system, a scheme of uniting all possible disciplines in a claim to encompass all possible knowing (Nicolescu 2005: 1). Given Jungian and archetypal psychology's scepticism about an all-knowing human subject, a far more productive theorizing of transdisciplinarity is that by Basarab Nicolescu and his insistence upon an open system of knowing, that knowledge can never be considered complete (ibid.: 1). Nicolescu gave a valuable overview in his talk at the Congress of Transdisciplinarity in Brazil in 2005, later published as 'Transdisciplinarity – Past, Present and Future' (Nicolescu 2005: 1). G. C. Tympas is probably the first to make extensive use of transdisciplinarity in Jungian research in his fine *Carl Jung and Maximus the Confessor on Psychic Development* (2014).

Nicolescu rejects the totalizing project inherent in Piaget's definition, and dismisses any possibility of a hyperdiscipline, one capable of subsuming all human knowing into a system of perfect knowledge, or ultimate truth. Rather, his structuring emphasizes what he calls 'beyond disciplines' in his transdisciplinarity, which appears to mean beyond the pretensions of any one epistemological construct to encompass all meaning. In this sense, a monotheistic demand for total knowledge gives way to a polyvalent polytheism of knowing.

> Transdisciplinarity concerns that which is at once *between* the disciplines, *across* the different disciplines, and *beyond* all disciplines.
>
> *(Nicolescu 2005: 4)*

What underpins Nicolescu's refusal to imagine a hyperdiscipline is his rejection of the traditional unified human subject of Western modernity, or, put another way, of rational consciousness as a sufficient and only basis for knowledge. For him, as quantum discoveries end the primacy of the dominant scientific method of repeatable experiments, he posits a new human subject for *all* research. Quantum physics discovered that, on the quantum level, measurements cannot be made using the criteria of objectivity: e.g., absolute separation between the observer and the observed, because the way phenomena are measured radically changes the results.

While on the one hand transdisciplinary does aim for a hypothesized unity in knowing, Nicolescu's radically 'open' unity means accepting that humans live on several levels of reality at the same time. It will never be possible to rationally know all psycho–physical realities, not least because some are neither measurable nor stable. These realities cannot be eroded or simplified (Nicolescu 2005: 4). Knowledge will always be in a state of dismemberment despite, or maybe because of, our legacy of a culture of only one divine body (of truth).

Nicolescu's recognition of irreducible differences in disciplinary premises moves his transdisciplinarity into three modes of research: it becomes theoretical, phenomenological and also experimental. As structuring principles to this paradigm–shifting enterprise, Nicolescu offers three axioms of transdisciplinary to replace those of traditional science that go back to Galileo.

Hitherto, many scientific disciplines adhered to the following axioms or fundamental assumptions:

i)   The universe is governed by mathematical laws.
ii) These laws can be discovered by scientific experiment.
iii) Such experiments, if valid, can be perfectly replicated.

> *(Nicolescu 2005: 5)*

Such a privileging of objectivity founds the traditional human subject of knowing as a creature of purely rational consciousness. All other unfortunate human qualities need to be screened out so that the naked empirical facts of the universe may be received without interference or bias. Nicolescu points out that this approach to knowledge has the unfortunate effect of turning the human subject into an object by stripping out feeling and values (Nicolescu 2005: 5).   FLATLAND

The problem lies in the positing of *one* level of reality as foundational to all others. This single way of structuring knowing (hyperdiscipline) then subsumes realities like society or the psyche to its objectivizing paradigm. Of course, objectivity and separation from what is studied, is not, of itself always problematic. Regarding such a posture as inherently superior to knowing based on feeling, body and imagination is. Without using myth, Nicolescu implicitly argues that Sky Father ought not to exclude or devalue Earth Mother consciousness as a basis of knowing and being.

By contrast, Nicolescu's transdisciplinarity explicitly disavows privileging objectivity based on separation because of the human subject's complexity, which exists in both simple and theoretical senses as we will see. Nicolescu's fundamental principles, or three axioms for the methodology of transdisciplinarity, are as follows.

i) The ontological axiom: *There are, in Nature and in our knowledge of Nature, different levels of Reality and, correspondingly, different levels of perception.*
ii) The logical axiom: *The passage from one level of Reality to another is insured by the logic of the included middle.*
iii) The complexity axiom: *The Structure of the totality of levels of Reality or perception is a complex structure: every level is what it is because all levels exist at the same time.*

(Nicolescu 2005: 6)

This approach to what we know and how we know it amounts to a paradigm shift from the competition of disciplines insisting on their unique perspectives to one that treats the universe as multidimensional. Reality is now complex. So are human beings. Nicolescu is emphatic that no one level of reality, such as sight perception, for example, can constitute a dominant position for knowing. No sense organ or academic discipline is capable of understanding all the other levels of reality in total. Knowledge in any of its forms is necessarily incomplete or open (Nicolescu 2005: 7). The god is in pieces. 'He' cannot be put together to make a perfect being modelled on an ego divorced from the other.

To repeat: *transdisciplinarity insists that academic disciplines cannot legitimately exist in a hierarchy where one is privileged above all the others.* One exciting implication here is that such an approach does away with the interior/exterior boundary of knowing.

Knowledge is neither exterior nor interior: it is simultaneously exterior and interior. The studies of the universe and of the human being sustain one another.

(Nicolescu 2005: 8)

As Nicolescu reiterates, his transdisciplinarity vitally undoes the classical subject/object division in favour of the ternary: subject, object, hidden third that is both subject and object (Nicolescu 2005: 8). This 'included middle' was explicitly prohibited by the previous rational paradigm, where A could not be also non-A. It does not, he notes, eradicate those types of logical knowing that do insist that A cannot be non-A. Rather, it shows them to be incomplete: they are one level of reality, not a primal truth framing all of them. Traditional objective science has its place as one *part* of the dismembered body of academic knowing that we call 'disciplines'.

Complexity, too, needs a context for its inclusion in Nicolescu's transdisciplinarity. Arguably, the development of Complexity Theory, or 'emergence' as an evolutionary paradigm towards the end of the twentieth century was a necessary prerequisite for Nicolescu's project. Complexity Theory, or emergence, suggests that evolutionary change occurred *and still occurs*, not by species competing for resources, but rather by the interpenetration of complex life systems. Moreover, in a move suggestive for Jungian studies, Nicolescu recognizes Complexity Theory's ancient lineage in making it indigenous to his transdisciplinarity.

> From a transdisciplinary point of view, complexity is a modern form of the very ancient principle of universal interdependence.
>
> *(Nicolescu 2005: 13)*

This hypothesis of complexity has been extended to Jungian psychology by scholars such as Helene Shulman and Joe Chambray. They look at how Jung's synchronicity and archetypes could connect with this new evolutionary perspective (Cambray 2012; Shulman 1997). Chapter 5 will consider further complexity evolution for Jungian symbols in psychology and literature. Symbols, as the rite of Ariadne and Dionysus, incarnate ensouled *zoe*. They do so in ways fruitful for revisioning literature and psychology beyond disciplinary competitiveness to another kind of interdependency.

In reality, everything is connected to everything else. For now, Nicolescu is concerned to preserve the openness of complexity theory to multiple and also non-rational modes of reality. So where some theorists are looking for a mathematical complexity, which would, in this notion of transdisciplinarity, limit the levels of reality that it could encompass, Nicolescu proposes the structure of horizontal and vertical axes.

> It is therefore useful to distinguish between the horizontal complexity, which refers to a single level of reality and vertical complexity, which refers to several levels of Reality.
>
> *(Nicolescu 2005: 13)*

Symptomatically, Nicolescu sees his three axioms as innately values generating. The hidden third, or included middle, emphasizes interdependence. Given that humans and the universe are regarded as mutually sustaining, we either have values or chaos. It follows that intelligence and education need a radical rethinking that moves them towards plurality. Transdisciplinarity requires at least three types of intelligence, including the conventional understanding of it as rational and analytical. Yet, added to what Jung would describe as Logos consciousness, are also intelligences close to his Eros, or Earth Mother, knowing: the intelligences of feeling and of the body. *para?*

Continuing on Nicolescu's path to transdisciplinarity, these revised intelligences demand that complexity be applied to the question of meaning. So here horizontal meaning is what most traditional academic disciplines do, situating meaning at one level of reality. By contrast, a transdisciplinary education would provide meaning vertically, at several levels of reality with none privileged over the others. Nicolescu suggests poetry, art and quantum physics as already providing vertical or multiple levels of meaning (Nicolescu 2005: 17).

To illustrate his revolution of knowledge, Nicolescu compares traditional disciplines providing fragments of one level of being to cultures and religions which anticipate transdisciplinarity by spanning multiple realities. What he calls 'techno-science', the alliance of instrumental technology with traditional science's repeatable experiments, is confined to the zone of the 'object' in his tripartite vision of subject, object and hidden third (Nicolescu 2005: 17). He calls for technoscience to become a 'culture', by entering into a dialogue with religion that would expand its zones of reality to all three (Nicolescu 2005: 17).

Nicolescu's portrayal of transdisciplinary education begins to look remarkably similar to the ethos of Earth Mother consciousness and its *articulation* into a dispersed Dionysus.

> The transdisciplinary education, founded on the transdisciplinary methodology, allows us to establish links between persons, facts, images, representations, fields of knowledge and action and to discover the Eros of learning during our entire life. The creativity of the human being is conditioned by permanent questioning and permanent integration.
>
> *(Nicolescu 2005: 14)*

By making hypothetical connections (that can never be one discipline taking over the reality proposition of an–other), transdisciplinary education generates Eros, feeling, perhaps even rejuvenation (*zoe*). Here is education in the framework of a theory of complexity that positions humans *within and part of* the creativity of non–human nature. Nicolescu's Eros is Earth Mother in knowing, and synchronous in epistemology.

In particular, the motif of subject, object and hidden third is a helpful image of the underlying shift in transdisciplinarity to what I have been calling dismembering and re-membering. It illustrates that knowing is both interior and exterior. Ultimately, these principles unite Complexity Theory with transdisciplinarity's challenge to the atomization of education in discrete disciplines.

For far from acknowledging dismembered Dionysus, traditional academic disciplines are all too used to rejecting any consciousness of each other as viable, yet different levels of reality. In the modern university, our mutually indifferent, or even antagonistic disciplines have no consciousness of themselves as dismembered parts. They therefore have no *zoe*, no dynamic life-force in their separate unacknowledged incompleteness.

What is needed is a vision, structure or image to sustain the radical dismembered openness of this kind of transdisciplinary future.

For transdisciplinarity, a Big Picture is not only possible but vitally necessary, even if it will never be formulated as a closed theory . . .
This does not mean the emergence of a unique planetary culture and of a
unique planetary religion, but of a new *transcultural and transreligious attitude.*

(Nicolescu 2005: 19 [italics in original])

Understanding transdisciplinarity, united with Complexity Theory, as embracing Jung and Hillman's vision of dismembered Dionysus is not to found a new
religion. Rather, it is a way to become conscious of the return of feminine, Earth
Mother potentials sorely needed in a Western-dominated modernity too addicted
to Sky Father dualism. Dionysus is one avatar of Earth Mother returned via the
recognition of knowing as divinely dismembered, not dissected and dead. When
Dionysus is re-membered by a transdisciplinary frame of knowing, then the god
regains his capacity for *zoe*, and transdisciplinarity gains a story that treats knowledge as open, as divine, in its disassembled parts.

Dionysus emerges in this millennium to figure Earth Mother in the shattered body of the old god whose marriage to Ariadne is an essential ensouling
of his dangerously fragmented being. For, as Kerenyi argues, *zoe* bestowed by
re-membering Dionysus is an absolute condition of instinctual life that is entirely
ignorant of its opposite, death or Thanatos (Kerenyi 1976: xxxii, xxxiv). 'Bios' is
the term for a creaturely life that includes a sense of its ending. *Zoe* is life without
end, pure instinct, and divine.

So human consciousness may long for rejuvenation from Dionysian *zoe* while
also being vulnerable to its inhuman, undifferentiated divinity. Kerenyi insists
that by marrying Dionysus and being elevated to the stars, Ariadne traces the path
of the soul reborn. Indeed, here we see both her and Dionysus as more characterized forms of Earth Mother.

If transdisciplinarity has its story, a history in Dionysian dismemberment and
marriage to Ariadne, then the divine fragments, those bits of different realities in
the disciplines, have their being in what Jung called symbols. In fact, the marriage of Ariadne and Dionysus is incarnated in symbols. Disciplines in Nicolescu's
transdisciplinarity are written in Jungian symbols because their language has to
remain open to the 'living mystery'. Disciplinary language becomes symbolic language, because to follow any discipline in a transdisciplinary (and Dionysian way)
requires a symbolic attitude.

To retain that vital 'openness', even so-called facts become symbols. As Jung
puts it, referring to symbols:

Whether a thing is a symbol or not depends chiefly on the attitude of the
observing consciousness; for instance, on whether it regards a given fact not
merely as such but also as an expression for something unknown. Hence it is
quite possible for a man to establish a fact which does not appear in the least
symbolic to himself, but is profoundly so to another consciousness.

(Jung 1921, CW6: para. 818)

"included"

can't the included media psyche study?

One can be disciplinary and reject a symbolic attitude, or be transdisciplinary and re-member Dionysus to evoke symbols in the language of knowing. It is time to look further at Nicolescu's invocation to the include middle, and how this might work for a transdisciplinary notion of psychology and literature.

Dionysus for psychology and literature: The included middle in Jung's symbols, archetypes and novels

As argued previously, Jung's *Collected Works* are closer to novels than to conventional scientific writing. Put in a transdisciplinary sense, they embody the included middle between psychology and literature: they are both. Moreover, I suggest that Jung's *Collected Works* are feminist novels in the sense that their animistic nature serves his project by turning to what has been marginalized in modernity as feminine. Such a feminine includes what he calls feeling and connection as Eros, as opposed discrimination and separation as Logos. It also summons the trickster androgynous plurality of Earth Mother and her complexity creativity that he named synchronicity.

Jung, the feminist novelist, is also Dionysian, as Hillman diagnosed in his two-stage dismemberment. First of all, there is dualism, the rending into oppositions that pepper Jung's terminology. More profound and more feminist friendly is Jung's second-stage Dionysian dismemberment into parts aware of themselves as parts, with an emphasis on Earth mother, embodied consciousness. Jung's trickster and animistic writing is the dispersed corporeality of the ecstatic god.

Taking this unlikely push of Jung into feminism further is to consider his writing as proto-transdisciplinary. Crucially, Jung's stress on the impossibility of complete knowledge given the indigenous mystery of the psyche is one factor that his work shares with Nicolescu. Here we can see that Jung has the potential to be a stabilizing force in Nicolescu's transdisciplinarity where the latter repeatedly warns against the trap of erecting some hyperdiscipline, as a pretension to control all meaning.

This is one example of how Jung might contribute to the transdisciplinary project. There are more as we start to perceive psychoanalysis and Jungian studies as intrinsically transdisciplinary in their acceptance of multiple levels of reality. Dreams, for example, in these psychologies, are real. They are also necessarily of a different order of reality than social engagement, historical events (no longer present to the senses), bodily perception or cultural representations. Psychologies of Freudian and Jungian persuasions have a particular expertise in working on multiple levels of reality as simultaneous and *complex* forms of knowing.

As an example of taking Jung's Dionysian feminism a stage further into transdisciplinarity, I want to consider the Jungian symbol further as an instance of the hidden third, here to be brought into knowing as the included middle. Jung writes about the symbol as a specific type of image, which is itself a manifestation of the unconscious as imag[e]-ination, the psyche as intrinsically image-making. Looking primarily at images in words, we recall that Jung called 'signs' those images standing for a relatively known or stable meaning, while 'symbols' are pointers to something relatively unknown, or not yet known (CW15: para. 105).

Symbols connect the conscious ego to the archetypal collective unconscious. They therefore are prime examples of Nicolescu's 'vertical', or multiple levels of reality, being at one level perceptual and on another intuitive, and on yet another spiritual, in the sense of pertaining to the immaterial unknown. Here I want to emphasize that Jungian symbols are far from icons of disconnection from the embodied world. Given that Jungian archetypes are inherited potentials, they have a bodily as well as spiritual pole (Jung 1960, CW8: para. 367). In transdisciplinary terms, symbols derived from archetypes operate vertically to manifest realities of body, feeling and spirit.

In this way symbols can activate all Nicolescu's intelligences of body, feeling and analytical intellect. They are the *third* term between the different levels of evoked reality. In terms of literature, the symbol of a rose in a love poem can be felt somatically and erotically as well as analytically. This symbol is also an idea about love in ways that are profoundly human and connecting, as well as divine and transcendent.

A Jungian symbol connects the psyche to what matters. It does so because it is the third that is both matter and psyche counteracting Sky Father binary logic that there is the human psyche *inside* us separated from matter *outside*. The symbol is the included middle. It breaks down the separation of subject versus object as the only basis for knowing. It is psyche activated by words in touch with the body, feeling, imagination, spirit. *manifested*

Finally we must notice that this symbol as included middle is an engine of complexity in the sense that it is a portal between human and non-human nature. Jungian symbols are scraps of the dismembered Dionysian body. They materialize *zoe*. They are the animated sparks that embody Earth Mother, the creatures that make the feminine texture of the novel. A symbol for Jung is an image of the deep psyche that stitches us into the cosmos as an act of feminine knowing. With symbols we know as Ariadne and we experience instinctual life as *zoe*. Such symbols are necessarily fragments aware of themselves as parts. *Mm!*

To continue this book's focus on Dionysus for literary studies as well as Jungian and archetypal psychology, we need to remember, and re-member, that more than the novel is implied in Dionysian transdisciplinarity. After all, this wild god also gave humankind its comedy and tragedy, two primal genres that will continue to haunt the ambivalent relations of psyche and literature, resurfacing in the writing of both Jung and Hillman.

The symbol is the included middle?

Dionysus for comedy and tragedy *or "psyche" is the included middle?*

Both comedy and tragedy as dramatic genres stem from Dionysian rites in Ancient Greece (Kerenyi 1976). While continuing to appear in play form, these dual modes of expression pervade subsequent literature, including the development of the novel. Moreover, Dionysian comedy and tragedy influence the formation of

subject / entity-that-is-both-subject-and-object / object

No — isn't the "3d term" the "included middle" the power is energy that enables the psychology itself, in particular those psychologies that pause before the instinctual unrestraint of the unconscious.

The archetypalist Kerenyi reports that both comedy and tragedy evolved into sacred dramas from songs and dancing in Dionysian festivals (ibid.: 321–42). Comedy included animals as characters. It demonstrated a universe of ecstasy in which social rules are unknown. Tragedy, a word meaning 'goat song', is a figuration of sacrifice to the god. Dionysian sacrifices are killed both *for* the god and *as* the god.

Therefore, in comedy and tragedy something primal about the relation of humans, animals and gods is renewed. When Athenians dismissed a play, they said that, 'it has nothing to do with Dionysus' (ibid.: 1976: 329). It is the presence of the god that guarantees *zoe*, the reborn instinctual joy of comic or tragic sacred drama.

In *Pagan Grace*, Ginette Paris describes the divine union of psychology and literature in these Dionysian plays by noting that the Dionysia had to be a *communal* rite (Paris 1998: 12). Festivals of Dionysus involved careful planning of their religious, psychological and practical components. In order to secure against a dangerous liberation of Dionysian unrestraint, the god must emerge from a culture or a community. The preparation must be psychological as well as practical, personal as well as collective, mundane as well as spiritual (Paris 1998: 12).

Athens inaugurated the festival of drama to honour the wild god. In this way, the meticulous planning of a major multilayered event in religious, social and artistic terms ensured that Dionysus did not escape the theatres. So the communal rites of Dionysus, plays reversing the so-called natural order, involved holding a dramatic competition, rehearsing actors and feeding crowds. Animals ruled, and women refused sex to men who continued to wage wars.

In the tragic hero's inevitable doom, we have the sacrifice and the god himself – dismembered. As Shakespeare later characterized Antony of *Antony and Cleopatra* in Dionysian terms, the hero when torn apart *became* the god:

> His face was as the heavens; and therein stuck
> A sun and moon, which kept their course, and lighted
> The little O, the earth.
> . . . His legs bestrid the ocean: his rear'd arm
> Crested the world: his voice was propertied
> As all the tuned spheres, and that to friends;
> But when he meant to quail and shake the orb,
> He was as rattling thunder. For his bounty,
> There was no winter in't; an autumn 'twas
> That grew the more by reaping: his delights
> Were dolphin-like; they show'd his back above
> The element they lived in: in his livery
> Walk'd crowns and crownets; realms and islands were
> As plates dropp'd from his pocket.
> *(Shakespeare 2011, Act V sc. 2, 93–112)*

The tragic hero is the dismembered god, and is the one dismembered as sacrifice to the god. Antony falls because he fatally refused to acknowledge that ecstatic divinity driving *his* lusts for power and Cleopatra properly belonged to another.

Above all, Paris stresses the *organization* essential to incorporating Dionysus successfully into the community. The god cannot be tackled alone, nor can he be approached casually by the group. To the Greeks, an individual's madness was actually a punishment of the god, not an acceptable part of the rite (Paris 1998: 19). Hence, dramatic literature is a vital and vitally communal conduit for Dionysian *zoe* as a collective act of sacrifice and celebration.

Perhaps this lineage supports the later genre of the novel's association with the animistic feminine? On the one hand, Paris asserts that Dionysus retains a link with an ancient feminine power shown by his visit to the underworld to rescue and restore to life his mother, Semele (Paris 1998: 30). The only successful resurrection of a human in Greek myth, Semele's return signifies the divine limitlessness of Dionysus's *zoe,* and also that she too incarnates Earth Mother qualities of death and rebirth, the cycle of the seasons.

Even more indicative is the role of Ariadne in the feminine novel taking on Dionysian energies from tragic and comic drama. Kerenyi suggests that she was originally an Earth Mother type of goddess of Crete (Kerenyi 1976: 124). As wife of Dionysus, she ensouls *zoe,* making instinctual life human and bearable. The novel, of course, marks a passage from communal rites of art to individual communion with a book. Hence Ariadne receives the ecstasies of tragic and comic heroes and ensouls them in a form bearable to the single embodied psyche. The novel is Ariadne's entry into our consciousness.

So now, Ursula Le Guin's treatment of the novel as a modification of epic hero stories of warrior poetry deserves another look. For she continues her criticism of singular dominating heroes into noting how modernity's dominant mode of rationalist science is so swayed by this persisting culture of war (Le Guin 1986). From archaic spear points emanates the drive to construct intercontinental missiles. The epic hero becomes the tragic hero of drama, in his destructive desire to conquer and rule. How might a psychology containing Dionysian drama start to change such a disastrous mind-set?

After all, literature bears witness to a challenge to the epic hero of inevitable and ongoing warfare. Fortunately, the hero myth of singularity and conquest, a prototype Sky Father consciousness through separation, meets Dionysus when thrust into tragic drama. A masculine god with some of the fluidity and corporeality of the more primal Earth Mother, Dionysus dismembers heroes who do not recognize his sacred mysteries. Greek drama is arguably a rite to negotiate the creation powers of myth, making the community more conscious. In the stone-built sacred container of the theatre, Dionysus draws in the community to experience his unbounded energies.

Later still, the novel privileges Dionysian comedy in the sense of fostering, animistically, many characters, and so a more diverse styling of the psyche. Comedy is rooted in Dionysian phallic-driven dances and songs. It celebrates sexuality, unrestraint, fertility and boundary crossing. While novels do contain tragic heroes who are dismembered to, and as, the god, they also, like Dionysus himself, retain a tie to the primal feminine in their animistic plurality of embodied spirits.

Here, Jung's Christian chicken is poised between comedy and tragic bathos:

> I happened to come in just as she was bringing back the decapitated cock and saying to my mother: 'He died like a Christian, although he was so wicked. He cried out, "Forgive me, forgive me!" before I cut off his head, so now he'll go to heaven.'
>
> *(Jung 1944a, CW12: para. 494)*

Dionysian comedy bursts the boundaries between human and animal kingdoms in the cause of divinity. Dionysian tragedy severs the bodies of tyrants like the wicked chicken, and shows them to possess souls that suffer alongside mere mortals. It is time to end this chapter by looking at another Dionysian quality that Jung, in particular, shares with literature, that of spontaneity and improvisation. This proves, unsurprisingly, to be bound up with the matter of the feminine.

Dionysus and spontaneity (return of the feminine)

> The anima has an erotic, emotional character, the animus a rationalizing one. Hence most of what men say about feminine eroticism, and particularly about the emotional life of women, is derived from their own anima projections and distorted accordingly. On the other hand, the astonishing assumptions and fantasies that women make about men come from the activity of the animus, who produces an inexhaustible supply of illogical arguments and false explanations.
>
> *(Jung 1925/1954, CW17: para. 338)*

This quotation is Jung in Dionysian mode, because it both deploys and exploits a *topos* of spontaneity. While both his concepts of anima and animus are defined in oppositional terms – anima as Eros and emotionality, animus as potential rationality – the flavour of this passage is not one of rational balance. Indeed, the indictment of all women as subject to ludicrous fantasies about men is comic in its lack of proportion. It is only a careful scrutiny of the semantic relations between these three sentences that offers something more than spontaneous irritable prejudice on the part of the male writer.

For in following the *logic* of these propositions, the excessive intensity of the 'inexhaustible' animus gives a hint of *zoe,* or life released from a dismembered psyche. The passage begins almost mimicking oppositional balance with 'erotic, emotional' answered by 'rationalising'. The speaker is ungendered, all knowing, and so the proper god-like rational progenitor of transcendent concepts.

Then, in sentence two, emerges a more immanent embodied perspective of a man whose view of women is biased by his internal anima. So who, from this starting point, speaks in the third sentence of those 'astonishing assumptions'?

To follow through the argument, it has to be the anima and not the writer's ego. Gender polarity dismembers the psyche so that the inner other may utter with Dionysian abandon!

What a reader cannot ascertain for certain is whether the anima's maenad like tearing apart a masculine target is truly spontaneous or not. Does trickster Jung set up the reader to see if we spot this minute performance of anima unreliability? Or, does he merely find her overcoming his better judgement in a Dionysian spontaneous riot? Either way, the rush of *zoe* experienced in the comic unrestraint of that third sentence is yet another instance, alongside the Christian chicken, of Jung's embrace of Dionysian comedy as an organ of his psychology.

Moreover, the several possibilities over the nature of the spontaneity here brings Jung's writing into the orbit of a literary genre recently outlined by Randy Fertel, in *A Taste for Chaos* (2015). Fertel identifies improvisation as a major generic tradition stemming from works as foundational as those of Homer, Milton's epics, novels such as *Tristram Shandy* by Lawrence Sterne, and modernist works like James Joyce's *Ulysses*.

Moreover, as will be considered in a later chapter, Fertel also includes Jung's *The Red Book* as a work of literary improvisation. However, Fertel's generic improvisation is not an unmitigated celebration of spontaneity. It does produce common, cross-cultural and trans-historical characteristics, but one of these is to discover limits to the unrestrained embrace of 'a poetics of presence' (Fertel 2015: 98).

While Fertel does not identify improvisation with Dionysus, he does emphatically discover the presence of compromise, or, in effect, in mythical terms the need for ensouling Ariadne to temper untameable *zoe*. When it comes to human inventiveness, casting out the fetters of reason and structure can only go so far. It falters before either discovering some fundamental pattering in the universe or, as he notes of Thomas Mann's explorations, becomes inhumanly savage; e.g., fascist (ibid.: 406).

Rather than push the re-invention of structuring into its least soulful mode (refusing Ariadne), I have been suggesting in this chapter that Jung's work *as a whole* draws in Ariadne as feminine soul, an aspect of invoking Earth Mother. We see this in microcosm in the tiny examples of his comedy, in the chicken and the vociferous anima.

Finally, I suggest that, just as literature mates the Dionysian with comedy and tragedy in the communal rite of theatre, and then stitches Ariadne animistically into the novel, so Jungian psychology ensouls *zoe* for a new age. It is time to look in more detail at how this *works* to re-member Dionysus for psychology and literature.

3

DIONYSUS IGNORED, OR HOW TO SAVE JUNG FROM *THE RED BOOK*

Introduction

Published for the first time in 2009, C. G. Jung's *The Red Book; Liber Novus* (here-after *The Red Book*), is a startlingly dismembered work. Conforming to no one literary or disciplinary convention, it places paintings, meditations and dialogues within the physical apparatus of a handwritten manuscript. While lamenting aspects of modernity, it visually resembles a medieval illuminated text. This chapter will examine early readings of *The Red Book* as they either emphatically resist the Dionysian elements of the text, or later move towards something that argu-ably anticipates the transdisciplinary Dionysian paradigm that may just produce academic renewal and *zoe*.

Re-membering Dionysus is above all a way of reading and writing that pierces the realm of instinctual life that is *zoe*. It invites the feminine soul as Ariadne to embrace its rejuvenating sacred powers. In the following examination of Jung's radically dismembered text by scholars and Jungians, we witness the struggle to contain, limit or even dismiss Dionysus, as in studies by Sonu Shamdasani and Wolfgang Giegerich.

Following these efforts of the heroic ego are different treatments by Jungians seeking to find disciplinary sustenance in *The Red Book*. These efforts see the work as evoking the sacred in ways plural enough to spot fragments of Dionysus in their writing. By responding to the text as a bringer of life to knowledge, they find its capacity for renewal, whether that be of something as disciplined as psychology, or for the expressions of the sacred of these times.

Ultimately, readings by figures such as Robin van Loben Sels, Sanford L. Drob and Walter Odajnyk glimpse and begin to re-member the wild god in his poten-tial for renewal. Such work constellates what could be liberation into Diony-sian transdisciplinarity, as I shall show. It offers a vision of Jung that saves him *for* the Dionysian rather than the imposition of a totalizing vision promoted by Shamdasani and Giegerich. To what extent has the publication of *The Red Book* itself facilitated a debate, as yet unrecognized, <u>for its *animation*</u>, its participation in anima or soul?

Re-membering The Red Book: *The debate*

Within three years of the publication of C. G. Jung's, *The Red Book*, surprisingly diverse opinions emerged of the implications of this radically unconventional text. These opinions range from Shamdasani's assertion that *The Red Book*, which he edited, is the 'single most important documentary source' (Shamdasani 2009: 95) and 'the key to comprehending [the] genesis of *The Collected Works*' (ibid.: 2), to Jungian analyst Giegerich's indictment that it represents Jung's 'fabrication' of the unconscious (Giegerich 2010: 389).

Rather than finding a consensus, first analyses have been revealing in their differences. There is as yet no broad agreement on the meaning of *The Red Book* in relation to either Jung's *Collected Works* or the practice of Jungian psychotherapy. This chapter will argue for the *productive* value of this field of dismembered parts or possibilities. Most suggestive of Dionysus, I contend, is the unexpressed transdisciplinary longing found in some of these readings. For example, in the preface to the first book-length study of *The Red Book* by Stanford L. Drob (2012), Stanton Marlan quotes eminent analyst and scholar Murray Stein on the challenges to reading posed by this unclassifiable text.

> It's not easy to get the proportion right or to find a way to talk about this strange work in a way that holds it but does not over or underestimate its value.
> *(Stein personal communication to Marlan in Drob 2012: ix)*

The suggestion of a polarization around the reception of *The Red Book* is also significant because of the unusual circumstances of its publication. In turn, these textual controversies are compounded by the form of the book not resembling anything else directly published by Jung. Handwritten with verbal and visual images indicating a wide variety of cultural sources, *The Red Book* was not authorized for publication during Jung's lifetime, unlike everything else that exists today in *The Collected Works*. Even *Memories, Dreams, Reflections* (1961), which was published after Jung died, was a project upon which he collaborated and contributed some specifically written material. If Jung's work is considered as some sort of whole, which it often is, then *The Red Book* is not so much a dismembered limb as a previously hidden organ, newly dug up (by others) and placed next to the previously collected scattered parts.

After all, in semi-autobiographical *Memories, Dreams, Reflections*, Jung alludes to *The Red Book* as abandoned due to its unsatisfactory aesthetic form (Jung 1963/83: 213). As a result, the relationship between what Shamdasani aptly calls 'a work of psychology in literary form', and the kind of writing that populates *The Collected Works*, is open to question (Shamdasani 2009: 3). These questions become more insistent when recognizing that *The Red Book* today satisfies no one literary or psychological genre. *The Red Book* is peculiarly Dionysian because it frustrates disciplinary divisions in its perverse fragmentation. This book poses questions to the history of writing and knowing in ways that could transform what is considered psychology and what is considered literature.

As an experiment in psychological writing, *The Red Book* is also an investigation into the parameters of art. As Drob remarks in one of the most penetrating valuations of its Dionysian quality in his *Reading* The Red Book*: An Interpretative Guide to C. G. Jung's* Liber Novus, such a multifaceted text invites ongoing and multiple meanings (Drob 2012: xii–xxi).

The next part of this chapter will deal with those readings designed to dismiss the spectre of Dionysian chaos. Such a refusal of the Dionysian is enacted by regarding *The Red Book* as a prelude to *The Collected Works*, and serves to limit the meanings possible in either publication. I will then show that more Dionysian approaches provide multiple relationships and fertile generativity between these texts, though a confluence of research in both depth psychology and cultural theory over 'field' thinking.

One aim here is to save Jung's plural possibilities of Dionysian re-membering from being curtailed by measuring his later works by singular interpretations of *The Red Book*. Having saved Jung from punitive readings of *The Red Book*, Chapter 4 attempts to save *The Red Book* from Jung in the sense of having its qualities restricted by constructing Jung as 'author'. Although no one doubts that Jung wrote and painted *The Red Book*, the notion of author in modernity is a cultural rather than natural one. By drawing upon literary disciplinary resources, I will show that *The Red Book* can be liberated from Jung as its 'authorizing presence'. It can, and arguably longs to be, re-membered as and through Dionysus.

In keeping with the theme of this book, that Jungian psychology and literary studies share an unconscious and unwritten history, it is worth noting the productive paradox that de-throning Jung as author actually serves to reinstate his core ideas on the value of decentring the ego in understanding. Applying literary scepticism about authorial control of meaning to Jung reveals the psychologist anticipating literary studies' challenge to conscious control of meaning in language. So it is appropriate to begin with the editor's peculiar positioning of *The Red Book* as requiring no outside interpretation at all (Shamdasani 2009: 32).

Saving Jung from *The Red Book*

Sonu Shamdasani's dream of history

Shamdasani points to the 'Epilogue' of 'Commentaries' within *The Red Book* itself as showing that the book contains its own self-explication from its author (Shamdasani 2009: 32). *Liber Novus*, as he always refers to *The Red Book*, needs no additional interpretation since it provides its own (ibid.: 32). This proposition is even more problematic than it might first appear to be, given that, for Shamdasani, it substantiates the notion that his own historical approach to the material effectively insulates *The Red Book* from any further outside analyses.

Put another way. Although Shamdasani's notion of history is both invaluable and irreplaceable in connecting Jung to his time and to his predecessors, it is also, perilously limiting. These limits are not confined to insisting on a singular account of *The Red Book* that refuses to liberate its nature as *parts*. Perhaps more significant is how Shamdasani's work rejects Jung's emphasis of the primacy of the creative unconscious. For at the heart of Jung's contribution to understanding the human psyche, I argue, is what James Hillman said of Pablo Picasso and Wallace Stevens:

> They realize that they are imagination before they are history.
>
> *(Hillman & Ventura 1992: 63)*

Shamdasani uses metaphors of the 'centre' and of 'genesis' to position *The Red Book* with regard to *The Collected Works* (Shamdasani 2009: 63, 95). While admitting the different form and even differences of content between *The Red Book* and *The Collected Works*, they nevertheless remain indivisible in his analysis. No dismembering between hidden manuscript and published papers is permitted.

> One is simply not in the position to comprehend the genesis of Jung's late work, nor to fully understand what he was attempting to achieve, without studying *Liber Novus*. At the same time the *Collected Works* can in part be considered an indirect commentary on *Liber Novus*. Each mutually explicates the other.
>
> *(ibid.: 87)*

As the 'centre' of Jung's oeuvre, as the editor's introduction begins, *The Red Book* was 'at the center of Jung's self-experimentation . . . nothing less than the central book in his oeuvre', so the introduction concludes; its circularity of vocabulary making the point inescapable (Shamdasani 2009: 95). In a revealing interview with John Beebe, published in the journal *Psychological Perspectives*, Shamdasani gives this notion of relentless centrality a human dimension by saying that here 'Jung becomes Jung' (Shamdasani & Beebe 2010: 421). Before *The Red Book*, Jung's publications show that he could have gone in the direction of comparative mythology, whereas *The Red Book* contains themes that Jung would elaborate for the rest of his career.

It is to John Beebe that Shamdasani explains his notion of history and biography in ways that channel understanding in a very specific direction.

> SS: I think the first task of any biography is reconstructing the subject's own self-understanding. That is what I tried to do in my introduction to *Liber Novus* . . . that's as far as I think one can go. One can reconstruct someone's

self-understanding: how the historical actors perceive their own actions, render the context intelligible and leave it at that . . . And not fill in the gaps with fantasy and speculation.

(Shamdasani & Beebe 2010: 414)

Beebe's reply to this definition of biography is to gently point out that Jungian analysts, by contrast, prefer a more liberated, even imaginative notion of interpretation; to which Shamdasani rejoins that such interpretation belongs in a different discipline (Shamdasani & Beebe 2010: 414). The motif of genesis and of centre provides a clue to the narrative by which Shamdasani is conceiving his own discipline. One could go so far as to say that Shamdasani is constructing an origin myth out of *The Red Book*. Crucially, it is one that refuses any connection to other disciplines. No re-membering of psychology and literature must pollute even this 'literary' (his word) psychology.

Alleging that Jung says that this work contains the 'nucleus' for his future psychology, Shamdasani positions *The Red Book* as the originating force, genesis as verb. In his three uses of 'genesis' in the Introduction, all are as verbs and not of Genesis as text, the first book of the Bible. 'Genesis' is what *The Red Book* does for *The Collected Works*. For that reason, *The Red Book* is 'primary documentation', and 'the single most important documentary source' even to much of what 'is written on Jung' (Shamdasani 2009: 95).

In effect, Shamdasani's *Liber Novus* is gateway to Jung as authorizing Father God of his psychology and writing. Just as Wolfgang Giegerich, with very different motives, ascribes a biblical fantasy to Jung's use of the term 'new book' (*Liber Novus* (Shamdasani 2009: 63, 95)), so to Shamdasani, *The Red Book* is the Bible, *Liber Novus*, to a significantly worded project of 'understanding' *The Collected Works*. To Shamdasani, *Liber Novus* means a new Bible, one that can provide an authorizing presence of Jung in his conventionally published work.

The Red Book as this type of bible, conceived as a record of a genesis-type creation of Jung's world, has implicit and important ideas for knowledge. For, by suggesting that historical biography should aim for the 'self-understanding' of the subject, Shamdasani infers that such knowledge is possible (Shamdasani & Beebe 2010: 414). To Shamdasani, *The Red Book* can supply crucial parts of Jung's self-understanding, especially when read as providing what is missing from *The Collected Works*, and vice versa.

Such an idea implies far more than that historical figures possess a sense of their personal and intellectual identity. For the notion of a reconstructable self-understanding relies upon the idea of a coherent stable self; and moreover, that such as self is to be found in writing. Even the term 'primary documentation' suggests that meaning in words is fundamentally fixed, can be ascertained by reconstructing historical and biographical context, and, crucially, has a subsequent stabilizing force on writing that is done later.

Primary documents are the material witness to the genesis-effect of *The Red Book* on *The Collected Works*. Therefore they must be read as vehicles of a stable truth of self, incarnated in language, with a secure, comprehensible and consistent meaning. Nothing could more determinedly banish fluid, liminal Dionysus, the god whose instability of meaning is so extreme that he is both the sacrifice and that which must be sacrificed to. In addition, Dionysus means polytheism, while fixed meanings imply a dualism based on a singular, totalizing god.

Given such a rationally monotheistic notion of writing in which the author becomes the father-god of the text, it is not surprising to find Shamdasani insisting upon *The Red Book*, not as experimental *writing*, but as records of scientific experiments. Experimental science took from monotheism its dualistic notion of truth, as inferred from experimental research in which words are transparent figures that merely record transcendent and stable truth.

Shamdasani tells his readers that *Liber Novus* follows the material in the preceding Black Books closely. In The Black Books are few dreams. Mostly the material stems from 'active imagination' that Shamdasani firmly calls 'records of an experiment' (Shamdasani & Beebe 2010: 24). The experiment is definitely not one of writing fiction, for he reports that active imagination to Jung requires fidelity to a source of images considered external to the will (ibid.: 30).

Shamdasani admits to some differences between the 'records' of the Black Books and the aesthetic qualities of *The Red Book* in Jung 'working' the material to differentiate characters. For example, Philemon speaks the 'Seven Sermons to the Dead' in *The Red Book*, whereas the 'I' figure does so in The Black Books. What Shamdasani characteristically does not do is to consider that Jung's noting of differences within *The Red Book* go further than his own. In the first place, Shamdasani does not examine the sentences in *Memories, Dreams, Reflections* in which Jung expresses dissatisfaction with the aesthetic fabulation within *The Red Book*. That Jung turned away from *The Red Book* in later life at the very least problematizes the whole idea of a coherent and consistent self-understanding.

If the Jung of the beautiful paintings and poetic writing of *The Red Book* in the early years of the century later changed his mind about this form of psychological expression, then Shamdasani's insistence on *Liber Novus* and *The Collected Works* as mutually completing *can only be partially valid*. The problem of relying upon an author as a stabilizing god of meaning is when the god gets capricious, as Jung knew well. If authors guarantee meaning, then it matters when they change their mind. Jung here more resembles scattered and dismembered Dionysus as writer than a controlling omniscient author.

Even more significantly, Shamdasani is condensing, as befits his genesis myth, the text of *The Red Book*, the writing and paintings, with the experiences that Jung said gave rise to them. In *Memories, Dreams, Reflections* Jung says that it is the experiences and the writing of the Black Books that provide the imaginal material for his future psychology. *After* the Black Books comes the aesthetic transformation of the material in *The Red Book*.

I had to draw concrete conclusions from the insights the unconscious had given me – and that task was to become a life's work.

(*Jung 1963: 213*)

Unlike Jung, Shamdasani conflates experiences plus writing them (in a form that is not aesthetic) with subsequent writing which is avowedly drawing on artistic techniques. To conflate experience with the making of an aesthetic work is to assume that artistic form can be separated from ideational content. It is another contentious instance of the notion that meaning in words is stable; here adding the condition that it is directly transmissible from psychic interiority to written text.

Ironically, one person who would disagree with Shamdasani on the divisibility of meaningful content from written form would be C. G. Jung. For despite his disavowal of the aesthetic when commenting on *The Red Book*, in the later work of *Aion*, CW9ii (1951), he testifies to the value of imaginative language as *precise* in representing the psyche.

> Therefore, in describing the living processes of the psyche, I deliberately and consciously give preference to a dramatic, mythological way of thinking and speaking, because this is not only more expressive but also more exact than an abstract scientific terminology, which is wont to toy with the notion that its theoretic formulations may one fine day be resolved into algebraic equations.
>
> *(Jung 1951, CW 9ii: para. 25)*

Preferring the dramatic and mythological over abstract scientific concepts could be construed as a refutation of Shamdasani's point. Aesthetic 'additions' to *The Red Book* that differ from material in the Black Books, and from the later *Collected Works* should not simply be smoothed away or disregarded as decorative accretions. Which of the two possible Jungs does Shamdasani want? Is it the Jung of *Aion*, who composed *The Red Book*, and whose aesthetic formulations could be imagined as even *more authentic* than the transcriptions of the Black Books, as he suggests in his preference for the mythological and dramatic? Or it is the Jung of the even later *Memories, Dreams, Reflections*, who ruefully admits to putting aside *The Red Book* because its aesthetic form seemed too disengaged with 'reality'? The god-author here is scattered within his writings, which possess the wild qualities of the Dionysian psyche.

By presuming a consistent Jung, Shamdasani's fidelity to a coherent 'self-understanding' starts to break down. We also note, in Jung's own wavering, an underlying unease with aestheticism and concerns with beauty. Aesthetics and its cherishing of beauty are seen as separable from what he means by myth, drama and poetic language. As Shamdasani rightly shows, key to Jung in the construction of *The Red Book* is his emerging theory of symbols; those images that, in distinction to signs, point to the unknown, or unknowable, aspects of the collective unconscious. As shown in Chapter 1, Jung is keen to dissociate symbols from wholly belonging to art or aesthetics.

Symbols are authentic portals to the unconscious, which has the status of psychic reality. Art may contain symbols, which contribute significantly to its autonomous nature, as Tjeu van den Berk explains in his fine book, *Jung on Art* (2009/2012). However, art in Jung's sense of it, is not primarily dedicated to in-forming psychic reality, or to transmitting the nature of our nature, as Jung believed of the symbol. Rather, to Jung art unites form and content to make a discrete and beautiful object In Jung's notion of the aesthetic, art is not in the service of psyche. Instead, he tries to preserve an ontological distinction between art and psychology.

It is for psychology that Jung is the mythographer and writer of symbols of the imagination. Symbols are for psychology. If a symbolic text slipped away from the path of psychology and into the bewitching beauties of aesthetics and art, then it might betray psychology's primary ontology or fidelity to the nature of the psyche as nature. In *Memories, Dreams, Reflections,* Jung seems to have come to the conclusion that the aesthetical dynamics of *The Red Book* detach it too far from the nature of the psyche.

> The anima might then have easily seduced me into believing that I was a misunderstood artist, and that my so-called artistic nature gave me the right to neglect reality.
>
> *(Jung 1963: 212)*

> In the Red Book I tried an aesthetic elaboration of my fantasies, but never finished it. I became aware that I had not yet found the right language, that I still had to translate it into something else. Therefore I gave up this aestheticizing tendency in good time, in favour of a rigorous process of *understanding.*
>
> *(Jung 1963: 213 [italics in original])*

The anima's accusation that he was making art seems to haunt Jung's composition of *The Red Book.* Significantly, Jung makes no attempt to reconcile or to marry this dissenting feminine voice. In the matter of nature versus art, he sees no Dionysian wedding. Here Jung misses aspects of this multi-talented god that could have taken him into a more transdisciplinary relationship with art.

Returning to Shamdasani; if his reconstruction of Jung's self-understanding omits some of Jung's own changes of mind, it also has a far more profound difference with Jung in the psychologist's defining conception of the creative psyche. Shamdasani's theory of knowledge is profoundly countered by Jung's adherence to the superior importance of the unconscious as fundamentally unknowable in extent, and as a constant destabilizer of knowledge and language. Jung wrote:

> Nobody drew the conclusion that if the subject of knowledge, the psyche, were in fact a veiled form of existence not immediately accessible to consciousness, then all our knowledge must be incomplete, and moreover to a degree that we cannot determine.
>
> *(Jung 1960, CW8: para. 358)*

Here we see why Jung valued the symbol and the practice of mythological and dramatic writing. Only the image that reveals that meaning cannot be fully rationally known. The symbol, or the narrative that structures relations to the other as unknowable, myth, can be paradoxically faithful to the protean quality of the psyche as a whole. The coherent self-understanding that Shamdasani aims for is far more indebted to the rational qualities of the ego than to the destabilizing influences of the collective unconscious.

This does not mean that Shamdasani's theory of knowledge is necessarily wrong; just that it is not fundamentally Jungian. In dividing off his historical research from Jungians doing interpretation of *The Red Book*, Shamdasani is positing a division in epistemology that is only sustainable if his history represses aspects of adjacent disciplines such as here, Jungian psychology; and, as I shall show later, literary studies.

Shamdasani is a wonderful editor of *The Red Book*, whose footnotes connecting the text to Jung's other published works and historical culture will be invaluable for scholars of many disciplines. However, it is important to see that Shamdasani makes claims for the future role of *Liber Novus* in Jungian Studies based upon a specific construction of a knowable subject in Jung. In effect, Shamdasani not only privileges ego (contra Jung), but does so by emphatically producing a version of the Judaeo-Christian myth of origins in *The Red Book* generative powers of 'genesis'. My point in *Remembering Dionysus* is that positing a rational god is not the only way to read Jung.

By privileging *The Red Book* in the Jungian canon, Shamdasani centres the rational ego in his historical epistemology. He connects this monotheistic ego to notions of science as a dominant paradigm, validated by experiments that point to a stable reality separate from the language representing it. Hence, form is divisible from content, and this historical way of knowing inherits the way Christian theology morphed into mainstream experimental science.

Both rational science and its antecedent in theology reproduce an ancient dualism and separation between spirit and matter: the father God as author who makes the world separate from himself. This is a separation between knowing and not knowing that is unbridgeable. It cannot be re-membered. Dionysus, as the dismembered psyche of the disciplines, as the ontology of our multiple knowings, is thereby thoroughly repressed.

By contrast, I suggest that Jung's work challenges this model of knowing as exclusive or superior. Even when looking at Jung's writing from the point of view of a rational authorial voice, we discern ambivalences and resistances to rationality as the dominant epistemology. Yet, in proclaiming the importance of the unknowable unconscious, Jung de–centres himself as author, and liberates his writing as texts that invite multiple readings. He is a Dionysian writer who invites the reader to re-member his work in a way that Nicolescu would call 'open', and Jung, 'symbolic', exposed to a mysterious cosmos.

I propose that Shamdasani is offering a dream of history; one that restates Judaeo-Christian monotheism as the only stable structure of truth. To Shamdasani, *Liber Novus* is the New Book, the bible of Jung's authorizing presence modelled on a singular god that represses all that is other to his rationality. Jung's

(margin note: God the Father vs. Dionysus)

psychology is aimed at undermining that very longstanding notion as the fantasy of an over-reaching ego that has lost touch with its 'other'.

Ironically, in seeking to retrieve Jung as an important psychological scientist, Shamdasani is devaluing Jung's most adhered to psychological principle: the effects of the intrinsic creativity of the psyche. Ironically, too, is that the Jungian critic who in many ways is most opposed to *The Red Book* as key to *The Collected Works*, Wolfgang Giegerich, similarly, although with different justifications, rejects Jung's sense of the unconscious as our indigenous creative nature. Both Shamdasani and Giegerich are the anti-Dionysians of *The Red Book*.

Wolfgang Giegerich and the swallowed world

Like Shamdasani, Giegerich deals with other critical opinions of *The Red Book* by relying upon an absolute division between academic disciplines. Unlike Shamdasani, although agreeing with its editor on the importance of *The Red Book* as documentary source in a historical sense, Giegerich regards the work as a 'fabrication' that is fundamentally at odds with genuine psychology, which requires 'logical form' (Giegerich 2010: 379). *The Red Book*, in Giegerich's superbly articulated indictment, is Jung's unwitting fantasy of dreaming a nature for the psyche; a nature that is untrue.

Here Dionysus is not dismissed for theological reasons, as in Shamdasani's absolute fidelity to the rationality of the Father God. 'He', as in the dismembered *Red Book*, is regarded as a mere pretence, a clown with no smile, by Giegerich. *The Red Book* falsifies the nature of the psyche as nature. It is 'absolutely esoteric', because it is only addressed to, and derived from, Jung; it is irrelevant to psychology because it lacks logical thought and general examples (Giegerich 2010: 379).

Giegerich begins this assault on the value of *The Red Book* by suggesting that it is not a book at all. Although Jung's copy is physically a book, now reproduced, *The Red Book* is not a *book* in the sense of being written for, and communicating with, a public. It is not Dionysian because it infers no audience except its author, so lacking that god's communal invocation of an audience. Here Giegerich implies more than disagreement with Shamdasani on Jung's hope for publication. He is denying value to the reception of the book, calling its style 'contraceptive', in a startling reversal of Shamdasani's genesis myth (Giegerich 2010: 363). *The Red Book* is an impossible book because its 'prophetic tone' insulates it from a general audience (ibid.: 363.).

Next, Giegerich demolishes a potential objection to his portrayal of *The Red Book* as insufficiently wrought by denying it the status of art. If *The Red Book* were to be considered a work of art then the peculiarity of the words and paintings might be attributable to a uniqueness that is its justification rather than its disqualification. Unfortunately for *The Red Book*, Giegerich draws on the philosopher Hegel to deny that possibility.

A work of art must figure its own origin, be aesthetically and formally self-sufficient (Giegerich 2010: 364). By contrast, *The Red Book* is tethered to Jung's

What's the whole point!

own fantasy world; it neither seeks nor achieves the status of Dante's *Divine Comedy*, or Augustine's *Confessions*, for these, despite personal content, are *formally* aimed at the public.

At this moment Giegerich anticipates the possible attribution of *The Red Book* to modernist art by suggesting that its medievalism, rather than being typical of modernism's transgressions, is rather evidence of the book's inauthenticity. I will return to the possibility of *The Red Book* and modernism later.

It is Giegerich's use of a geographical metaphor that is revealing of his own attitude to making knowledge. By comparing Jung's claim to be 'finding' the unconscious psyche as 'real' and a potential source of meaning to the exploration of previously unknown physical territory, Giegerich gives a cultural history to his own ontology and epistemology (his belief in what is real and how to construct and justify knowledge from it).

> The new locus of truth that was needed could not simply be discovered and made use of by Jung, the way America was discovered and then settled by millions of Europeans. He had to fabricate it, and fabricate it as he was making use of it.
>
> *(Giegerich 2010: 389)*

Giegerich uses a colonial metaphor. The unconscious, to him, is not a place to be discovered as America was by Europeans. What is fascinating about this particular use of metaphor is its revealing perspective. 'Discovered' is an old-fashioned word to use of America, given that it was already settled by complex societies that had been in situ for thousands of years. More precisely, the metaphor is Eurocentric and modernity-centric. It assumes a history of knowledge that pays no heed to counter-histories of the way knowledge takes political form, for example, in colonial expansion.

Giegerich's colonial metaphor of the discovery of America is a two-way mirror. It figures his point about Jung wrongly positing the unconscious as a pre-existing real entity. It also uncovers his singular adherence to Western modernity as the only valid perspective. It constructs knowledge as *singular*, a monotheistic conception of knowledge-culture as coherent and admitting of no challenge from outside itself. The well-known existence of Native American societies does not disrupt the notion of America being 'discovered', because they offer no significant challenge to the knowledge-making practices of the Europeans. Dionysian fusion with the wild is not native to this critic.

Similarly, Giegerich is not denying the unconscious as an aspect of the human psyche. Rather, he is denying it the status ascribed to by Jung, one that emerges here in *The Red Book*. To Jung, dreams are real in a way external to the ego. They are evidence of an autonomous part of the psyche, an independent and *natural* activity. Images outside the control of the ego, in dreams and active imagination, are where human nature becomes impossible to differentiate from non-human nature. They are Dionysian in nature. For Giegerich, dreams are not nature. While being outside the ego's control, they are nevertheless dynamic parts of a psyche that wants to become integrated as logical thought.

> [Dreams] are . . . my dream thoughts, produced by me, only by me. They are thoughts and not events of nature.
>
> *(Giegerich 2010: 400)*

Here we see Giegerich's assertion that the human psyche is fundamentally separate from the external world. Unlike Jung, 'nature' is not an 'other' that is a productive contributor to making meaning, whether nature is the human unconscious or the planet that houses it. To Giegerich, nature does not think. So the unconscious psyche is incapable of originating dream images. Non-human nature is without intelligence or animation. Dionysus is denied; or, as Jung might put it, ignored.

What is foundationally at odds between Giegerich and Jung is their incompatible construction of the 'other', whether that other refers to other cultures, the unconscious, or non-human nature. Put another way, Giegerich is essentially monotheistic in believing in only one conscious centre of psychic being, one way of producing knowledge, and one planetary species capable of meaningful animation.

By contrast, Jung's founding dualism gives way to a dialogical relationship between oneness and manyness, in his sense of a psyche populated by animated creatures who cannot be restricted to the human. Jung both respects and enacts Dionysus. His dismembering writing also re-members, and so enables Ariadne as soul to return to us. While Jung's monotheistic tendencies find dualistic expression in his concern with the Self archetype as totality and centre of meaning, his animist intuitions remain, in the way his unconscious fractures *any* secure notion of knowledge. To Jung, the psyche is too mysterious, too diverse, and too wild to be restricted to Giegerich's far more coherent and totalizing ideas.

Giegerich himself comes to a similar conclusion about Jung when identifying what he sees as the defining flaw of *The Red Book*. This heretic text, Giegerich contends, is vitally wrong because it violates psychic unity. It is dis-membered. The fabrication of the unconscious is not a neutral term, as if Jung were weaving or making cloth (fabric). It is rather a falsification of an underlying monotheistic vision of what a human being is.

> *The Red Book*'s fatal fault is that it tears this unity (the unity of the soul's logical life) apart and distributes its two moments, subjectivity and objectivity, to two. . . separate ontological realities, the I and nature, the I and 'the unconscious' – and even . . . the I and the self (as a real Other).
>
> *(Giegerich 2010: 401)*

Giegerich sees *The Red Book* as Dionysus, and does not like him. Where Jung regards what he calls the objective psyche as a separate reality, Giegerich sees it as a different mode of an essentially unified, or unifiable, psyche. To Giegerich, Jung's notion of the self is a huge mistake. The self as Jung expresses it is not the goal, centre and totality of psychic being. It is rather 'the swallowed world', in which mind has been wrongly reconceptualized as inside (Giegerich 2010: 396). Such mistaken interiorizing by Jung constructs a different outside, which can attract the status of an-other reality.

So, *The Red Book* to Giegerich is an historical novelty. It is 'primary documentation', but in a very different sense to Shamdasani's use of the term. Yes, to Giegerich *The Red Book* is evidence of Jung's developing psychology, but primarily in terms of errors before the greater evidence of logical thought in *The Collected Works*.

On the other hand, both Shamdasani and Giegerich demonstrate a modern monotheistic structure in their ideas about knowledge. The notion that this religious myth can both exalt and dismiss *The Red Book* in relation to Jung is arguably a sign that the underlying motif both rely upon, Jung as author-god, is also open to question. Perhaps it is time to be more flexible about God or the Gods? Might other early critics of *The Red Book* be more sensitive to its Dionysian qualities?

Changing gods in The Red Book

Three Jungian scholars offer intriguingly diverse perspectives on *The Red Book* while remaining focused on a monotheistic God as envisioned from Jung's Christian-educated position. Indeed, the notion of a religion as possessing cultural, historical and even geographical definitions is one that Ann Belford Ulanov, Lionel Corbett and Walter Odajnyk all regard as one of *The Red Book*'s significant contributions. Although religion, by definition, is bound up with questions of ultimate realities, these scholars see *The Red Book* as marking an important realization that the transcendent requires roots in immanent, embodied and contingent living. Moreover, to a greater or lesser extent, *The Red Book* demonstrates that a religious tradition, if it is to play a role in a healthy psyche, needs critical examination for the way it is always affected by often unconscious cultural biases.

Of these three scholars, Ulanov's 'God Climbs Down to Mortality', is most embedded within traditional theology as a study of the Divine (Ulanov 2010). She calls *The Red Book* an 'ur-source', which is similar to, yet not identical with, Shamdasani's notion of 'primary document' (ibid.: 71). Whereas Shamdasani's use of 'document' is meant to stabilize the book as a wholly comprehensible guarantor of historical verification, 'ur-source' signifies a more primal, less entirely rational approach to origination.

An ur-source is never a straightforward prior text. True, it does possess a generative, genesis quality; it is nevertheless one subject to scholarly debate. An 'ur-source' will not wholly authenticate nor stabilize the meaning of another piece of writing such as Jung's *Collected Works*. It will exert influence on interpreting the succeeding work without determining its meaning. Interpretation is invited rather than forbidden. Even in the midst of Ulanov's Christian faith, Dionysus peeps out.

As if to substantiate Dionysian visions, Ulanov's ur-source myth of *The Red Book* is far less singular than that of Shamdasani. An ur-source implies that historical understanding contains a good deal of what is not subject to conscious knowing because so much relevant material is not recorded. Ur-source gives history an unconscious. It is a disciplinary unconscious with a Jungian twist that leaves space for other fruitful arguments to flourish in Dionysian miscellany.

Unsurprisingly, Ulanov's designation of *The Red Book* as ur-source is in keeping with her main proposition of a radical change to the image of God. She sees *The Red Book* as embedding transcendence within human beings (Ulanov 2010: 64). Whereas Christianity has had a long history of portraying God as outside of the human, now God is within (ibid.: 67). By dealing with God in the form of the Divine Child, *The Red Book* marks a shift in human subjectivity (ibid.: 73). Ulanov notes the role of contemporary catastrophe in the images of World War One. Part of the revelation of *The Red Book* is to demonstrate that outer divisions in the world have inner counterparts, a point echoed by other Jungians.

So the question of the relation of human-embodied immanence to transcendence is collective as well as personal. Is war an aspect of religious breakdown? Ulanov's analysis opens the way for other cultural and historical interpretations, some of which will be examined later in this chapter. For example, both Corbett and Odajnyk see *The Red Book* as offering a treatment of contemporary Christianity that still has real psychological and social value in this new century (Corbett 2011; Odajnyk 2010).

In 'Jung's *Red Book* dialogues with the soul: Herald of a new religion?', Corbett scrutinizes the religious content of *The Red Book* against the allegations of Richard Noll in his two books, *The Jung Cult* (1994) and *The Aryan Christ* (1996), that Jung was trying to found a new religion in the context of pre-fascist Germany's neo-pagan, spiritual and political movements.

Corbett is convincing in his criticism of Noll's literalism. Episodes in *The Red Book* of Jung apparently acting out Christ-like events are not actual self-deification (Corbett 2011: 19). Rather, Jung is figuring, literally *figuring out*, individuation as a process of relating to what can be an overwhelmingly creative unconscious. Corbett sees Jung in *The Red Book* as respecting Dionysus, not becoming him. The tension between the god as sacrificed and sacrificed to is maintained by the 'I' figure.

Noting the relation between 'salvation' and 'salve', Corbett argues that *The Red Book* brings religious and psychological healing together, and not in a way that structures Jungian psychology as a religion. Jungian psychology neither provides acts of worship nor prescribes a fixed set of ideas about the transcendent; it offers no creed. What it can do is provide a spiritual practice by testifying to the psychological reality of experiences of the sacred.

Hence Corbett is suggesting that *The Red Book* is a work in which psychology, a word that never appears its text, is primarily enacted through the medium of spirituality. Such an approach is implicitly transdisciplinary, as explored in Chapter 2. Corbett is implying that *The Red Book* may pose a disciplinary question as to the boundary (or not) between psychology writing and that of religious studies (when encompassing spirituality as well as the study of actual religions). Such a topic is endemic to the Jungian field, given the determination of the many volumes of the *Collected Works* to treat religion as a major factor for the psyche.

Odajnyk's two papers, first published in *Psychological Perspectives* (2010), are concerned with exploring the religious dynamics of *The Red Book*, as they illuminate Jung's companion work of the period on psychological types. In this sense, Odajnyk is treating *The Red Book* as an unproblematic source of Jungian ideas, if not the only one.

What is particularly striking about Odajnyk's approach, however, is first of all his implicit challenge to Giegerich's alternative reading of *The Red Book* refusing to offer a path to the rest of us. Secondly, Odajnyk locates the work's religious significance in the context of addressing the perils of the collective in the twenty-first century. *The Red Book* is without a specific creed, yet it embodies an urgent contemporary psychological, cultural and political truth.

So where Giegerich sees *The Red Book* as explicitly refusing to teach anything of value, saying that the way of 'I' is not for anyone else, Odajnyk, by complete contrast, sees this very notion as the core of the text's healing function. As a vital stage in this deceptively straightforward argument, Odajnyk is more sure than either Ulanov or Corbett that *The Red Book* is primarily psychological, rather than religious. By firmly associating Book One of *The Red Book* with an essay written at the same time ('The Transcendent Function', Jung 1916), Odajnyk is able to locate, or re-locate, *The Red Book* as pointing to psychology (Jung 1960, CW8: paras. 131–93). Perhaps fortunately, it is a psychology of freedom to roam as opposed to pre-scribed pathways.

Containing significant elements for the theory of psychological types, 'The Transcendent Function' subsumes *The Red Book*'s vision of the divine child into a theoretical concept (Odajnyk 2010: 17). Odajnyk is therefore able to turn this argument of *The Red Book* as source for Jungian ideas around. He employs Jung's types to stabilize his reading of *The Red Book* as providing valuable persuasion for what Jungian psychology can offer the conflicted world of today. Types, he argues, are hugely important in accounting for human intransigence.

The types to which we are psychologically predisposed have a strong influence on the kind of ideas, politics and practices that we are prone to endorse. In this sense, the intractable quarrel between Jung and Freud that may have precipitated some of the ingredients of *The Red Book*, Odajnyk says, remains a vital lesson for today (Odajnyk 2010: 3). For by understanding this tragic breakdown in relations as typologically structured, we may begin to perceive the psychological dimensions of what appears to be wholly external and immutable. As Odajnyk memorably puts it:

> All religious, ideological, national, ethnic, political and cultural disputes are at heart externalizations of conflicting forces within our individual and collective psyche.
>
> *(ibid.: 21)*

Here Odajnyk shows the value of assimilating religious, along with other, trauma into psychological conflict. He is constructing *The Red Book* as a source for Jungian psychology, insofar as it provides ways of understanding the world today. In this, he differs significantly from Shamdasani's notion of historical source as generating intellectual content rather than possibilities for applying it.

Odajnyk's vision of Jungian ideas is a practical and socially engaged one, offering today's readers a new understanding of, and possible solutions to, what ails society. He wants *The Red Book* to foster a new collective consciousness that might just save the world. *The Red Book* can help rebirth the collective psyche *because* it does not set out a specific creed or teaching, not in spite of it. He places psychology as a re-membering of a dismembered world.

This is a fundamentally contrary position to the one Giegerich takes. Less obvious is the way Odajnyk echoes Shamdasani in regarding *The Red Book* as source for ideas in *The Collected Works*, while transforming the implications of a 'source' from historical verification to participating in the crises of the twenty-first century. Saving the world cannot happen by telling people what to do, Odajnyk suggests. It can only come about by a collective change that responds to an inner transformation of human souls. In offering *The Red Book* as a potential catalyst for just such a new consciousness, Odajnyk is proposing that changing our ideas of God via *The Red Book* changes both Jungian psychology and its afflicted subject, human psychology. It is a change that insists upon Dionysian plurality and mutability of the world if it is to be saved.

Changing (Jungian) psychology

In 'The Mark of One Who Has Seen Chaos: A Review of C. G. Jung's *Red Book*', Nathan Schwartz-Salant manages to diagnose Jung and Jungian psychology (Schwartz-Salant 2010). In doing so, he proposes a seamless transition between the primal 'experiences' that *Memories, Dreams, Reflections* calls the seeds of a lifetime's work and their 'faithful' rendition in *The Red Book* (ibid.: 12). The value of such an assimilation of troubled psyche and its written counterpart is evident in Schwartz-Salant's radically different treatment of the 'chaos' of *The Red Book* from that by Wolfgang Giegerich.

Both Jungians note that whatever the theoretical Jungian elements of *The Red Book*, its immersion in irrational images gives a different flavour to the *Collected Works*. Where Giegerich sees the adherence to patterns of order in the latter volumes as evidence of the logical thought of psychology proper, Schwartz-Salant believes that it has led analysts to overemphasize finding order at the expense of allowing for the rich possibilities of disorder. In essence, Schwartz-Salant celebrates the Dionysian quality that Giegerich rejects.

On the other hand, Schwartz-Salant also regards the 'I' of *The Red Book*, as identical to the historical Jung, and sees him exhibiting a narcissistic resistance to the feminine and the body (Schwartz-Salant 2010: 26). The work is a 'wisdom teaching', even though the Jung within it fails to recognize some of the potentials of, for example, meeting Philemon. This figure possesses mythical resonance as half of a long loving marriage, and yet *The Red Book* omits Baucis, his wife, as a voice.

Schwartz-Salant sums up the connection of *The Red Book* to the *Collected Works* as one in which the genre 'wisdom teaching' allows for a more candid exploration of chaos and more idiosyncrasies of personal psychology. While containing many seeds of future concepts such as archetypes and the transcendent function, *The Red Book* neglects the mystery of the body and feeling relationships (Schwartz-Salant 2010: 34).

By contrast, psychologist Sanford L. Drob makes a point of offering multiple perspectives on *The Red Book* in his invaluable *Reading The Red Book* (2012). He is both incipiently Dionysian and transdisciplinary. In a fascinating final section he considers the work as a dream, a dream of a *discipline*, of psychology itself. Crucially, he offers *The Red Book* as a compensatory dream; one that implicitly challenges and augments the biases of psychology trying to squeeze into the confines of rational cognition. A study of *The Red Book* allows Drob to suggest what possibilities are suppressed in the mainstream of twenty-first century psychology.

> Psychology . . . has essentially become separated from its philosophical, literary, and theological roots, and has carried itself out as a specialized science with clear boundaries from other social sciences and much sharper ones from the humanities and such disciplines as anthropology and history . . . What Jung, in *The Red Book*, referred to as 'the spirit of this time' (the scientific, hyper-rational mode of thinking) is, within the discipline of psychology, gaining a stranglehold on the academy and profession.
>
> *(Drob 2012: 262)*

Drob sees *The Red Book* as compensating an over-rationalized discipline in a number of key ways. Its imaginal depths offer so much more than the simple cognition in the discipline today. It is an implicit warning against regarding psychological knowledge as an unproblematic cumulative progression with its conjuring of past styles of knowing. *The Red Book*, if regarded like Shamdasani does, as emanating from an 'experiment', is far from the rationally defined research projects sanctioned today. Indeed, while this argument seems to evoke Nicolescu's transdisciplinary paradigm, it more precisely laments the narrowing of psychology itself from its Dionysian and animistic potential in *The Red Book*, to a subject that refuses to value the irrational.

Importantly to Drob, *The Red Book*, and Jung's work overall, is prepared to question the assumptions made by psychological knowledge, and to assert that no one framework can encompass it all. Its god cannot be wholly in the realm of consciousness. Dionysus is too present in *The Red Book* for Drob to see reason as the sole basis of psychology. *The Red Book* is a testament to the psyche's other, nonrational voices and their potential to add to a meaningful life. As a result, *The Red Book*, according to Drob, is a striking compensation for psychology's isolationism.

It amounts to a refusal of psychology to relinquish other disciplines; other ways of knowing and being.

> This not only means that psychology should reopen its boundaries to other disciplines, including those that are artistic and literary, but . . . that it should also consider the possibility that things of great psychological significance can be better or only expressed in modalities such as music, art, and literature that are neither scientific nor rational in the narrow sense of the term.
>
> *(Drob 2012: 264–5)*

In the end, not even an expanded psychology can invoke all the mysteries of the psyche as indicated by the wild, Dionysian *Red Book*. In a revealing comment, Drob suggests that contesting the boundaries of the discipline might detach psychology and psychiatry from its largely unacknowledged splicing into economics and socio-cultural factors (Drob 2012: 268). The fantasy that disciplines can be wholly separated from the powerful forces surrounding the world of knowledge is part of the limitations of adhering to one ontological and epistemological model.

Drob ends by saying that if *The Red Book* can be viewed as a dream of a discipline it is one to be interrogated rather than simply accepted (Drob 2012: 271). With such a robust attitude to *The Red Book* and its multiple possibilities for transforming psychology into a more Dionysian and transdisciplinary model, I now turn to one of Drob's most potent suggestions; that psychology open its borders to the humanities via the bewitching images of *The Red Book*.

Imagining/imaging the dead historically, cross-culturally and in literature

John Beebe's insightful paper in the journal *Quadrant* describes 'The Red Book [as] a Work of Conscience' (Beebe 2010). Later in his interview with Sonu Shamdasani, in *Psychological Perspectives*, he calls *The Red Book* 'writing for psyche', where Jung was becoming a psychological writer in a uniquely imaginative manner (Shamdasani & Beebe 2010: 422). I suggest that Beebe means something different from what might be conventionally called psychology writing, or writing *on* psychology from an external, public stance. Rather, Beebe's own paper shows *The Red Book* to be structured around the treatment of collective and persona trauma in ways that override any distinction between inside a person known as 'C.G. Jung', and outside him, in the world. NO!

The Red Book memorably stages the death of the young male hero in the killing of Siegfried, mythical son to a 'Sigmund'. Beebe suggests that this startling event embodies a dual necessity; that Jung felt it necessary to kill his 'sonship' to Sigmund Freud, and that with Europe descending into massive warfare, felt a necessity to kill its own heroes on the battlefield. For the heroic attitude is a threat to the soul (Beebe 2010: 45–6). Dionysus is no hero. The European catastrophe of World War One must be answered by coming to terms with such irrational chaos in the soul. What drives *The Red Book*, according to Beebe, is the acknowledgement of an ethical obligation to address the inner roots of this war (ibid.: 48).

> [T]o do anything less is to endorse the spirit of the times that is ruining the world.
>
> *(ibid.: 48)*

As a result, *The Red Book* turns away from modernity in far more than just horror at its literalization of technology on the battlefield. It is in this work that Jung accepts the irrational as a source of knowing, and carves out a critical revision of Christian teaching, memorably summed up by 'you did not live your animal' (Jung 2009: 294). Such a charge effectively summons Dionysus from his hiding place in the wild woods of the Christianized psyche.

The culmination of this work of conscience, Beebe says, is to serve the haunting refrains of the dead by finding a way to live religiously that honours the physical part of human beings (Beebe 2010: 54). Although Beebe does not explicitly say so, the role of the embodied feminine in *The Red Book* is arguably to enable Ariadne as feminine soul. She will re-member and wed Dionysus as the god torn apart and the god of being torn apart.

Beebe's analysis of *The Red Book* does not locate it as history, as either a study of the past, or as originating, a pre-text, for a set of ideas. In conversation with Shamdasani, Beebe suggests that the present is also a time that resembles pre–World War One. For us too, *The Red Book* is 'a reminder of the danger of neglecting the depths' (Shamdasani & Beebe 2010: 432). Just as on the one hand the work shows an eradication of boundaries between collective and personal soul, so to Beebe, it is not sealed in the past. *The Red Book* is alive to, and for, the psyche of today.

In this way, the interview in *Psychological Perspectives* sends tendrils into the journal that testify to the psycho–active nature of the text. The journal itself becomes Dionysian in its wandering amongst the deep roots of unconscious instinctual life. For example, Nancy Furlotti, in 'Tracing a Red Thread: Synchronicity and Jung's *Red Book*', speaks of magical feeling coincidences in the production of the work (Furlotti 2010). Intimately involved in the scanning of the book in Zurich, she was afflicted by migraines and dreams that were strangely prescient.

> At the time. . . I had no idea of its content. . . what only revealed itself later was the appearance of three key motifs from *The Red Book* in my dreams: killing and being killed; the red one; and recovery of the feminine soul.
>
> *(Shamdasani & Beebe 2010: 477)*

Similarly, Stephen Martin, whose work with Sonu Shamdasani in setting up The Philemon Foundation was instrumental in the publication of *The Red Book*, speaks of being read by it (Frantz 2010: 392). Cynthia Ann Hale refers to a conversation with Sandra Vigon, also involved with the physical production emphasizes a numinous sense of birth about the book, occurring at the same moment as a

Jungian friend was dying in the same city (Hale 2010: 491). These accounts of *The Red Book* echo with the theme of the psyche coming alive *now* through its publication. They do not endorse linear time or history. Dionysus returns via its pages.

Moreover the notion of *The Red Book* coming alive over questions of war and death occurs in another anthropological paper by Robin van Loben Sels in the *Quadrant* volume (van Loben Sels 2010), in which she offers a context from outside Western modernity for the urgent and urging presence of the dead within *The Red Book*.

Van Loben Sels considers *The Red Book* from the perspective offered by Haiti, which, like the war-torn Europe of Jung's time, has suffered recent humanitarian disasters. Unlike Europe, Haiti possesses a religion in which the dead are treated as fellow inhabitants of the everyday world. Such a non-Western insight into ways of psychically acknowledging the dead prizes open a gap in our conventional assumptions about what is real. This gap enables van Loden Sels' fascinating essay to re-position the psyche and *The Red Book*. For, if the vivid culture of Haiti is imbued with ancestral spirits, we, too, mobilized by our dominant myths of evolution, should revere our own ancestral (pre)humans, including animals, plants and perhaps even stones.

Quoting anthropologist Paul Shepard, van Loben Sels invokes our 'great grandparents . . . the mighty trees' (van Loben Sels 2010: 82). In this cross-cultural and Dionysian sense of belonging to a web of life and death, *The Red Book*'s distinctive theology of the dead is a major contribution to a growing revolution in consciousness. Full of lament, *The Red Book* provides a home for the cries of the dead from a ruptured world, from the atrophied 'spirit of these times' that has lost touch with 'the spirit of the depths', the underworld residence of the dead.

In modernity's adherence to rationality as the only valid structure of consciousness, what is 'other' has been killed in a way that denies psychic energy to the lingering spirits. So here *The Red Book* is a vehicle by which what is primitive and embodied, ancestral and daimonic, in ourselves can be renewed. Effectively, van Loben Sels traces what I am calling the Dionysian dynamic of *The Red Book*. Feeling and spirit are reconnected, suggests van Loben Sels, which return in us a capacity to value connection to the wild (van Loben Sels 2010: 89). Above all, *The Red Book* teaches us that consciousness is not found, but rather made – collectively, by imbuing the spirit of the times with the depths enacted by the dead. It is re-membered, as we remember them.

Like Beebe, van Loben Sels sees in *The Red Book* a necessary death of masculine heroic consciousness. It is here imaged for her in the Grail Legend. Perceval is the knight who has to learn to ask a question with the spiritual discernment to make it the *right* one. Until masculine discrimination can do this, the Fisher King's grievous wound, the sick Western psyche, will remain unhealed.

Van Loben Sels and Beebe are united in perceiving a historical element of *The Red Book* as that which takes it into the mythic time of the psyche. What is in one way a motif of Jung's terrible wounding over his quarrel with Freud, the appalling horrors of World War One is, in the same moment, the death of an heroic knight and the festering wound of a world in which masculine and feminine have been too long severed, Dionysus too long denied.

The Red Book, concludes van Loben Sels, is a revelation of the sacred quality of our immanent, embodied being: '[w]e are always "on Holy Ground."' (van Loben Sels 2010: 92). Sensing this work as transcending historical specificity through scrupulously enacting it gives *The Red Book* the quality of the Jungian symbol. It stands for that unmappable yet necessary transformation of collective consciousness in the twenty-first century. It is what I have been calling, remembering Dionysus.

The Red Book *as modernist literature?*

Modernism, is, in its way, another historical framework for *The Red Book*. For it associates the work with contemporary revolutions in culture, theory and the arts, now known as modernism. Mathew V. Spano is probably the first to examine what the generic dismembering of modernism means for Jung's radical text in 'Modern(-ist) Man in Search of a Soul: Jung's *Red Book* as Modernist Visionary Literature', on the cgjungpage.org website (Spano 2010).

He points out that *The Red Book* contains many of the defining characteristics of modernist painting, sculpture or literature in its themes of uncertainty, its structuring around a quest for meaning and soul, its existential angst and fascination with myth. Less prominent in Spano's analysis is modernism's revaluation of the irrational as potentially valuable. He also does not go into modernist scepticism about the efficacy of traditional forms of art in the face of unprecedented change.

Using Jung's own division of art into 'psychological' and 'visionary', Spano finds the latter an apt description of *The Red Book*. 'Psychological' denotes literature primarily concerned with consciousness and the known, while 'visionary' works are made with symbols, and so draw on the unknown collective unconscious (see Chapter 1). Spano looks at *The Red Book* through its editor's account as composed via the Jungian technique of active imagination. He explicitly adheres to Shamdasani's notion of *The Red Book* as 'primary source, cause and progenitor of Jung's theories', while departing from the editor's refusal to sanction any other disciplinary framework as equally viable.

In suggesting literary value for *The Red Book*, Spano is going further than Shamdasani's 'work of psychology in literary form' (Shamdasani 2009: 3). Instead, he proposes that although both Jung and, after him, Shamdasani define active imagination as a means of psychotherapy, not art-making, one might still choose to consider *The Red Book* as art. The book is thereby given a literary ontological, or reality value, apart from its author and his future work.

Spano's conceptual move here, which I wholeheartedly delight in, is not spelled out as the disciplinary transition it actually is. Whereas many historians and psychologists instinctively regard Jung as the best arbiter of what *The Red Book* is, Spano is making use what is tempting to call at this point, Jungian psychology's 'evil twin', Literary Studies, in which literature *is its own justification*. The author cannot limit, just as he or she cannot definitively know, the meaning and ultimate nature of the work. The Dionysian text is unchained from its writer's ego.

how to re-experience history
and myths as personal,
as subjective?
Dionysus ignored **65**

In fact, what Spano's insightful literary modernist reading of *The Red Book* shows is that revisioning of disciplinary boundaries, which ultimately suggest the *related* nature of imaginative art and the psychology of the imagination. Put another way, transdisciplinary and Dionysian implications emerge from reading *The Red Book* as discrete, explicitly challenging disciplines. Pointing out that in the early twentieth century, artists and psychologists of the unconscious read and influenced each other, Spano makes a persuasive case for *The Red Book* participating in a modernist revolution of consciousness, specifically around the structuring of academic disciplines.

For example, *The Red Book* shares with its literary contemporary, James Joyce's novel, *Ulysses*, both a diagnostic and compensatory use of myth. Spano calls the episode of Izdubar (or Gilgamesh), a diagnostic use of myth in uncovering the loss of meaning in the contemporary psyche. The encounters with 'The Red One', by contrast, compensate for something missing. Other instances of modernist literary modes proliferate, such as the different voices and styles manipulating the narrator and narration, linking episodes by image rather than by plot, the preference of subjective renderings of experience over rationally presented external plotting, giving a layering of consciousness not wholly dissimilar to works by Virginia Woolf.

In addition, *The Red Book* shares with modernist art an urgent need to manifest and contain elements from the past, including archaic or medieval forms of consciousness. By encapsulating 'the past' in artistic structures, *The Red Book* achieves one of its goals: the birth of a new god in re-membering the psyche as historical as well as personal. In re-membered Dionysus, Ariadne can find her thread. Soul returns.

Spano is persuasive in his ground-breaking comparison of *The Red Book* to modernist art. Indeed, I suggest that his work goes further than he makes explicit, in breaking the ground for fertilization between those so-called singular disciplines of psychology and literature. As others unwittingly find in *The Red Book*, it dreams transdisciplinary dreams in the imaginative re-membering of this wild text.

Saving The Red Book *from Jung: 'Field answers frame for Dionysus'*

In the various constructions of *The Red Book* can be discerned what philosopher Jacques Derrida memorably termed, in *The Truth in Painting* (1987), the problem of the frame. He pointed out that for a painting hanging upon a wall the 'frame' that contains the art is more problematic than it appears; for the frame is neither inside nor outside the painting itself. The frame is rather the device that makes it possible to posit an inside and outside.

In doing so, the frame-as-device in a quiet way serves to underpin all kinds of unprovable notions, or what Derrida considers 'transcendent' ideas because they cannot be derived from within their system of meaning-making. So the frame marking the outside of a painting, is 'step by step, from the whole field of historical, economic, political inscription in which the drive to signature is produced includes and belongs to the general text of the history of being as presence' (1987: 61). Picture frames are essentially religious icons. They give the illusion of innate boundaries, as if inside and outside were natural universal laws. Instead, Derrida insists, frames mark divisions that his philosophy of deconstruction calls arbitrary.

By marking off space into different qualities of 'art' and 'not art' the frame instates a whole series of orderings between 'interior' and 'exterior', 'outer' and 'inner', 'above' and 'below'. Importantly, not all frames are made of material substances. Frames occur when *anything* is used to delineate the inside and outside of a work, including a written and visual work such as *The Red Book*. In this sense, each of the readings considered above are, in their own way, 'framing' *The Red Book*. For example, in literally coming between the reader and the text, Shamdasani's Introduction places *The Red Book* in a mythical frame of genesis, and also by presenting to us a unique individual with a distinct set of ideas.

In particular, Shamdasani's 'frame' that *The Red Book* is the 'single most important documentary source' (Shamdasani 2009: 95), is a peculiarly apt example of instating what Derrida calls 'meaning as presence' (Derrida 1987: 61). By collapsing the historical personage Jung, who placed some intangible personal psychic experiences into writing that he did referring to these events, Shamdasani is relying upon an ancient notion of meaning in words as stabilized by their author.

Inherent in Ancient Greek dualism is Plato's idea that speaking is more authentic than writing, because of the presence of the person uttering the words. By contrast, Derrida proclaims the reverse epistemology: that writing is more valuable than speech because it does not pretend to an *authorizing presence* that is illusory, since speech rather depends upon writing, upon the properties of the language system, to signify.

In fact, Shamdasani's overt naming of *The Red Book* as possessing 'genesis' powers is revealing of exactly the religious basis of the system of ascribing stable meaning to authors that Derrida is disputing. Derrida would say that Shamdasani's metaphysics of presence frames *The Red Book* in two senses: first in offering to position the text in a way that it can be seen for what it is – this is Shamdasani's claim, which to Derrida is framing as in a picture frame. Secondly, Shamdasani frames *The Red Book* as a forger might, by producing the very meanings of the work that he is purporting to reveal.

Put another way, rather than introduce *The Red Book* in its naked truth, as he claims, Shamdasani is placing an interpretative frame over it that aims to modify what we understand by it. In this sense, his Introduction is both inside and outside the work (the signifying *work*) of *The Red Book*.

Similarly, and more openly, Giegerich frames *The Red Book* by setting up his own version of monotheistic presence, here defined by its relative absence in the fabrication. By refusing any valuing ontology to the unconscious, any sense that its existence consists of a reality that deserves a significant place in psychology, Giegerich provides a frame that dismisses the volume as merely a source of irrational material of no real value to the knowledge known as psychology. Hence, *The Red Book* is not a book. Its relevance to Jung's own psyche is merely of passing interest, for its symbolic matter does not *matter* to anyone else.

In Giegerich's review there is a similar framing through what Derrida would call 'presence', but the construction of 'Jung' in the work is very different. Instead of an author-god *originating* his later psychology, as Shamdasani would have it, we have the essential psychologist (who for Giegerich is the Jung who makes his soul logically) abdicating the scene. It is the relative absence of real presence, here defined as the logic of soul, which condemns *The Red Book*. Giegerich frames the book by subjecting it to a reality test that it fails, miserably, in his estimation. His metaphysic is of an absent author-god, and therefore *The Red Book* is a trivial work.

Without necessarily revisiting all the previously discussed interpretations of *The Red Book*, it is possible to see that each possesses a disciplinary or ontological/reality perspective that frames *The Red Book* in ways critiqued by Derrida. By calling *The Red Book* 'psychology', or 'literature', an essay is not merely putting the text in a particular setting or epistemological landscape. Rather, by giving the text a context, *The Red Book* itself is changed, reconstructed into a work incompatible with other contexts, other disciplines. The frame wobbles between outside and inside.

One might take this framing perspective a stage further by noticing how it dismembers so-called stable disciplinary boundaries. After all, if the different senses of being and truth-making in disciplines such as psychology and literature are merely frame devices, then their claim to be discrete, potentially unified sources of knowledge is radically undermined. Yet this taking apart of the fiercely defended structures of academia can be applied to the mythic psyche as well. Does deconstruction's dismembering banish Dionysus or liberate him? Perhaps the already deconstructed nature of *The Red Book* can help.

The frame is not stable because it rests upon a metaphysical principle linking the words to the writer as authorizing presence, and so becoming a god-like authority in the text. To deconstructionist philosophers like Derrida, what the essayists are doing is not writing about *The Red Book*; they are re-writing *The Red Book* with every publication. For the division between text and commentary also relies upon the notion of a stable duality, a system of original work and secondary analysis. Instead of books remaining obediently between their covers, writing for deconstruction is an unstable mutually contaminating system often called 'intertextuality' (Eagleton 1983/2008: 111–22). The signifying property of writing slips and slides; it is, as literary critic Terry Eagleton puts it, in 'a flickering of presence and absence' (ibid.: 111).

Two key consequences result from looking at the diverse readings of *The Red Book* as providing alternative and multiple frames. One is to allow us to interrogate claims to have decoded *The Red Book*, to have found a singular, ultimate meaning, or to proclaim only one kind of importance for it. Even more interesting and Dionysian, I suggest, is the extent that Jung's own conceptualizing, or framing of the psyche, legitimates or anticipates such an approach.

Of course there is an irony in taking a justification from Jung's ideas to look at his work deconstructively. Such a practice is, paradoxically, to embark upon the very authorizing project that deconstruction is against. On the other hand, in defence of such activity, I assert the theme of this book, which is that depth psychology and literature can stop pretending to be strangers.

So I would suggest that Derrida's notion of language as a flickering field of signifiers that makes up what we call reality (for language cannot be confined to words once it escapes from page or screen), suggestively resembles Jung's overall vision of the psyche as that which envelops and, yes, frames our reality. The psyche frames reality because it produces our sense of the world through processes we call conscious and unconscious.

Archetypes are the body and creative psyche dynamically energizing, yet not determining, conscious experience. Because so much of the psyche escapes conscious, or rational, control, language remains radically unstable. Our frames only pretend to stabilize writing as one kind of knowledge or another. After all, Derrida's own argument is itself a frame, and in both senses. The paradox of deconstruction is that, like Giegerich on *The Red Book*, it insists upon a falsification of everything but its own claims. Put another way, Derrida does not in this way succeed in abolishing transcendence, for he finds it returning via the very drive to dismember the divisions of rational modernity.

Divine energy survives deconstruction. What is left are frames of reality dismembered. So psychology and literature cannot continue to fantasize their absolute separation. Where might Dionysian re-membering occur? After all, the rational Father god has been taken apart by his own Other, those Dionysian energies of immanence, and a body so long marginalized. What is needed is a new figuring of post-deconstruction's lack of frames, one that includes an unknowing unconscious psyche.

Led by our re-writing of *The Red Book*, it is appropriate, for both the world of deconstruction and of the Jungian psyche, to consider the text as open to wild nature participating in a psychodynamic field.

The Red Book *in the field*

In *The Cosmic Web: Scientific Field Models & Literary Strategies in the 20th Century* (1984), N. Katherine Hayles explains that what she calls 'the field' of reality is a metaphor derived from the implications the science of relativity, particle physics, quantum mechanics, and their consequences for language.

'The field' emphasizes that everything is interconnected. What is significant here is that 'everything' includes the consciousness of any observer. Its second most potent characteristic is that languages pre-structure, pre-scribe, what we construe as reality. We are used to words apparently denoting autonomous events 'out there', such as the separation between text and reader. In fact, this reflects not reality but the deep structure of Indo-European languages. These languages are oriented towards a mechanistic ordering of reality (1984: 16). Inherent in our language perspective are two prerequisites: that there is a separation between observer and observed, and that time flows in one direction.

By contrast, quantum theory proposes that any separation between subject and object is an arbitrary distinction (1984: 31); while relativity theory proposes that what we perceive as real depends upon which frame we are standing in. Moreover, cause and effect are multidimensional. The world is a quivering, dynamic living whole. As such, it cannot be understood by human reason alone. We are always within the cosmic web of language and nature or reality; there is no way to look at it from the outside. This indeed is a vision that calls for a transdisciplinarity and the open system of knowledge, as Nicolescu suggests.

Jungian psychology enters this dynamic, interactive field via Jung's notion of synchronicity. His description of synchronicity is as a coincidence between a psychic event and a material one connected by meaning, rather than a straightforward cause and effect. It is also called by him *acts of creation in time* (Jung 1952/1960, CW8: para. 965). Synchronicity presupposes a reality of psyche and matter as not fundamentally separated; a reality liable to self-ordering or patterning in ways that abolish the distinction between self and world. Synchronicity is Dionysian, or, as I have argued elsewhere, a property of Earth Mother in the fundamental structuring of the cosmos (Rowland 2005).

Such a notion of the Jungian psyche as part of transpersonal archetypal patterning has been substantially developed by Michael Conforti and his Assisi Institute (Conforti 1999/2003). He refers to this work as 'archetypal ethology', or the study of natural patternings in which the ways animals behave, studied by traditional ethologists, are expanded to include human beings, their societies and environments (ibid.: 90–135). Here is liberation from the frames of singular or monotheistic disciplinary approaches to *The Red Book*. Archetypes as dynamic field properties does not pretend that there can be understanding that is perfectly neutral, objective, unhistorical, unbiased, non-mythical or not pre-conditioned by a set of ideas or discourses.

We cannot escape the effects of the patterning qualities of nature, whether psychically or materially defined. Its patterning is to be found in our cultures, psyches and dreams. Put another way, we can escape neither from the history that has formed our ideas and our consciousness, nor from our embodied psyches with their evolved patterns and meanings (archetypes), nor from the fundamental systems in nature and the cosmos. The implications of Conforti's work, I would argue, is that it is to carry on the Jungian project to consider *The Red Book* as a dynamic constituent within an interactive field of psyche and matter, language and creative soul.

Where *The Red Book* differs from other evocative works is that its revolutionary, discipline-defying nature reveals it to *be* nature, our nature. It reveals our nature, dis-membered among disciplines but looking for re-membering in multiple readings, different frames that form a never completed whole.

The field perspective also, I suggest, augments literary studies. We witness a text within a field of language as inseparable from matter and body. Literary studies can be Dionysian as well as psychology. Archetypal patterning is a way of understanding reality as possessing innate ordering qualities that do not amount to determining structures. It implies that the cosmos is impossible to predict; and it is also creative, tending to development of greater complexity. Reality is in this sense unmappable because of its protean qualities, and yet textual in its underlying tendency towards self-organizing systems. Further implications of Dionysus *in the field* are explored with complexity theory in Chapters 2 and 5.

My approach is Dionysian. It is an argument for transdisciplinarity *with* the gods. Here the singular frames provided by the essays discussed previously are parts of a multifaceted and never-completed open system of knowing. What *The Red Book* tells us is that there will always be other framings, or creative interventions, into the nature of *The Red Book*. It is in this spirit that the following chapter carries out another (mis)reading of this remarkable working of the field of language and the creativity of the embodied, nature-embedded, emergent soul.

4

DIONYSUS REMEMBERED, OR SAVING *THE RED BOOK* FROM JUNG

Introduction: *The Red Book*'s taste for chaos

Chapter 3 on Jungian treatments of the Dionysian *Red Book* ended with the evocation of 'the field', taken from sources as various as Jung's synchronicity and N. Katherine Hayles's notion of language as 'cosmic web' (Hayles 1984). This field suggests a radical unsettling of assumed separations between readers and books, self and world. It figures Dionysian liminal boundaries and incipient transdisciplinarity. Just as Derrida's notion of the frame argues that every writing about a book, for example *The Red Book*, is a re-writing of it, so the field suggests that we are perpetually caught up in a web of language and being that implicates self (in both ego and Jungian sense) as inextricably woven into world.

Chapter 4 will look more deeply into the dismembered literary and psychic limbs of *The Red Book*, by offering the Dionysian field two further frames. These are the literary criticism of Jung's (and *The Red Book*'s) contemporary, M. M. Bakhtin; and the medieval mystery play, arguably, a Christian survival of ancient polytheistic and Dionysian festivals.

> The scene of the mystery play is a deep place like the center of a volcano.
>
> *(Jung 2009: 178)*

> It is exactly like the modern novel, where one often does not know where the direct authorial word ends and where a parodic or stylized playing with the characters' language begins.
>
> *(Bakhtin 1981: 77)*

However, first of all I want to consider further the element of boundary-breaking spontaneity in *The Red Book* in the context of Randy Fertel's superb study of the surprisingly literary lineage of improvisation (Fertel 2015). After all, as a work built

[handwritten margin notes: "and deserving", "A I a disciplined, spontaneity", "different from amplification", "A I invites forward creativity", "difference between Nietzsche and Jung"]

from extensive active imagination, in which the image is permitted to come alive as autonomous, even articulate, *The Red Book* could be said to be a re-working or re-membering of disciplined spontaneity. Jung's later account of active imagination testifies to its conjuring of psychic immediacy.

> I therefore took up a dream-image or an association of the patient's, and . . . set him the task of elaborating or developing the theme by giving free rein to his fantasy. This . . . could be done in any number of ways, dramatic, dialectic, visual, acoustic, or in the form of dancing, painting, drawing, or modeling.
>
> *(Jung 1960, CW8: para. 400)*

By such means *The Red Book* fulfils most of Fertel's generic requirements for improvised literature, as he himself elaborates in a chapter devoted to Jung and his contemporaries, James Joyce and Thomas Mann (Fertel 2015: 367–419). Yet it is fascinating that earlier in his book, Fertel outlines a topos of spontaneity that both does, and does not, apply to Jungian active imagination (ibid.: 61).

Improvised literature provides a topos of spontaneous composition distinguished by the following: carelessness or effortless outpouring; a direct transcription of experience; writing by chance; invoking a found object; using an intimate or unthreatening setting; and writing flowing in an inconvenient situation or under the influence of drink, drugs, divine possession, or some other external power.

While active imagination as a whole, and *The Red Book* in particular, emphasizes immediacy and spontaneity in allowing the psychic image its autonomy, it is also, I suggest, *a discipline*, and not careless or free flowing at all. The discipline lies in forging and maintaining distance between the ego, with its drive to manage the psyche, and the image as 'other'. The external power of active imagination is usually construed as an internal yet separated power, with the ego corralled so as not to mute the voice of the spontaneous image. The psyche in active imagination is a dismembered one.

More apt are Fertel's other generic characteristics of improvisation, in his use of the Fool or Trickster persona, and stylistic conventions of simplicity, free association, digression, enumerations, formlessness, fragmentation, imperfections and a move from tradition, or towards biographic realism, as we will see (Fertel 2015: 80, 84). Moreover, Fertel articulates what is potentially transdisciplinary about *The Red Book*, when he says that it violates Jung's own sense of the aesthetic (ibid.: 376). For in setting this text within the large category of improvised literature, *A Taste for Chaos* opens Jung's rough red work to being re-membered in disciplinary parts. No longer would psychology and literature be foreign fields to each other.

As Fertel says of the chorus of ghosts late in *The Red Book*, their lament 'favors the Dionysian at the expense of the Apollonian' (ibid.: 388). 'Jung's whole project was balance and integration', he adds, in what is for him a crucial ingredient of improvised literature: its discovery of limits to the irrational or chaotic. Such an interruption to spontaneity is succeeded by the desire to re-found reason on a broader basis (ibid.: 388).

To Fertel, *The Red Book* is never more faithful to improvised literature than in its insistence upon renewing the spirit of the times by immersion in the spirit of the depths. He sees *The Red Book* as exemplary in its renunciation of chaos, in which one key feature is the aesthetic patterning that Jung later gives as a reason to reject the volume as psychology. What is on the one hand a retreat from spontaneity is on the other hand an entry into the transdisciplinary that is for Jung a step too far.

Active imagination in *The Red Book* is in this way entirely faithful to improvisation, in both its psychic liberation and its disciplining in the sense of a learned craft practice. The discipline is within active imagination itself, in allowing the spontaneous god to appear, and in the re-membering afterwards, as Jung shaped his dialogues with imaginal persons into *The Red Book*. However, what Fertel does not go on to say, is that *all* of his improvised literary texts from Homer to specific modern novels are Dionysian.

I suggest that the drive to improvisation in literature is Dionysus dis-membering and re-membering consciousness in the cause of renewal by participation in *zoe*. Jung's *Red Book* is here a focused example of active imagination as Dionysian discipline: the sacrifice (of ego control) to the god (psychic image) that gives him life, or 'blood', as we will see. In turn, the god/image in active imagination enters into a dialogue with the sacrificed ego, and allows 'his' divinity to be manifested.

In the end, the divine god/image will also be sacrificed, or dismembered, in the processes of active imagination, as the soul or whole psyche is re-membered. Dionysus is both sacrificed *to*, and sacrificed *for*, renewed life, for he is the god of rebirth. His unmediated *zoe* is too great a divinity to be sustained by an embodied creature. So the soul as Ariadne, abandoned by heroic modernity (in Theseus mode), is re-membered. She returns via Dionysus *in* active imagination and *as* active imagination. Let us see how this is done in *The Red Book*.

Bakhtin's remembering and The Red Book as Dionysian mystery play

In a former book, *Jung as a Writer* (Rowland 2005), I considered the strikingly parallel work of C. G. Jung and M. M. Bakhtin in the 1930s. In these years Jung was writing the texts that were to become his book *Psychology and Alchemy* (CW12), and Bakhtin was writing the essays that were later published in English as *The Dialogical Imagination* (1981). While it is highly unlikely that the work of a Russian literary critic and a Swiss psychologist were known to each other, it is far more likely that both were responding to a climate of new thinking about space, time, psyche and language.

Previously I suggested that Jung's notion of an archetypal psyche could be understood as providing the psychology for Bakhtin's portrayal of language as dialogical, meaning inter-animated by social use and a vehicle for all kinds of power.

Bakhtin's theory of language relies upon an *a priori* notion of a fundamental universal tension between centripetal energies and their opposite, the dispersal due to centrifugal forces. Hence, language is polarized between a centralizing tendency of power to standardize and perfect, versus a reverse tendency for it to become more idiosyncratic in actual social use.

This, to Bakhtin, is the 'dialogical imagination' in which power is both internalized and resisted by social interaction. Here dialogical means more than just dialogue, but as a tension innate to every verbal expression and use of language in writing.

Here Jung steps in to supply a psychology that would be capable of producing such a profound dialogical and productive tension in language and culture. Archetypes are in this way dialogical in Bakhtin's sense, for their centripetal intrinsic distilling of meaning exists in consciousness only in tension with centrifugal forces diluting meaning, as the primal psychic archetype is embodied and historicized in actual social use. Archetypal images that make up language and culture are the structuring organs of the dialogical imagination.

Moreover, Bakhtin sees the embodiment of language in social interaction as working through repeating patterns of forms of time-space, or what he called 'chronotopes' (Bakhtin 1981: 84). Such an idea resembles the way archetypes structure culture, as their images become dialogized by social forms of authority in everyday life. Put another way, both Bakhtin and Jung place dismembering and re-membering at the heart of how language and power operate within the psyche and its culture. The dialogical imagination is a Dionysian one.

What this could mean for *The Red Book* is a way of framing it in a field that enables close scrutiny of its unique dialogical form in a number of useful social, psychological, historical and spiritual contexts, without privileging any as the 'real' meaning or purpose. Dialogical here goes beyond the sense that has myriad dialogues, such as between 'I' and The Red One, 'I' and the Soul, or 'I' and Izdubar. Rather dialogical, in Bakhtin's *The Dialogical Imagination*, signifies that all language makes meaning only in dialogue with an-other.

There is no single authorizing source; no author as a god controlling the meaning of his words. All language only exists in use, and is perpetually in a dialogue between the specifics of that particular expression *and* the powerful codes in a society – political, religious, ideological – that work by concentrating meaning in words. No one person owns or authorizes their meaning, because words are intrinsically dialogical. They exist in a dismembered and re-membered Dionysian field.

In such a context, Jungian psychology proposes that no one person owns their deepest psychic impulses or dream images, for these are dialogically construed through a universal inherence of archetypes in tension with the unique psychic circumstances of any one moment. With this parallel of Bakhtin on language and Jung on psyche, it is perhaps significant that the one literary genre that *The Red Book* mentions twice is one of the most 'dialogical', in both Bakhtin's understanding and in the everyday sense of consisting only of dialogues: the medieval mystery play.

A form generated on the margins of religious practice in Christian Europe, the mystery play is symptomatically in keeping with the medievalism of *The Red Book*, yet also far removed from the ethos of the apparatus of the illuminated manuscript form. Whereas the medieval book with illuminated paintings suggests a religious culture of elite trained monks speaking Latin in the unchanging language of religious rituals, the mystery plays were partly improvised, events in the charge of crafts guilds, performed and written collectively. They are a perfect example of Bakhtin's dialogics, since they exemplify the ultimate text of power, the Bible, in dialogical tension with the vernacular life of the people. Mystery plays were dramatic renderings of biblical stories performed by working people as part of Easter celebrations.

Since even the Bible of this period was in Latin, mystery plays provided a significant break from, as well as continuity with, official culture. For mystery plays were in the language of the people, in earthy tones, with jokes, clowning and interpolations, as well as being sacred drama. Most mystery plays were performed in huge cycles over several days, and told for their audience the story of their spiritual universe: from God's Creation and the Fall of Man in Eden, to Christ's crucifixion and promise of paradise.

Perhaps here is a relevant analogue for *The Red Book*. For example, the original mystery plays acted out a participation in Christianity that was mostly denied to the common people. As Bakhtin stresses, medieval literature as a whole was essentially of the carnival, a festival associated with the sacred that insisted on a temporary overthrow of the strict hierarchy of social and religious authority.

> All the parodic travestying forms of the Middle Ages . . . modeled themselves on folk and holiday merrymaking, which throughout the Middle Ages bore the character of carnival and still retained in itself ineradicable traces of Saturnalia.
>
> *(Bakhtin 1981: 79)*

The effect of carnival as a whole and mystery plays in particular was to enable a brief abolition of controls that were equally *external* to the people in church and state authorities and *internal* in the power dynamics within their language. Religion became momentarily incarnate and anarchic. Dionysus returned. As Ginette Paris argues about Dionysian festivals, these were carefully prepared so that the ecstasies of performance did not spill over into frenzy of the maenads (Paris 1998: 12).

Such extremes occur when Dionysus is denied, and thus sacrifice gets out of hand. The mass tearing apart of human bodies in World War One is suggestive here. By contrast, mystery plays are charged with a uniquely intimate and corporeal dialogism between sacred text and vernacular expression. Dionysus emerges in dramatic guise, so that sacrifice can be ritual, not literal. The formal structure of the plays and playing liberates the Dionysian spirit within the plays and the people.

In a world in which religion was a strictly controlled manifestation of social hierarchy, carnivals and mystery plays were concrete dis-memberings of the language of power. The words of everyday and licentious behaviour became, for a short time, the manifestation of their god. After these wild celebrations, with their taste of *zoe*, the re-membered world was also spiritually reborn, along with Dionysus. Perhaps the mystery play of *The Red Book* takes place where there is also a profound gap between the language of religion and the discourses of everyday living. Where Jung laments that Christian symbolism no longer knits together the collective psyche, *The Red Book* seeks to be a mystery play for our time, re-incarnating the Dionysian spirit in the textures of living. It is time to turn to that dismembering work in more detail.

Placing of the hero and the word in The Red Book

Of course, one way in which *The Red Book* is not like a medieval mystery play is that there is no getting away for the fact that we know who composed it, C. G. Jung, who additionally possesses a complex legacy of authorized texts published in his lifetime. Mystery plays, on the other hand, were handed down within craft guilds, and the idea of any one writer having a *personal* stake in the writing would have been nonsensical. The plays were a communal relationship with the sacred and, crucially, with a particular time and place. They were saved from year to year, yet also expected improvisation unique to their ritualized performances. They were, in spirit, Dionysian festivals.

So, on the one hand, *The Red Book* is not at all like a mystery play in its historical location in a modern era of named authors and the importance of the individual. Yet, conversely, *The Red Book* is about a psychic construction of time and place, I suggest, requiring the inter-animation of collective voices. It is worth recalling the insightful analysis by John Beebe of the death of the hero-son as being simultaneously a collective and personal dramatization (Beebe 2010). The dead son is both Jung, the man who has fallen out with his mentor, Freud, and those many sons being slaughtered on World War One's battlefields.

Here *The Red Book* is chronotopic in Bakhtin's terms, because it is animated by *topos* or themes defined partly by their historical and cultural *location*, where location is both metaphor and literal setting. The death of the warrior hero, Siegfried, in *The Red Book*, forms a *topos* in its association both with the writer's personal history, and with his younger contemporaries in the trenches.

Moreover, the incident with the hypnotic drive to shoot fated Siegfried proves pivotal to a major theme in *The Red Book*, for it is said to result from the requirement to murder the god within (Jung 2009: 162). An overwhelming necessity to transform religion, literally to re-form it, dominates the whole work. Transformation is the dismembering and remembering Dionysian necessity. In this sense *The Red Book* truly continues Jung's Protestant Reformation heritage. Devoted to mobilizing spiritual change, the slaying of the hero is prerequisite for ending heroic beliefs to be defended by the sword. Such hero-ego beliefs include those about specific meanings of words.

At one level, the dialogism of *The Red Book* explores that liminal aspect existing in the work of Jung and Bakhtin, on how psyche and language do, and do not, work together. Put another way, it is the question of images as defined by depth psychology. Can words be charged with imagination in the way dream images are often said to be? Another way of expressing this issue is the debate between meaning in language as essentially stable or unstable. What Jung's text enacts here, I suggest, is a Dionysian solution to the issue of stable meanings: that the psyche's polytheistic energies offer meaning as a *process* that is never wholly stable. Rather, it is dismembered, re-membered and reborn.

An overt attempt to deal with the problem of meaning in words is Jung's distinction between signs and symbols in literature (see Chapter 1). A sign has a conscious, known and hence stable or reliable meaning, while symbols, being charged by unconscious energy, offer possibilities of unconscious, unknowable dimensions. Ultimately, one could call this a disciplinary and therefore cultural question, in that some types of writing are 'supposed' to have stable and coherent meanings, such as science and the law, while others are expected to be playful and challenging, such as with literature and poetry.

What is fascinating about *The Red Book* is that the work as a whole enacts a dialogue that serves to open up rather than close down possibilities of how far imagination is liberated or constrained by language. For example, not only the young warrior hero is dead, so too is a whole ordering of words that has deprived soul of life (ibid.: 129). Then the text turns to dreams as an authentic language of soul, and so perhaps withdrawing the psyche from verbal expression (ibid.: 132, 143). Yet what *was* said by the ancients through images in the desert is that the 'word is a creative act' (ibid.: 143). So perhaps language can regenerate? Do we need to re-member those desert ascetics as Jung does in the figure of unhappy Ammonius?

Meeting the iconic figures of Elijah and blind Salome brings about a memorable exchange over thoughts and symbols. Elijah insists on comparing thoughts to trees and animals in their independence (ibid.: 186). Nothing is to be gained by calling Elijah and Salome symbols, for they are as real as other people, he says (ibid.: 187). Much later, of course, the 'I' meets this pair again and discovers that they do not know of his adventures. Interestingly, the conversations between these three are truly dialogical in the Bakhtinian sense, in that no one of them has complete control of the meaning of *The Red Book*. Neither the 'I' voice nor Elijah are so overwhelmingly convincing as to settle once and for all who is in charge.

'I' is not 'Jung', if by Jung we mean the typical imagined author of modernity who is supposed to know everything about his work. Neither is Elijah, nor Salome, nor any other individual voice in *The Red Book*, a stand-in for such an author. That author-ity figure has been killed imagistically by eliminating Siegfried, for he alone is the type of character to insist upon heroic command of this work. Although young, Siegfried is also the aged sky father god who is so actually dis-membered in the horrific mud of the trenches. 'Father' dies over and over in the suffocating earth he has abandoned for too long. On another level, he is also torn apart for his fantasy of controlling all possible meanings in words and books.

The slaughter of millions of young men in World War One is at least partly due to traditions of heroic masculinity directly related to monotheistic ideas of singleness of meaning formed by rejecting all that is other. The death of Siegfried is the death of certainty, because such singularity of meaning requires a warrior to defend it. Dionysian savagery stalks this field, in which drowning in the muck of the war is not separate from the ruthless elimination of Siegfried in *The Red Book*.

Where is a feminine that might transform and form anew these horrific Dionysian sacrifices to a more bearable embodiment? Where is Aphrodite, who is feminine sexuality uniting nature and culture in love as an art rather than as chaotic excess, as Ginette Paris memorably describes (Paris 1986: 19)? Perhaps the fundamental narrative drive in *The Red Book* is the seeking of a feminine to tame and ground dismembering Dionysus.

Meanwhile, the struggle over dismembered meaning continues. *The Red Book* gives another portrayal of the tragic consequences of the drive to perfect meaning in the sufferings of Ammonius, the Anchorite. He is stranded and tortured by the many meanings of words. He longs for the Divine in a word that is holy because defended from limitless possibilities (ibid.: 250). Only a god can know all the possible meanings of words, and so Ammonius dreams of a word to protect him from the slippage of signifying. That word would be a protective god to him. Or, as is suggestively offered, that word would be 'protective magic against the daimons of unending' (ibid.: 250).

Effectively, to want to escape from multiple possibilities in words is to want to escape from the Dionysian psyche itself. *The Red Book* develops an interesting dialogue between images, words and magic that is also part of its counterpointing of Christianity and its predecessors. In the section 'The Three Prophecies', the soul is said to give war, magic and religion. The enigmatic and powerful figure of Philemon emerges to embody magic, rather than offer explaining words about it. He says almost nothing. Indeed, magic appears to be anti-verbal in the silence of Philemon's teaching. The silence is potent when Philemon finally says that magic is the opposite of what one can know; it is not about understanding or knowledge (ibid.: 401–2).

So the one who is adept in magic is one who unlearns reason, and no longer insists upon a stable, coherent, knowable meaning to words (ibid.: 401–2). Magic seems to be a way of integrating with the world that absorbs the creativity inherent in language, when it is regarded as embodied and not limited to human utterances. For here, 'I' is deemed by others to have learned magic from Philemon by being seen in his company. Magic is bestowed by Dionysian processes of re-membering the physical body. It incarnates the rejuvenating properties of *zoe*.

Above all, something has died when *The Red Book* begins. Killing Siegfried seems to be what 'I' does, and also what has already been done to 'I'. Siegfried is the hero within, dying in the war that is fuelled by a system of belief in fixed meanings and ideas that is now dead. Can *The Red Book* revive the psyche through developing a dialogical sense of magic and religion? If modern consciousness and its science is dis-membered, who can re-member it now?

in the name that it to know is to be able to formulate

Re-figuring god through Dionysus

In the first section of *The Red Book* we are told of a spirit of the times and one of the depths (ibid.: 119). It is this latter force that provides the essential ingredient for 'supreme meaning' when sense and nonsense are combined (ibid.: 120). A world dismembered between 'the times' and 'the depths' must learn to re-member them. Whatever is indicated by supreme meaning is therefore not a straightforward correspondence between word and significance.

Indeed, an underlying purpose of the whole *The Red Book* seems to be to conjoin supposedly rational modes with a variety of narrative styles, poetic voices, and symbols, in order to find a new language of the sacred. A 'supreme meaning' is dedicated to finding religion within the psyche not outside it. In this sense *The Red Book* re-places the old god of modernity with a renewed divine through, and also as, Dionysus. God is alive in psyche and embodied being, rather than transcendent of them.

A repeated image of replacing a god is the emergence of the divine child, another Dionysian motif. As a child Dionysus was hidden amongst nymphs, perhaps reminiscent of the many personas of the feminine in *The Red Book*. It is also as a child that Dionysus is twice-born, the second birth being from the thigh of his father, Zeus. In *The Red Book*, the god is reborn from the dying bodiless father-god via the struggles of 'I' to invoke Dionysus in his daimonic encounters, as we will see.

By wedding order and disorder in the text, the holy child identified as the supreme meaning is born (ibid.: 139). In a typical narrative structure for Jung, this idea of giving birth to god-as-child reappears throughout *The Red Book* in a spiral form, repeated in a way that develops its resonance. It gets closer to embodied nature, and is more Dionysian. So important is the notion of god as Dionysian child that it arguably drives the unusual romance between the 'I' and Salome, one of the key characters of the text.

In 'The Conception of the God', we are told that the divine child is born in 'I's soul, then behaving like a virgin (ibid.: 171). In what could be a rejection of Oedipal thinking, the soul has already insisted that she is not mother to 'I' (ibid.: 144). Perhaps it is worth noting here the second birth of Dionysus from his father's thigh, which eliminates a mother's womb. Dionysus then travels to the underworld to release and deify his mother, Semele. This same narrative trajectory occurs in the way the Jung persona is forced to rescue, or 'cure', his feminine in *The Red Book*.

Like Ariadne, the first incarnation of the feminine soul is capable of trickery. Salome appears first of all accompanying Elijah, and is blind. The 'I' figure is not impressed by her. He repudiates her in horror of her history of bloodshed. We might recall that Ariadne made the murder of the Minotaur, her monster brother, possible (ibid.: 176). A section follows labelled 'Instruction', in which Elijah insists on the reality of himself and Salome, and 'I' accepts her as his soul noting the 'cruel Goddess' of his inner being (ibid.: 190).

Acknowledging the violent history of Salome as his own soul seems to propel the three characters of Elijah, Salome and 'I' into a ritual by which Salome is healed of her blindness and calls 'I', Christ (ibid.: 197). The scene is also enlivened by huge serpents, another repeating image associated with this particular soul. In fact, at the end of *The Red Book,* in 'Commentaries', we learn that the soul has three elements: serpent, human and bird (the latter indicating the most ethereal aspect).

Innate to the transformation of the divine within the psyche is its expansion of the sacred to include the human, animal and superhuman in one Dionysian ecstatic communion. Here the deification ritual of 'I' has a profound effect of again generating the vision of god as a divine child. Divinity emanates from this union with Salome and heals her blindness (ibid.: 204).

Late too within *The Red Book* is the reference to mystery play images. We are told that the old man accompanied by a young girl is Logos in the presence of Eros, whose blindness must be removed (ibid.: 563). So it is unsurprising that these core principles occur also in a romance novel setting in a castle in a forest, and also later with the mystic Simon Magus who travels with Helen, whom he found in a brothel. Simon and Helen merge into Philemon and Baucis in their mythical role as hosts of the gods (ibid.: 552). Both the old man and the girl are said to be eternal figurations in the human spirit (ibid.: 563).

Evidently, *The Red Book* confounds conventional expectations about coherent characters as well as by colliding rational and irrational forms. When in human figuration, *The Red Book*'s soul is usually feminine, erotic and even sexual in relating to 'I', very like Ariadne with Theseus and Dionysus. However, in perhaps the most extreme Dionysian enactment (and contrary to traditional Christian ideas of a soul), 'she' compels 'I' to eat a piece of a murdered child (ibid.: 320–5).

Forced into the role of a Dionysian maenad, here indeed is a dramatic realization of 'I''s initial repugnance towards Salome as bloodthirsty. A female figure declares she is the soul of the dead girl and insists 'I' eat a piece of her liver. After doing so, 'I' is told that this woman is his very own soul. 'I' has eaten from the flesh of a child now called divine: the sacrifice to the god that is also the god.

As elsewhere in *The Red Book*, flesh, blood and sexuality are returned to sacred rituals. At this point, 'I' still has trouble accepting god as present in body and the irrational. Before he can accept the body as the place of soul open to a god, he will need to meet more feminine sponsors such as the fat cook (ibid.: 333).

Above all, 'I''s encounters are a kind of Dionysian pilgrimage dedicated to finding a god within the psyche, allowing the Dionysus aspect of the human psyche to be renewed. God has to be re-placed, given another context rather than replaced in *The Red Book*'s radical adherence to Christian culture as capable of admitting Dionysus. Put another way, *The Red Book* is Christianity in Dionysian mode, in the sense that the story of the birth, miracles, sacrifice and resurrection of Christ are re-presented as essential psychological structures of individuation, or of psychic regeneration.

Jung is indeed the psychologist of integration. The old gods did not die, and thus must be acknowledged if Christian culture is to survive in a viable psychology.

The Red Book is a radical adherence to Christianity, because it insists that lingering Dionysian traces are necessary for psychic health. Hence, the embrace of paganism in figures such as The Red One and Izdubar as *vital*; literally, conferring vitality. The need to come to terms with these figures is metonymic for a larger, hidden-in-plain sight, re-membering of Dionysus.

Again, a crucial element of the Jungian psyche is its tearing down the bound-aries between human and non-human nature, such as when 'I' sprouts leaves and becomes a green leaf daimon (ibid.: 216), also in the dynamic role of serpents as parts of the soul. In re-placing God with the Dionysian aspects of our psyche, the divine in our nature is also the nature of the whole planet.

In bringing body, sexuality and the feminine into the nature of the sacred, *The Red Book* ultimately embraces a natural regenerative process of all kinds. However, this is not to suggest that the theme of spiritual renewal is merely a rational pro-gression of learning to love bodily existence. That would be dangerously reason-able for a work dedicated to finding a supreme meaning, or divine, that conjoins rational and irrational. It would not be Dionysus. Rather, 'I' and his readers have to follow the path of the enterprising god. In rescuing the feminine/soul we visit Hell and traverse its diabolic geography.

Hell and the diabolic underworld

In a statement reminiscent of Bakhtin, Jung's *Psychology and Alchemy* gives an astute diagnosis of the connection between hell and the kind of dialogical, dismembering/remembering writing that is *The Red Book*.

> The medieval carnivals . . . were abolished relatively early . . . Our solution, however, has served to throw the gates of hell wide open.
>
> (*Jung 1944b, CW12: para. 182*)

In *The Red Book* 'hell' is a particularly resonant term. Drawn from Jung's native Christianity, its identity with a place of torment after death is radically revised. For example, 'I' encounters hell first of all in his sense of combining movement with being: travelling to hell is becoming hell (ibid.: 156). Here in what appeared to be empty desert creatures are absorbed into 'I' and change his form into a daimonic predatory animal (ibid.: 157). Now 'I' is both killer and victim in a union of oppo-sites that makes no sense at all. It is, of course, Dionysus as the sacrificed and also the divinity who demands his death.

Later, when encountering the anchorite Ammonius, 'I' seems to have deepened his identification with hell in being taken for Satan himself (ibid.: 258). Of course Christianity ascribed many of the chaotic qualities of divine Dionysus to the new trickster figure of the devil, including the splicing of animal and human in his body. On the other hand, Ammonius may be a poor guide on this spiritual quest. He is having trouble with the apparatus of living, in being unable to tolerate shift-ing meaning in words. His 'word' on who 'I' is may not be wholly convincing.

Perhaps that is what 'I' indicates by reflecting that accepting one's inner darkness may entail appearing as the devil (ibid.: 262). Indeed, while seeming Satanic to Ammonius, 'I' has in fact abandoned a division between self and world. His inner life has fled into an animate earth. Eventually he becomes a tree, or, in a later section, 'a leaf green daimon' (ibid.: 272). This transition marks a stage in 'I''s opening of psyche to embodying the divine animal who is undifferentiated from the world; a Dionysian confusion.

Ammonius is again a dissenting voice in calling 'I' Satan, while his new friend, 'The Red One', calls 'I' a pagan. Yet hell has far from finished with the twisting narrative of *The Red Book*. In a section bluntly labelled 'Hell', a tangle of bodies is relieved only by a maiden driving a fishing hook into the eye of the devil (ibid.: 315–18). In this place, too, a woman forces 'I' to eat part of the flesh of a murdered girl child: another Dionysian transgression. First she is the soul of the child, then announces herself as the soul of 'I' (ibid.: 322–4). 'I' concludes that God wants this intimacy, whereas he would prefer rationality (ibid.: 325). Hell is a state of being forcibly identified with predatory and Dionysian violence in human nature.

At this moment in *The Red Book*, there seems to be no disassociating from the terrible action of Dionysian maenads. We remember that the tearing and eating of human flesh occurs when Dionysus is not respected. Such horror engendered by eating a child's flesh happens when Dionysus has been repressed by structures of reason and psychic division for too long. 'I' has to become a maenad before he can rescue the torturing feminine soul before him. She herself cannot deal with hell without cruelty. She blinds the devil by fishing for him.

Moreover, accepting hell as part of human Dionysian nature means accepting ourselves as part of nature in 'I''s incarnation in green. Of course it is the essential nature of *The Red Book* that we remember its dialogical structure in which the word of 'I' cannot be taken as the ultimate truth of the text. In the section 'Nox Tertia', 'I' is taken to a madhouse and proclaimed to be hell by some inmates (ibid.: 350). The Soul insists that madness should be lived and incorporated into psyche. That way madness is divine, renewing Dionysus. Unfortunately at this point in *The Red Book* the so-called mad are being locked up (ibid.: 348–50).

So now hell inheres in words that drag up the underworld (ibid.: 351–2). 'I' senses that by accepting what is that underworld in himself, such as what begins *The Red Book* as the voice of the Spirit of the Depths, the diabolic splitting can be healed. Accepting the low is to plant a seed in Hell which can grow into a tree of life, uniting the infernal regions with Heaven (ibid.: 356–60). God is no longer a distant detached spectator. He is rather Dionysian human nature that plants us in nature with a renewed connection to instinctual life, or *zoe*.

This Tree of Life is what Jung defines elsewhere as a symbol, an image pointing to the not-fully-known, uniting conscious to unconscious psyche. Here in *The Red Book* we are told that salvation leads through gates that are symbols (ibid.: 392). While Elijah has previously insisted that he and Salome are real, not symbols, now the symbol is that word rising from the deep to conjure a wholeness of being.

Different approaches to symbols are further indications of the multiple perspectives in *The Red Book*. Similarly, plural is the feminine soul. As I suggested in Chapter 2, symbols are psychic soul-stuff; they are Ariadne married to divine Dionysus.

Vital to *The Red Book* is its emphasis on the embodied psyche and the need to stop that diabolic splitting characteristic of modernity, such as between intellect and soul, mind and body, humans and nature. Such splitting is often imaged as our essential identity regarded as separate from the world, from our place of being. Who we are is not part of where we are.

By contrast, *The Red Book* concretely re-figures our psychic sense of being as a body in a space. Yet when 'I' is unable to maintain the division between inside and outside, being and place start to signify each other. Hell is place as being; its suffering annihilates any spark of self as apart from its own overwhelming contamination. *only then can we be at home in the world*

Hell is a state of being that includes being embodied in a space. Perhaps this is one the essential aspects of Hell that we need to re-connect to in order to be whole. Hell begins as a journey into Dionysian being when 'I' says that to travel to Hell is to become it. Hell continues as the more substantial madhouse in which inmates envision it as the diabolic underworld.

Here the Fool agrees entirely with the Professor figure that 'I' belongs in the mental institution. After all, only in the madhouse is Dionysian boundary confusion such as total identification with a god permitted to exist. Such an agreement between those in charge and those in their charge might be a clue as to the way *The Red Book* is handling characters.

If 'I' at times realizes (in the sense of making real) that he is not separate from the Dionysian nature of his human nature, then what about his division from his fellow characters in the text? Are figures such as Ammonius, The Red One, and formidable Izdubar not so much individual characterizations as perspectives in dialogue that have their essential location within one psyche? Could the characters in this named mystery drama re-present different types of psychic being found within and between people, and within and between people and planet?

'I' is both dismembered and re-membered for and as Dionysus. So is the whole of *The Red Book*. The colliding, communing, incomprehension and dissentions between the characters are all a Dionysian confusion, a con-fusion for and within the god.

Put another way, if the way to salvation is through the gates of symbols, then Elijah's point about being real and not symbols could be neither right nor wrong, just premature. Symbols as Ariadne are the gates to Hell and the way *out* of Hell. She took Theseus into the labyrinth, then revealed hell to him in the Minotaur and in his murder. She then gets Theseus out. But now her own nature is too much of a betrayal of her *own nature* in what she has done to her brother.

She has to experience violent loss, disconnection from the killer in herself, before she can meet her divinity in wedding Dionysus. By planting the seed in Hell that is to become the tree uniting Hell and Heaven, *The Red Book* animates language by drawing upon ever larger and more powerfully imaginative meanings. *The Red Book* makes symbols real by invoking Dionysus, imbuing them with the powers of Hell, and of Heaven.

I suggest that in this way, *The Red Book* answers the later point from *Psychology and Alchemy* about opening the gates of Hell in a world without carnivals. *The Red Book* is mystery play and carnival in which hell is demonstrated to be present within the world of today in our violence and madness. Only by accepting the irrational within can we contain our own capacity for making a hell. We must sacrifice to Dionysus in order to be connected to him, and receive renewal through *zoe,* but also in order not to be wholly possessed by him.

What is particularly noticeable about this particular pilgrim's progress in *The Red Book* is how much it stresses the need to listen to other voices, to voices *being other* to conventional notions of sanity, of God and of established genres of writing.

Strangers: The cook, with and without her Christian chicken, and Izdubar/Gilgamesh

The progress of 'I' in *The Red Book* is one of multiple encounters in diverse settings. From desert to romantic castle in a forest, madhouse to garden, a hellhole with a pile of corpses, serpents, birds, alluring young women, a library and a kitchen with a fat cook, 'I' takes on aspects of the place and the characters as both part, and not part, of his being. He experiences himself as dismembered by seeing himself in human others and nature's others. Notable amongst the human figures are those with whom a respected psychologist of the early twentieth century might not usually converse. These include a one-eyed tramp who later dies (ibid.: 232–6), and the fat cook with whom he discusses a book, *The Imitation of Christ* (ibid.: 333).

Both these figures from the lower classes provoke spiritual reflection. The one-eyed tramp prefers towns because they have cinemas that enable him to see someone carry their head under their arm (ibid.: 233). 'I' recalls such feats previously performed by saints, and wonders if technology has replaced miracles (ibid.: 234). With the blood of the dead man on his hands, 'I' reflects upon the man's life of poverty, violence and love as having lived the 'human myth' (ibid.: 236). Destitute, this man is and is not part of 'I'. Yet, in the subsequent passages 'I' sees that this tramp is part of his own being, leading him down into the depths.

The fat cook is a more comfortable figure, whose kitchen is 'the realm of the mothers' (ibid.: 362). Interestingly, these mothers, at least, are readers with *The Imitation of Christ* a gift from the cook's mother (ibid.: 333). From both the tramp and the cook 'I' gets divine intimations. The cook is evidently substantial nourishment for the body, yet her reading points her towards the other feminine voices in *The Red Book* who are all associated with the soul. The realm of these mothers is not Hell, and not without the sacred. Or perhaps the heat of the kitchen reminds us of Hell and Hell's necessary, even ultimately nurturing function in *The Red Book*?

The fat cook has another counterpart whom we have met before

'But only people have an immortal soul and a religion,' said my mother, equally astonished. 'No. that's not so,' replied the cook. 'Animals have souls too, and they all have their special heaven, dogs, cats, and horses, because when the Saviour of men came down to earth, the chicken savior also came to the chickens, and that's why they must repent of their sins before they die if they want to go to heaven.'

(Jung 1944a, CW12: para. 494)

In Chapter 2, I suggested that this unorthodox cook with her talkative chicken was a novelistic, animistic, Dionysian and feminine excursion in Jung's examination of psychological alchemy. Here in *The Red Book* we encounter a similar woman with a simple religious faith, this time enlivened by a contemplative religious book. It is rather 'I' in *The Red Book* who is beset by animals as indivisible from the sacred.

I do not want to speculate on how far either incident stems from Jung's memory or how accurate that memory might be. Instead, I want to comment on the fluid relations between the feminine in terms of supplying food, reading, animals and the sacred. 'I' in *The Red Book* and in CW14 eats divine flesh in the divine child's liver, and the Christian chicken who will become Sunday dinner. Together these events stage a Dionysian ritual of dismembering and re-membering, one that includes reading the sacred in words as well as ingesting it in flesh. Jung's writing in these episodes renew the old world of books by re-membering the even older world of bodily incorporation.

Removed in tone from the homely and devout cook is the part-god, devout Izdubar (ibid.: 277–309). A literally larger than human life, hyper-masculine hero, he is better known today as the Gilgamesh of epic poems uncovered in the nineteenth century (Mitchell 2004). As in the murder of blond warrior, Siegfried, 'I' proves remarkably potent in the world of Izdubar. By telling him about science, 'I' destroys his religion and almost eliminates the man–god altogether.

Indeed the effect of 'I' on Izdubar is striking, given the impressive stature of the battle-scarred king who is part divine animal with horns growing from his head (ibid.: 277). Izdubar claims to be sickened by 'I' telling of Sky Father, Science, of humans as being separate from world. Learning of modern technology, where men can fly like winged creatures, sacrifices his life spirit. He perceptively asks if there are two kinds of truth, only to be told that there is an external truth of science and an interior one of his religion.

Unfortunately, this dismemberment of the world into radically opposing perspectives leads 'I' to say that he has only words, and Izdubar to decline into a death-like depression (ibid.: 287–93). 'I' realizes that he cannot abandon Izdubar, who is in some sense his god. By coming to the understanding that Izdubar is a fantasy, he is able to carry him as weightless and enclose him in an egg. When Izdubar 'hatches' he tells 'I', that he feels he has had an experience of cosmic expansion. His rebirth is an initiation into *zoe* that perhaps only a god can fully bear.

The Izdubar episode is yet another Dionysian ritual. It enacts again, in Jung's typical wheel-like narrative, the dismembering and re-membering properties of

The Red Book. Here it is explicitly the split psyche of modernity that is dismembered, revealing the mythical unconscious devastated by the detachment of modern scientific principles from psychic reality. The thin voice of rational science as the spirit of the times literally meets the spirit of the depths, and the result is a psychic death. Fortunately, this psyche is Dionysian, capable of death and re-birth through fantasy. 'I', or the brittle modern ego, discovers that imagination can revive even where faith has been destroyed.

Literalism, as in the collision of science and ancient polytheism, kills. Izdubar and his gods are not real, as science says the material world is. Yet Izdubar and the mythical depths can be saved by the concrete, rather than the literal. By taking Izdubar as real in fantasy instead of the narrow literalism of science, the god–man is reborn from an egg. 'I' declares to have saved his god by calling him a creature of his imagination. God, he suggests, cannot be left outside to die in his own hell of modern science, stripped of his imagination by literalism (ibid.: 296).

Taken inside as imagination, God can flourish (ibid.: 295). Izdubar provides the mythical polytheism of an ancient land, and his joyful rebirth is an infusion of *zoe*. The encounter dramatizes a process of suffering into knowing of the divine within as dismembered and dismembering Dionysus. *The Red Book* is a space for many voices. Its drama is divinely Dionysus, providing a temenos, or container, where the sacred may arise out of its dialogical nature. The book is a dialogue with the depths that evoke Dionysus via its diverse limbs of cultural and religious languages.

The Red Book and literary forms

Just as the characters play out the dismembered voices of *The Red Book*, so too does its assembly of literary genres. Along with the mystery play, liturgical language, the cadences of the Bible and its psalms, dramatic and dramatic encounters, there are the sentimental tones of romance novels in the castle in the forest, dream stories reminiscent of medieval literature, ghost stories, a fairy tale of the king and a jar of otter fat, the madhouse episode; and, of course, the whole form of *The Red Book* as illuminated medieval manuscript. While there is material here for many book–length studies of the literary ingredients of *The Red Book*, one evident quality is its opening to the collective through the use of multiple, *recognizable* genres.

The Red Book remembers Dionysus in the modern psyche by dramatizing voices and styles of language that incarnate psychic scraps of being (see Chapter 6 for more on scraps of paper). These styles, or genres, are collective structures crafted from imagination's needs; they are moulded anew to adapt to social and psychic changes. By weaving together characters not limited to human beings, and genres not limited to those designated psychology, *The Red Book* strives to embody more psyche than is usually permitted to psychology. *The Red Book* re-members Dionysus as the modern psyche.

Therefore, basic to its Dionysian nature, *The Red Book* never offers a single voice or image as the one meaning or symbol for all of it. 'Overmeaning' is not singleness of meaning. It is rather a term that advertises its clumsiness to deny such a possibility. It is Dionysian in its awkwardness, like a divine animal that does not know how to behave within the human city. Overmeaning is mobilized in *The Red Book* by symbols and their articulation as the stuff of the feminine as soul. Only by accepting the feminine as 'his', that the soul as Ariadne is vital to navigating the labyrinthine underworld of *The Red Book*, can 'I' find renewal by contact with *zoe*.

Symbols in the Jungian sense are the psychic union of language and psyche, or soul: they are 'her' language. Symbols image psyche; they are psyche as imaging or imagining. In asserting his and Salome's reality, Elijah says that calling them symbols does not invalidate their status as being as real as other people (ibid.: 187). Symbols are real in the psyche; they are the soul's marriage to Dionysus. After this conversation, 'I' reflects that symbols are transforming. He sinks into a symbol in order to change 'from my one into my other', so asserting the many voices of *The Red Book* as those of the psyche (ibid.: 190).

Put another way, *The Red Book* as carnival and mystery play is vitally animistic, in remembering Dionysus as wedded to soul. Whereas privileged rational genres of modernity strive for coherence in the multiple possibilities of words and hence monotheistic oneness of meaning, *The Red Book* lets loose the many voices of its genres and creatures. Animism is here used to mean a religious and psychic system of many voices that exist in dialogue without any one dominant spirit.

Animism is a mode of Earth Mother consciousness that bases consciousness on connection, embodiment, sexuality, and being part of non-human nature, not separated from it. It therefore remembers Dionysus in the dismembered registers of *The Red Book*. Finally, in figuring a psychic rebirth for modernity, *The Red Book*, is most truly Dionysian when listening to the voices of the dead.

Conclusion: The dead and the way of what is to come

Late in *The Red Book* three dead shades approach. Philemon eventually delivers to them 'Seven Sermons to the Dead' (ibid.: 507–28). Even at this point the multiple voices of *The Red Book* do not agree. The soul suggests building a community with the dead so the past will co-exist with present, while Philemon insists the soul is not to be trusted (ibid.: 492–5). Is Philemon here a Theseus-like masculine inability to trust a tricky feminine? The last shade to approach is described as blue, and in the Black Books is identified with Christ. After speaking of suffering, the voice of the blue shade ends the narrative of *The Red Book*. It is followed by a section of commentaries and reflections (ibid.: 562–79).

In the commentaries we are told that 'I' is an Odysseus who wanders before returning to his wife (ibid.: 569). The three dead, on the other hand, have returned from Jerusalem unsatisfied. Who are these dead shades asking for blood? In some sense they are collective voices of a historical location, the dead hero Siegfried as metonym for the dead heroes of the European war. Dead too is so much of the psyche of 'I', whose science has not nurtured him and whose modernity is beset

'I': learning how to subscribe to a symbol

with dead words. Dead, too, is the mythical realm of Izdubar and The Red One, if 'I' cannot find a form to connect its psychic vitality to the present.

The dead demand blood. They invoke blood as both death in sacrifice, maiming and dismemberment; and also as life, as the life-blood of endless instinctual *zoe*. They demand to be remembered in blood, to be *re-membered*.

The unfulfilled dead stand for the many voices and creatures of *The Red Book* desperate for renewal in *zoe*. They also represent the wasteland that is both World War One's trenches and withering modernity, whose Jerusalems of knowledge and power do not feed the soul. Perhaps one of the insights of *The Red Book* is that the dead cannot be ignored. They *must* be remembered. For the wasteland to regenerate they must be incorporated, bodily re-inscribed, into the world. So the dead as the dead voices of modern languages of science, rationality and religion demand blood: the blood of connection to the Dionysian body and earth that they have lost.

Early in *The Red Book* is proclaimed 'The Way of What Is to Come' (ibid.: 119). What comes in the text are dialogues of diverse voices demanding re-integration into what modernity has thrown away: body, sexuality, nature and myth imaged, imagined as Dionysus. The dead are a metonym for that in us that must be revived because they cannot be ignored. They are the languages of power and dominance that have no life without being embodied through a dialogic enactment with symbols of body and earth.

Ultimately, *The Red Book* goes further than Bakhtin, in representing the necessity for power and knowledge to be dialogized, to be embodied and enacted in everyday living. *The Red Book* shows that Dionysian renewal must be collective as well as personal. It also suggests that Bakhtin's dialogical imagination, stemming, as he admits, from the social enactments of carnival, is also, and at root, a Dionysian festival at the heart of language, being and communities (Bakhtin 1981: 70–79). Dionysus here embraces what is 'literature' and what is 'psychology' by refusing to wholly separate them. There is blood between them in *The Red Book*.

The Red Book offers no single or coherent meaning. Even its 'overmeaning' is animistic and Dionysian in its multiple capacities to incorporate the irrational. It summons the dead in the dying voices of our age. The breathing reader gives them blood as *The Red Book* assists us in facing the war-torn and ecological wastelands of the twenty-first century. It tells us why we need to re-member Dionysus.

The Red Book's plural voices foster a creative complexity in the mind of the reader. It directs our world to the matter of complexity theory and the Dionysian marriage with symbols as figured by the god's wedding to the abandoned feminine, Ariadne. Two further chapters of *Remembering Dionysus* will consider the *zoe* glimpsed between the disciplines in the sublime scraps for Jung and Jacques Lacan (Chapter 6), and magic in close reading as active imagination (Chapter 5).

In the final chapter I will explore James Hillman's major work in rejuvenating both the psyche and its logos, *Re-visioning Psychology* (1975). I show how his dismembering of Jung's monotheistic preferences into exuberant polytheism is an embrace of Dionysus that offers sparks of renewal in the separated limbs of psychology and literature.

5

DIONYSUS AND MAGIC

The *zoe* of 'active imagination' for/as 'close reading'

Introduction: Two disciplines and the *zoe* of Dionysian remembering

Remembering Dionysus argues that academic disciplines such as psychology and literature can be understood as parts of what has been severed in Dionysian dismemberment. Such a revision will facilitate their and our renewal via participation in *zoe*, or endless instinctual life. So what might that look like for the disciplines themselves? How does *zoe* transform through Ariadne soul-work? Where previous chapters have looked at Dionysus within Jung's ideas and writing, Chapter 5 will consider Dionysus in terms of method.

Through remembering disciplines as *related*, as parts of one divine body, psychological method can become reading that simultaneously remakes being and knowing. Both disciplines are renewed via forging this relationship, although the new methodology will look different from each disciplinary perspective.

Here Dionysus dismembering and re-membering epistemology or the ways we make and justify knowledge, is able to reconnect the abandoned feminine soul of modernity to *zoe*, or as the pre-moderns called it, 'magic'. Specifically, we move from Jung's active imagination as text-making, as in *The Red Book* of Chapters 3 and 4, to active imagination as knowledge-making, which is a Dionysian methodology. Such a shift permits figuring dismembered Dionysus in comparing something similar in literary studies, the epistemology of close reading (see pages 94–8).

> Active imagination . . . means that the images have a life of their own and that the symbolic events develop according to their own logic – that is, of course, if your conscious reason does not interfere.
>
> *(Jung 1968, CW7: para. 397)*

> "No, it is not art! On the contrary, it is nature."
>
> *(Jung 1963: 210)*

> The Intentional Fallacy is a confusion between a poem and it origins . . . The Affective Fallacy is a confusion between a poem and its results (what it is and what it does), a special case of epistemological skepticism.
>
> *(Wimsatt & Beardsley 1954: 21)*

Dismembered and unremembered, active imagination is a kind of therapy not specifically directed to a way of knowing. Close reading in literary studies is a way of knowing originally designed to be objective. It was designed to provide knowledge of literature as an object wholly separate from the observing psyche. Re-membered in a Dionysian relationship to active imagination, close reading offers *zoe* for psychology as a hermeneutical practice of reading that can create knowledge. For literary studies, re-membering reading with Jungian psychology engenders a Dionysian expansion of being.

Dionysus is the loosener. *Zoe*, or magic, is invoked, since Dionysian remembering of these disciplines loosens their equal and opposite repressions. Jungian psychology insists on active imagination as nature, refusing its Dionysian dramatic properties as art. By contrast, literary studies clings to close reading as an art that forbids crucial aspects of literature's roots in nature.

In close reading, particularly in its starting point in New Criticism (as I will show), literary studies corrals Dionysus, refusing to allow his chaotic nature as well as his union with non-human nature to be expressed in reading. Literary studies needs Jungian psychology to find nature in reading, while literary close reading has the capacity to release Dionysian arts within psychology's active imagination.

For it is seeing both the similarities and differences between active imagination and close reading that reveals the hairy limbs of the god in the wilderness of the untrammeled, undisciplined psyche. Seeing active imagination for/as close reading as relatable yet *not the same*, discrete, enables that relationship to be in touch with the endless fertility of Dionysian *zoe*.

I argue that both Jungian psychology and literary studies are rejuvenated by the playful wild god revealed as indigenous to these core practices. *Remembering Dionysus* in active imagination and close reading demonstrates how Dionysian transdisciplinarity can work to figure an open system of knowledge that summons a multiple, polytheistic reality. Moreover, via this untamable god, that which has been marginalized as feminine, nonhuman nature and the embodied soul, are hereby re-membered. We begin with the problems and opportunities that the unknowable parts of the psyche give to reading as a path to knowing.

Reading, knowing and the unknown psyche

In this chapter, I want to re-member Dionysus through methods or practices that deserve to be oriented towards research, or making knowledge. Such a project will take C. G. Jung and reading into contested spaces about the formation of academic disciplines via their mythical antecedents in magic, alchemy and esoteric practices.

Such a history remembers the evolution of academic disciplines differently, along with a more Dionysian notion of evolution itself.

Relatively recent forms of academic study, such as psychology, were constructed by dividing a heritage along lines of 'respectable' proto-scientific ideas and magical practices better forgotten and left in the dark. Unfortunately, these lost magical arts took with them ways of relating to symbols, images and words that are arguably too valuable to discard. After all, how we approach images is fundamental to reading texts of all kinds. In turn, reading texts, which do not always have to be as/in words, is crucial to what we know and how we know it.

The act of reading might therefore be defined as the interpretation of words and other signifying material, such as dream images, opening up large spheres of knowledge; for example, hermeneutics, the study of imaginative literature, and in pre-Enlightenment eras, reading arts such as alchemy and magic. We are accustomed to the presence of tricky Hermes in hermeneutics, with his unreliable darting about, as expressing the volatility of words. This chapter will consider other gods in texts, primarily Earth Mother's wilderness son, Dionysus, with his capacity to dismember and re-member being.

When it comes to the shift from active imagination as text-making, as in *The Red Book* (see Chapters 3 and 4), to active imagination as *method*, leading to reading and epistemology, I suggest that that Jung proposed a way of working with unconscious images, active imagination as he called it, that was simultaneously an act of liberation and repression. Comparing active imagination with its historical parallel from the discipline of vernacular literary studies, close reading, makes visible this structure of reduction and expansion.

As offered by Jung, active imagination represses its *nature* as an art, while proposing a psychic expansion of reading sorely needed by literary studies. In turn, examination of close reading and its antecedents reveals a structurally similar, and opposite, repression, that of the creative psyche, while expanding the role of readings as an art of *making*. In this way psychology and literary studies may re-form each other to show both active imagination and close reading as acts of Dionysian magic for the twenty-first century. *MAGIC ≡ PSYCHE ≡ " INVISIBLE" ?*

It is helpful to begin with Jung's insistence on the unconscious as a factor that cannot be ignored in being and knowing. Such a standpoint subverts conventional assumptions about reading. Words and images are not unproblematically paired with meaning if part of the psyche resists conscious control. Jung devised active imagination, to read images generated primarily by the unconscious.

For him, those images shaped by the partly unknown psyche retained some of its mystery. These images he called symbols. In a previous chapter I suggested that they incarnate the human soul as feminine Ariadne wedded to Dionysus. Symbols thereby supply psychic renewal through contact with *zoe*. In this chapter I will show how *zoe* and Ariadne arise by re-membering these two disciplines via their esoteric, philosophical and Dionysus-entangled histories.

For is it rather suggestive that active imagination arises contemporaneously with another recently founded academic discipline. The newness of literary studies as a degree in higher education has often been overlooked because literature in Latin and Ancient Greek was traditionally the staple of universities. However, literary studies differs radically from the Classics, in constructing *vernacular* literature as a basis for knowledge. It is a degreed subject invented, like psychology, in the nineteenth century (see Chapter 1).

After all, more than disciplinary liveliness is at stake in re-membering disciplines to facilitate transdisciplinary Dionysus. By such incorporation, we may be able to figure – individually, socially, culturally and historically – how to be members of one planetary body, with the instinctual life of *zoe*.

Furthermore, I will show that this cross-disciplinary comparison allows active imagination to be re-imagined as a *skill to be practiced*. Active imagination becomes soulful magic, soul-fulfilling magic, while, and partly by means of, converting close reading to Dionysian reading. For it becomes an image-native re-weaving into the body of the earth. Next, an excursion into the undisciplined wilderness.

Literature and psychology: Wild and (un)disciplined

For centuries, literary scholarship meant the examination of classical texts and their languages. By the close of the nineteenth century, emancipatory pressures generated the requirement to open the universities to new categories of students, such as women and middle-class men. They were admitted with anxiety about their fitness for such robust study as the Classics. Therefore, as a compromise, a new degree of literary studies was invented using the students' own vernacular and literary history (Eagleton 1983: 15–35).

In a sense, both the psychology of the unconscious and literary studies began in previously neglected 'wild writing' and set about 'disciplining' it as quickly as possible. Psychoanalysis began to listen to the feminine voices in hysteria, while literary studies had to consider the feminine domesticities of native fiction. Wild writing is a term taken from the poet Gary Snyder, who argues that language is rooted in the human body, and is therefore 'wild' in its essence (Snyder 1992). However, it becomes cultivated by practice, education and artfulness, and thereby transitions into culture.

Human language is, in this construction of it, a medial realm by which boundaries of nature and culture are negotiated. Art, and in particular the intensities of poetry, may open up the roots of language in the nature of our biological being. This bodily being is shared with other creatures, who themselves have languages we can only dimly appreciate. Dionysus emerges within human and non-human articulation as befits a god who spans human and wild nature.

Jung is important here in the context of his drive for cultural as well as individual healing. His concern for the psyche in an age of accelerating technological change can be traced back to the literary and philosophical anxieties of late eighteenth-century Romanticism. These tensions are explored in Ross Woodman's magnificent study of Romanticism and Jungian psychology, *Sanity, Madness and Transformation: The Psyche in Romanticism* (2005). His work compares literature a century prior to its vernacular 'disciplining' to Jung's very similar treatment of the wild in writing. Revealingly, Woodman starts with Jung, and Northrop Frye, a literary scholar rooted in process of making the new discipline of literary studies.

Influenced by Jung, Frye was equally fearful of breakdown in the collective psyche. Both Frye and Jung therefore adopt the term 'archetype' to offer a new understanding of symbols as healing containers of psychic energy. However, there is a crucial difference between Jung and Frye. While both agree that the decline of Western Christendom has dangerously weakened social health, Frye finds alternative sources of the sacred in Romantic poetry, notably that of William Blake.

As Woodman explains, Frye, also like Jung, identifies the mythopoetic imagination with the experience of the numinous (Woodman 2005: 5–21). However, unlike Jung, Frye believes that existing symbols generated by the psyche remain communicable to the world. Literature can still save us. Frye's archetypes are entities contained in great literature and evoke 'presence', that intensity of meaning that endows the receiver of the symbol with authentic being.

Frye identified the presence of the mythopoetic in Romantic literature with the Logos of Christ. He finds his new Gospel in existing literature whose symbols remain potent in stabilizing the personal and collective psyche. Thus, I want to consider further Woodman's distinction between Jung and Frye on the symbol and its social function. What is more symptomatic of a fractured psyche than the failure of the great codes in religion and the arts? If they are no longer read in a way that knits the collective together, then society is indeed fragmented. Dionysus dismembered in this context is the shattered soul incapable of regaining vital being.

> From Jung's point of view, Frye's notion of the archetype as 'the communicable symbol' ignores the historical fact that the symbol is no longer communicable. The unified and integrated symbolic life embodied in the Catholic Church, he argues, has been squandered by, among other things, the Protestantism that replaced it . . . 'Only an unparalleled impoverishment of symbolism,' he then goes on to explain in *The Archetypes of the Collective Unconscious*, 'could enable us to rediscover the gods as psychic factors, that is, as archetypes of the unconscious.'
>
> (*Jung 1968, CW 9i: para. 150*) (*Woodman 2005: 11*)

Woodman therefore makes an important point that Jung's notion of the archetype inheres in humanity through the body's connection to the psyche; while for Frye it can still be found in the reading of great vernacular literature. For Frye, literature re-members Dionysus. For Jung, society no longer has the means to both *be* the god and be dismembered by him. We face utter ruin, as loss of contact with the divine unleashes his maenads upon us.

> Herein lies the difference between Frye's notion of the archetype and Jung's: whereas Frye locates the archetype in 'the metaphysics of presence,' Jung locates it in the unconscious operations of the human body.
>
> (*ibid.: 104*)

In this analysis, Frye invokes literature as a source of the mythopoetic numinous to counter the abyss of un-signifying that is the unconscious. Woodman regards Jung as more realistically offering the human body as repository of archetypal energies of patterning against the abyss. While finding Woodman's reading of Frye and Jung persuasive, I want to offer two counter-arguments as more optimistic responses to Jung's appreciation of the unconscious void.

Making the symbol communicable

Woodman's acute sense of Jung's psychology and Romantic literature as built upon the absolute void (the absence of signifying in the unconscious) is powerfully explored by him through the cultural theory of deconstruction, and the work of Jacques Derrida in particular.

> Not until my immersion in deconstruction during my final teaching years did I fully confront the depth of the 'secret unrest' that . . . gnaws at the roots of Romantic being, or recognize in Jung's psychological views of the archetype the way in which Frye's essentially Christian view aesthetically insulated him from the global psychosis that threatened to invade it.
>
> *(ibid.: 15)*

This convincing portrait of the radically deconstructive nature of Jung's unconscious provides a starting point, I argue, for two countering notions of how this terrifying void has an-other kind of being altogether. These two notions are, firstly, the role of the unconscious *as productive*, in magic and myth that re-members as well as dismembers. A second route from the abyss draws on potentials in Jung's work on relations with nature as the imbrication of the human body in the non-human through evolutionary complexity science. Both of these arguments provide major recuperative frameworks for reading symbols with the body and nature.

Active imagination and amplification v. new criticism and close reading

Both active imagination and what I have been calling close reading are responses, in different disciplinary locations, to the perceived loss of the communicable symbol in culture. They are equally strategies for recovering meaning and, ultimately, for making knowledge. Even though these hermeneutic practices differ because they are based on different ideas about what is more real, psyche or language, each have something to offer the other as re-membered other. It is time to look at these practices in detail.

Of course Jung does not present active imagination as a theory of reading, but as a way of encouraging the spontaneous growth of psychic images, and of using them as a mode of healing. When a patient is depressed or overwhelmed by a feeling of dread, he or she is prompted to allow the sheer power trapped in the unconscious to produce an image, or to meditate upon a potent dream symbol. By relaxing conscious control, the overwhelming other will develop images on its own accord.

> But active imagination, as the term denotes, means that the images have a life of their own and that the symbolic events develop according to their own logic – that is, of course, if your conscious reason does not interfere.
>
> *(Jung 1968, CW7: para. 397)*

EGO MUST NOT INTERFERE

Either with the analyst or alone, patients work on finding a rapprochement with this active, previously alien, part of themselves. Ultimately, the active in active imagination encompasses ego as well as the unconscious. In this sense, active imagination is a way of improving and enhancing individuation, that healing development of an ever deeper connection between ego and unconscious archetypal energies.

Amplification, by contrast, calls upon the image to be considered alongside parallel or congruent images from culture or mythology (Jung 1954, CW18: para. 178). It is emphatically not a matter of personal association to the image. Rather, we are called to research the image in another resource. The aim is to find the image in its collective setting, the collective consciousness that is the emanation of the collective unconscious. Even more pointedly than in active imagination, the ego is put aside for the objective, or collective, archetypal resonance.

We can also see both active imagination and amplification as a Dionysian process of ego sacrifice, a dismembering and re-membering of the psyche that ultimately facilitates rejuvenation by *zoe*. The ego, fearful of the chaotic god in the overwhelming images, submits to finding the image *real*, other, creating of being, and thus divine. The image takes on Dionysian divinity, not only because it is other to the ego in a destructive sense, it is also constructive because, in allowing it to *be* itself, it sponsors an exchange, a dialogue with the ego-persona. The image is (Dionysian) god because it gives of its energy. It re-members the divided psyche in the intimacy of exchanges between *parts*.

Above all, the ego's relationship with the divine image is forged so that something of the energy of the other unites permanently with the ego. This is the advent of *zoe* as the participation in instinctual life without limit. *Zoe* is without limit because it belongs to the divine image in his realm: active imagination is a dismembering re-membering that binds a touch of *zoe* into psychic being. Again, Dionysian initiation is to both be sacrificed to the god, and to briefly *be* the god by being rejuvenated by *zoe*. Active imagination is a submission to the dismembering divine image that offers the gift of being re-membered for, and as, the god.

None of this looks like reading in its everyday sense, except for the insistence on beginning by treating the other as distinctively other. Active imagination is a kind of reading when it insists upon symbolic images being treated as *the text of another.* So where, in the course of the process of these symbols being integrated into ego individuation, does it cease to be a kind of reading? In fact, active imagination remains symptomatically allied to reading if the resemblance to depth psychology's fraternal, e.g., non-identical twin, literary studies, is pursued.

Contemporary to Jung in the early twentieth century there arose, c.1900–1960, another response to the loss of the communicable symbol, a literary theory known as New Criticism (see Chapter 1). The New Critics pioneered the method known as close reading, a practice still indigenous to literary studies , and therefore influencing the teaching of literature in schools and colleges throughout the Anglophone world. I suggest that recognizing the resemblance of close reading to active imagination would be beneficial to both psychology and literary studies. It would be a way of re-membering disciplines as parts of a divine body that would bestow contact with *zoe*, as I shall show.

New Criticism is a theoretical label applied to American and British scholars with a range of attitudes to vernacular literary study, including, in Britain, I. A. Richards, T. S. Eliot and F. R. Leavis; and, in the United States, J. C. Ransom, Cleanth Brooks and W. K. Wimsatt (Eagleton 1983). What linked those theorists was the belief that a work of literature forms an organic and semantic whole that is transcendent of its origins in an author, or a historical context.

To the New Critics, a literary text needs nothing outside itself. It is autonomous as to its meaning. New Critics are by default liberal humanists, because they argue that a literary work can speak to an attentive reader in any historical setting by reason of its communicative ability to a common human essence. What holds potential conflicts of meaning in a work together is the power of symbols operating as verbal icons.

Fascinatingly, rules proposed by critics W. K. Wimsatt and Cleanth Brooks, in the terms Intentional Fallacy and Affective Fallacy, serve to isolate the fragment of literature in ways suggestively resembling active imagination's strategy with regards to the image.

> The Intentional Fallacy is a confusion between a poem and it origins . . . The Affective Fallacy is a confusion between a poem and its results (what it is and what it does), a special case of epistemological skepticism.
>
> *(Wimsatt & Beardsley 1954: 21)*

The Intentional Fallacy means: do not interpret literature according to how you guess that the author intended it. The author is no god. Rather the words alone, regarded as entirely severed from their origin in a human being, are generative. Similarly, the Affective Fallacy means that the emotional response of the reader is to be discounted altogether. How it makes us feel is irrelevant. Put another way, literature is an entirely objective, autonomous object.

As in traditional science, the subjective being of the researcher must be eliminated. New Critical close reading aims to be rigorously objective with absolute separation between the object of study and the reader. Dismemberment in knowing is certainly achieved given that the reading psyche's non-rational faculties must be ruthlessly suppressed. The resistance of the theory to re-membering literature as part of the personal and social world is part of why this critical orthodoxy has fallen out of favour. As a mitigating factor, New Critics were united in seeing their literary images as symbols capable of assimilating complex or opposing forces of meaning *within* the literary work itself.

While faith in the symbol to transcend conflicts of meaning in the text is seductively close to Jung's notion of a psychic symbol possessing a transcendent function, the New Critics disowned psychology all together. As mentioned, they dismissed the psyche of both the author and the reader in interpreting a work of literary merit. It is not their approach to the reader that brings them to depth psychology, but to an act of reading that so resembles active imagination.

In effect, the New Critics endorsed active imagination technically, yet not ontologically, because the psyche is ignored. For in order to restrain a literary work from spilling its meaning into the reader's conscious mind, or to expose it to historical or cultural considerations (all anathema to New Critics), close reading was developed as a way of *othering* the text. Close reading is a perverse counter-intuitive practice for the modern person. It involves focusing on words, phrases, their sounds and shapes on the page to invoke their almost infinite possibilities to spark interpretations.

For close reading, everyone's interpretation of a particular text will be different. Exactly like active imagination, the text is the image that must be allowed to come alive of itself. In knowledge-making terms, it is a god as a generator of meaning and being. It is partially Dionysian, in demanding the dismemberment of the reader from psyche. Yet the New Critical close reading is not Dionysian, because it refuses the next Dionysian move: to re-member its reader. Only the image-text-god gets to be remembered as whole, and wholly separate, from the reader. No *zoe* for the New Critical reader!

It may be perverse to suggest a link between literary theorists who insisted upon ignoring psychology and a psychology of the unconscious. However, I want to forge a connection between close reading and active imagination beyond and despite the New Critics' insistence in ignoring the reading psyche.

In particular, I want to look for a link between close reading as a technique (once New Critical theoretical orthodoxies have been left behind), and active imagination plus amplification. The New Critics invented close reading, but the practice survived their dominance of the academy. A fuller Dionysian remembering, I suggest, is possible in later articulations of close reading as a practice shorn of assumptions about the text as object.

For even as new theories emerged to leave their mark upon the junior discipline of literary studies, the perverse closeness of the reading has survived. It has been severed from New Critical doctrine and modified by all subsequent literary theories, such as Freudian psychoanalysis, Feminism, Marxism, structuralism, cultural materialism, Queer Theory, poststructuralism, postmodernism, postcolonialism, ecocriticism, etc. Close reading remains a valued, even central, research method supporting various epistemological diversities. Above all, the major change from

New Critical close reading is permission to follow the signifying of the text beyond its boundaries.

In effect, close reading today has added Jung's method of cultural amplification of the symbol to its active imagination-like generation of its own, or *othering*, significance. Indeed, I would suggest that close reading has survived in literary studies, at least in part, because of its underground kinship to active imagination, its cloistered history in the psyche. In turn, an exploration of this hidden Dionysian impulse may have something to offer psychology. *Remembering Dionysus* is to discover disciplines as parts of a never fully stitched together body, since knowledge has to remain open.

For while the methodology of close reading represses a conscious role for the reading psyche, it actually draws upon the structural precepts of active imagination and the symbol as understood by Jung. In close reading, the literary work must be allowed to manifest its own imaginative powers. In contemporary literary studies, the term 'symbol' has fallen out of favour, but the notion that literature is language that possesses multiple, hidden or repressed directions for making meaning is inescapable.

Like active imagination, students of literature are directed to put aside their conscious concerns and allow the text to speak through them. Here is a more complete, yet psychologically under-theorized, Dionysian mode of reading as dismembering and re-membering text and reader.

In literary studies close reading, post–New Criticism, personal associations to the text are still discouraged, while cultural and historical connotations are encouraged. In this way, amplification is added to the initial active imagination, or allowing the words on the page, the *symbols*, to manifest their own power and energy. What follows from active imagination (when it is called psychology) is a new synthesis of psyche through the activity of images imbued with unconscious energy.

What follows with close reading (when it is called literary studies) is the students' own written interpretation. This will also be a new synthesis, different for each person, and should be guided by the symbolic power of the text, not the ego of the reader. A Dionysian process is enacted, one dedicated to knowing (but little aware of psyche for literary studies), another formed for therapy (but reticent on its potential for knowing), for psychology. A consideration of the antecedents of both close reading and depth psychology in Romanticism may provide further clarification of this secret kinship. In fact, it provides evidence of a foundational disciplinary severing.

Romanticism and the creative imagination

I have been describing the basic technique of close reading as it evolved from the New Critics. Early on it was recognized that New Criticism itself derives from Romanticism, but it deliberately cast off those Romantic theories of mind, theories that in turn re-emerged in depth psychology. In 1952, the critic, R. S. Crane examined New Criticism in general and the work of Cleanth Brooks in particular (Crane 1952). His essay focused on Brooks' debt to, and divergence from, the Romantic poet S. T. Coleridge. The latter was the author of *Biographia Literaria* (1847), a work of Romantic aesthetic theory that anticipated a psychology of archetypes. In particular Coleridge theorized that the imagination was innately, even divinely, creative.

Crane found New Criticism wanting for its unwarranted diminishing of the category of imaginative writing into fictional literature only. To the Romantics, as to Coleridge, poetry was a larger category than could not simply be confined to the making of poems. Poetry is a quality of writing that emerges from the creative imagination, whether it is directed to scientific, philosophical or literary ends. In fact, Coleridge's view of the imagination is very close to that of Jung, in seeing it as a creative power added to the conscious will, or ego (Crane 1952: 89). Coleridge argues:

> The reason that 'poetry' comes into being, no matter what the medium, whenever the images, thoughts, and emotions of the mind are brought into unity by the sympathetic power of the secondary imagination.
>
> UNCONSCIOUS *(ibid.: 87)*

For Coleridge, the 'secondary imagination' corresponds to what Jung later called the unconscious, for it is the creative force in humans not always accessible to the rational faculties. Primary imagination is the creative energy of God: it makes the world. Crane points out that for Coleridge, and by extension the Romantics, three kinds of knowing are needed for literary study: logic, grammar and psychology (ibid.: 93). By the era of Cleanth Brooks, and by extension, the New Critics, only grammar is needed for literary criticism. Unable to locate an originating cause in the human psyche, they are reduced to positing the origins of imaginative literature in the properties of language (ibid.: 93). *language all the way down*

Through disciplinary negotiations and formation, New Criticism and Jungian psychology divided the heritage of literary and philosophical Romanticism. New Criticism was founded in order to structure literary studies via its practice of close reading. In doing so, it denied the discipline an epistemology in the psyche conceived of as intrinsically imaginative. New Criticism took this path because of its urge to separate 'literature' from other kinds of writing.

Arguably, this collective insistence can be traced to a founding anxiety about the academic credentials of the new discipline of vernacular literary study. For how could examining imaginative works in their own language be justified as *knowledge*, e.g., epistemologically, if literature were not in some way a special category? Disciplines that could be regarded as helpfully allied, such as literature and psychology, were firmly dismembered by the demands of the early twentieth-century academy (see Chapter 1).

What was achieved, I suggest, by this thankfully short-lived denial of psyche in literary studies, was a concentration upon technique. Indeed, it was the very perversity of the exclusion of the reading psyche from reading that lead to the corresponding energy being applied to the words on the page. As a result, bequeathed to subsequent theories of literary study is the notion of developing a counter-intuitive skill. Close reading remains in literary studies as a skill, an art that has to be learned over time by consciously repressing parts of the ego and repressing conventional ideas about what pleasurable reading is actually for.

Close reading does its (founding) disciplinary job of converting reading literature from an act primarily given to pleasure to a mode of exegesis. It is this achievement of expertise, skilfulness and art that keeps the practice vibrant in literary studies today. No longer confined to the text as discrete object, close reading remains the most common epistemological practice. I also suggest that this characteristically disciplinary development of epistemological skilfulness has something to offer the idea of active imagination.

Remembered as previously of one body, skilful close reading and numinous active imagination might provide *zoe*. In order to re-member literary studies and depth psychology as allied and alive in Dionysian arts, I need to go further back into their mutual lineage and recall the mythical realms of hermeneutics and magic.

Hermeneutical problems, magical texts

R. S. Crane noted that Coleridge's Romantic theory of mind was indebted to Plato for his thoughts on imitation. Plato erected a dualist sense of the world through an ultimate reality of transcendent forms that would be imperfectly imitated by humans. Following him, Coleridge gave us a secondary imagination by which we might learn to mimic the primary creative imagination of God (Crane 1952: 85).

Hermeneutics, the art of creating meaning from texts and its epistemological philosophies, also contains a Platonic notion in its various ideas about recollection. Plato described a process of 'anamnesis', or learning about the unknown by recognizing it as, or through, the already known. Such a strategy becomes a principle in hermeneutics, where meaning is constructed by placing the unknown within an already known context (Gallagher 1992).

Another key to the development of hermeneutics is the notion of the 'hermeneutical circle', which, although having roots in Plato, was actually formulated by Friedrich Schleiermacher in the nineteenth century (Palmer 1969). Here textual apprehension moves from concentration upon parts to realizing its context in the whole work, and vice versa. Such a dialogue between a dismembering and re-membering activity is surely not coincidentally Dionysian. By erecting an ongoing exchange of epistemological acts, the hermeneutical circle extends Plato's concept of recollection, placing the unknown in the text in the context of the known.

In his book, *Freud and Philosophy*, Paul Ricoeur made a significant redefinition of hermeneutics by re-focusing the practice on the interpretation of texts, and by incorporating some psychology of the unconscious. It was Ricoeur who famously announced a 'hermeneutics of suspicion' congruent with Freud's assertion that a dream *conceals* a wish. By contrast, he also announced a 'hermeneutics of trust', which is closer to Jung's belief in treating an image as meaningful in itself, thus building meaning by amplifying it (Ricoeur 1970).

Already in Ricoeur we see hermeneutics learning from depth psychology. Less recognized is New Criticism's close reading's debt to the hermeneutic circle, with its tradition of placing the unknown in the context of the already known or rec-ollected. Close reading in New Criticism depended upon the literary text being regarded as an autonomous entity whose meaning could be gleaned by scrutinizing its parts minutely in the context of the entire work. It re-membered texts while refusing to admit any psychological animation embedded within the process (no *zoe*).

Just as in the hermeneutic circle, close reading needed to move from parts to whole and from whole to dismembering parts. New Critical close reading emphasized even more acutely the requirement to stick within that circle, for the boundary of the text was indeed 'sacred' to it. Post–New Critical close reading is free to expand the hermeneutic circle of interpretation beyond the text, and even, ultimately, into the psychic dimension of the text's symbols.

Now it is time to look at what we might call 'the psyche' before psychology and Romanticism, in Renaissance magical lore. Here Dionysus was free to roam between art and science, since disciplines such as literary studies and depth psychology had not yet begun to dismember him.

Magicians and readers

In *Eros and Magic in the Renaissance* (1987), Ioan P. Couliano draws on Freudian depth psychology to a greater degree than that of Jung. He therefore applies Ricoeur's hermeneutics of suspicion to those master magicians of the Renaissance, whose arts of darkness he likens to the hucksters who now bewitch the public with advertising and mass media's manipulative techniques.

While appreciating Couliano's moral distaste for those who manipulate people by controlling psychically potent symbols, I here advocate for a role for his research on magic in a 'hermeneutics of trust'. For the Renaissance treatment of psyche may reveal a magic potent enough to revise close reading with/and active imagination. In magic we find Dionysus now be ready to return to enliven our disciplines.

Like hermeneutics, Couliano traces a lineage for Eros and magic back to Plato and his separation of true reality in an imperceptible realm of ideal forms from their imperfect shadows in everyday light. By the Renaissance, this dualist heritage had become what today could be recognized as a sophisticated, if metaphysical, psychology. For man possessed a soul that was in essence *phantasmic*, not of the substance of the body, and not destroyed by death.

The human phantasmic soul shared something of the inaccessibility of Plato's ultimate forms. The soul did not understand the body's language, which was dependent upon the physical senses. The soul only comprehended a language made of phantasms, one that the body did not know. A faculty called the intellect had the capacity of perceiving phantasmic language as well as the sensual. Again we return to the problem of communicating symbols, because they are the organic form or matter of the esoteric phantasmic language. Too much dismembering, be it of society, or of knowledge, renders symbols mute to each other.

As Couliano puts it:

> Fundamentally all is reduced to a question of communication: body and soul speak two languages, which are not only different, even inconsistent, but also *inaudible* to each other. The inner sense alone is able to hear and comprehend them both, also having the role of translating one into the other. But considering the words of the soul's language are phantasms, everything that reaches it from the body – including distinct utterances – will have to be transposed into a phantasmic sequence. Besides – must it be emphasized? – the soul has absolute primacy over the body. It follows that the *phantasm has absolute primacy over the word*, that it precedes both utterance and understanding of the linguistic message. Whence two separate and distinct grammars, the first no less important than the second: a grammar of the spoken language and a grammar of phantasmic language. Stemming from the soul, itself phantasmic in essence, intellect alone enjoys the privilege of understanding the phantasmic grammar.
>
> *(Couliano 1987: 5–6)*

Significantly, here intellect is of the soul and phantasmic. It is far from the rational ego of post-Enlightenment reason. In Jung's view, this rational ego is fallible because it has been constructed through cultural discourses of reason that repress too much that is other. It has been dismembered from the body in a way that forbids re-membering. Jung calls for this ego to re-make its relation with the unconscious by converting a strategy of repression into one of relationship. This is individuation, and a nice illustration of Jung preferring a hermeneutics of trust to that of suspicion (that distances the other). Hermeneutics in his individuation of trust re-members the psyche in the cause of invoking *zoe*, or greater life.

Here we can see why Jung was so attracted to Renaissance symbolic practices such as alchemy. For with a soul-full intellect that is phantasmic in essence is a corresponding ego deeply rooted in what he liked to call the Self. In finding symbolic texts prior to the historical elevation of logical rationality, Jung sought to heal modern psychic splitting by evoking a past with another, and an other architecture of psychic being. For the Renaissance psyche, re-membering is neither impossible nor devoted wholly to assimilating other energies. Notably, in placing so much importance on alchemical texts, Jung is implicitly structuring active imagination as a kind of reading.

Couliano's explication of phantasms offers more understanding of the Renaissance alchemist's sense of working simultaneously in body, psyche and material substance. In this era, the phantasm is a language, *and* a material realm of being in which the soul can be manipulated by the intellect of a skilled practitioner. This

'Art', as it was called, encompassed what we now call science, for it also operated on, and from, the material world. For the Renaissance practitioner of the art of phantasmic manipulation, it was possible to change of material substances, and even to affect the world at a distance. In one sphere it was 'alchemy', a word that stems from the Egyptian *Khemia*, 'land of black earth'. In another kind of work, such manipulation was magic.

Central to the notion of phantasms and magic is the belief that there is no essential separation between an individual human and the material and spiritual cosmos. Phantasms offer the individual a soul that engenders an intellect, which is, after much study, capable of apprehending it. Soul and intellect (ego–with–self) also belong to a cosmic unity that is structured through and with the stars. Hence, the individual soul is caught up in a dynamic universe of subtle, part material, part spiritual potential entities. As Couliano explains:

> [M]agic makes use of the continuity between the individual pneuma and the cosmic one.
>
> *(Couliano 1987: 23)*

> Reciprocity or the principle of inversion of action, is the guarantee that a process that takes place in the phantasmic mind and spirit of the individual will result in obtaining certain gifts the stars grant us by virtue of the con-substantiality and intimate relationships existing between us and them.
>
> *(ibid.: 27)*

That Jung had a very real sense of this aspect of Renaissance alchemy is shown by his depiction of the subtle body, in fact, the dimension of psychic and material phantasms.

> The singular expression 'astrum' (star) is a Paracelsan term, which in this context means something like 'quintessence.' Imagination is therefore a concentrated extract of the life forces, both physical and psychic . . . But, just because of this intermingling of the physical and the psychic, it always remains an obscure point whether the ultimate transformations in the alchemical process are to be sought more in the material or more in the spiritual realm. Actually, however, the question is wrongly put: there was no 'either-or' for that age, but there did exist an intermediate realm between mind and matter, i.e. a psychic realm of subtle bodies whose characteristic it is to manifest themselves in a mental as well as material form.
>
> *(Jung 1968, CW12: para. 394)*

Fascinatingly, we see here Jung using imagination for what Couliano terms Renaissance intellect, and what in depth psychology's language might be called the ego individuated into the numinous unconscious. Not only is this an era in which there is no universally accepted division between the sciences and imaginative arts, there is also little sense of psychic differentiation between these activities. Dionysus has yet to be dismembered into disciplines such as 'scientific' psychology and literary studies.

Taking his *Collected Works* as a whole, Jung of course remains wary of what in his era would be seen as the shocking departure of endorsing magic. Much of his depiction of alchemy relies upon the post-Cartesian division of self as intrinsically separate from world. In particular, Jung began by basing his conceptual scheme on his inherited dualism of conscious versus unconscious, with terms like ego, archetype, anima, animus and shadow that belong on either side of the divide. Even though he came to accept an intermediate realm between mind and matter, much writing recognizably adheres to the underlying dismemberment of his age in post-Platonic dualism.

Yet evidently at the heart of his project are processes such as individuation that signify a momentous *undoing* of dualism within the psyche and between psyche and material world. There is in Jung's whole project, as I have argued elsewhere, an underlying drive to re-member the modern psyche to include what has been termed 'feminine', and designated in this book by the Dionysian (see Chapter 2). Regarding alchemy primarily as psychic projection is Jung's contrary retention of epistemological respectability. He is dualist on alchemy when suggesting that for Renaissance alchemists the psyche was projected into matter.

It is in Jung's later work on synchronicity that we find his more authentic alchemical and, I suggest, magical and Dionysian sensibility. In synchronicity, mind and matter reveal themselves as intimately interrelated. Jung describes as synchronous, phenomena in which a psychic event and a material one reveal a meaningful, not causal, connection (Jung 1952, CW8: para. 864). For example, I dream of a long-lost relative whose e-mail arrives with the information that it was typed *while I was dreaming of her.* To Jung, synchronicity reveals the possibility of a universe similar to the one invoked by the Renaissance alchemists and magicians.

Perhaps it was Jung's insistence on moral reservations that preserved the difference between his work on synchronicity and Renaissance magic. Synchronicity is a revelation of a property of reality, whereas both alchemy and magic were *arts*, thus deliberate attempts to manipulate actual conditions. As arts they embody the Dionysian heritage that reveals the artist as born of the magician and the shaman. Given that Dionysus is not Asclepius, the god of medicine and physicians, it is no wonder that Jung, the psychotherapist, did not want to expose his doctoring role to a god who inspired dismembering maenads.

Jung can equate his healing-directed psychology with Renaissance alchemy as long as he holds onto projected individuation as the key link. Provided alchemy shows the possible individuation of an individual psyche, it is safe from the moral dubiousness of magical attempts to intervene in the physical world. It is also safe from those successors to Dionysian magic who conjure matter: artists who put their Dionysian god above the well-being of persons around them.

Couliano is explicit about what he calls Eros and magic as manipulative practices against unknowing populations. Today we possess, and are possessed by, 'magicians' who manipulate, even sculpt our embodied psyches, in the magical *[handwritten top margin: Pauli saw that modern science SINFULLY excluded the psyche (matter is meaningless w/o psyche, and potentially immoral)]*

symbolic images of the media. In the manipulative arts of cinema, television, the internet and its social media, we are all wandering in the wilderness of Dionysus, stumbling upon heaven knows what god, or gods.

So Jung, preferring a hermeneutics of trust, cannot explicitly consider the proximity of individuation to magic. In *Memories, Dreams, Reflections*, his rejection of art to explain the voices in his psyche, is emphatic.

> "No, it is not art! On the contrary, it is nature."
>
> (Jung 1961: 210)

[handwritten: 3/29 .... /18 fb] *[handwritten: dreams that seem pointed at urging me (moral) to be open to & synchronicities and also providing symbols to "affect," "instruct," "show to read the signs"]*

By clinging to nature in order to drive art away, Jung commits a founding dismembering that forms his psychology on one side of the post-Renaissance divide between the arts and sciences. He severs Dionysus, cutting away his artistic energies from his psychic ones. Here is truly Jung the trickster and Dionysian writer. For he formally pushes art-making beyond the boundaries of his therapeutic psychology. Yet, simultaneously Jung summons wild creativity in order to incarnate as much as possible of Dionysus within his ideas of psyche.

Therefore, I argue that active imagination, another process by which a dualistic psyche surmounts its dichotomy, is friendly to a magic that comes by way of literary studies' close reading. Such a re-membering can liberate both disciplines with an experience of instinctual life, or *zoe*.

Close reading and magic: Making active imagination an art

Nothing could be further from the intentions of the devisers of close reading than the rediscovery of Renaissance magic. Denying the creativity of psyche in the reading process, New Critics repressed all the esoteric possibilities of the hermeneutical circle to that of language regarded as a disembodied system. And yet, the stripping of psyche from language created the essential psychic perversity embedded in close reading. Subjecting the reader to an impersonal system dissolves individualized psychic identity. Close reading is a defeat of the ego, or it is *not close enough*.

At this point it is time to recall one of Jung's dualisms: his binary division of literature, and, by extension, of art. (Jung 1968, CW15: para. 139). One category is confusingly called 'psychological', and refers to literature where the psyche's potential for mystery has been fully processed into the work. Psychological literature knows its own world and builds it out of signs: images that denote a stable conscious meaning. In effect, psychological literature is that of the dismembered modern over a rationalized psyche.

Opposing the psychological is 'visionary' literature, saturated by the raw symbols of the collective unconscious. Visionary literature is dangerously Dionysian. Less noticed than this stark division is Jung's acknowledgment that literature may change categories over time. A work of art may be read as visionary in one era, psychological in another, and vice versa. This leaking of categorization into the *circumstances* of reading has inspired me to propose a revision of Jung's psychological

[handwritten right margin: better, to Reality as synchronistic]

[handwritten bottom margin: "EROS EBO" is an ego state in which one is deliberately attuned + open to synchronicities)]

and visionary into *modes* of reading which could be applied to any work of art, not just literature, and of any time (Rowland 2010).

'Psychological reading', therefore, reads art for its conscious intervention into psyche and the world. It reads for the collective consciousness, for respecting the dismembered categories of psyche of our times. 'Visionary reading' reads for symbols that point to the unknown, not yet known or unknowable. To read in a visionary manner is to read in the service of the collective unconscious, to allow the work to *work*, in re-membering the soul.

Of course these two types of reading are epistemological strategies that either preserve or defeat a dualistic expression of psyche and world. Psychological reading adheres to faith in consciousness as separable from unconsciousness, if not wholly distinct from it. Visionary reading is a process by which an ego, considering itself as separate from the unconscious, is, through reading symbols, integrated into it. Visionary reading invites Dionysus into the psyche. It makes a divine marriage with the instinctual god through Ariadne, in symbols (see Chapter 2).

Furthermore, visionary reading is Dionysian because it cannot retain a psyche distinct from body or non-human nature. For visionary reading describes a practice of working with symbols in art that are simultaneously *known* in the body, and through the body to the non-human, and signifying cosmos.

Here I must insist that visionary reading requires the practice of close reading in order to be visionary. It is close reading in the visionary mode that deconstructs the ego as a disembodied island of rationality. The ego is sacrificed to Dionysus in order to become Dionysus, in re-membering the psyche through symbols.

Moreover, vital to my argument is close reading as an acquired skill. As taught in literary studies, close reading requires little in the way of natural aptitude. Anyone with a normal attention span can learn to do close reading, to let the words of the text become alive and guide the reading psyche, rather than vice versa. (Although it is a skill that of course benefits from years of study and practice).

Overarching the notion of learning skills is the great theme of evolution in both natural and cultural terms. In particular, theories of evolution have generated a new ecological complexity science, arguing that creativity and skilfulness are not reserved only for homo sapiens. Evolution, in this sense, has gone Dionysian, in not limiting creativity to human beings. We are no longer forever dismembered from animals, from plants, from nature in general, from the cosmos. What follows for reading in the context of magic if signifying and creative enmeshment means embracing the whole planet?

Magic through complexity science: Symbols as nature speaking

Jung's synchronicity implies an ordering in nature accessible to the human psyche. A parallel perspective is to be found in Wendy Wheeler's *The Whole Creature* (2006). Wheeler draws on notions of carnal tacit knowledge, such as craft skills, to re-situate the body in nature as an organ of knowing indivisible from the psyche.

She argues that art and culture advance through intuited embodied knowledge. It is through the incarnated creative unconscious that the 'new' happens. Tacit bodily knowledge means a complexity greater than that comprehensible at the time. This complexity is not confined to cultural change. Instead, complexity is now regarded as innate to evolution in nature.

Here is an important development in the theory of evolution after Darwin. Evolved nature is not so much a result of competition between species. Rather, nature changes through ever more complexly interpenetrating environments.

> Complex systems evolve via the emergence of strata of increasing complexity. Biological evolution proceeds in this fashion, as, we have now seen, does human culture and human knowledge. Human discovery and invention – human creativity – proceeds via tacit knowledge and our sense that we are in contact with a complex reality of which there is more to be known.
>
> *(Wheeler 2006: 67–68)*

What Wheeler does not say is how far Jung, particularly with reference to synchronicity, anticipates her fruitful 'biosemiosis', the signifying systems of non-human nature. Biosemiosis means that plants and animals communicate within and across species. Sometimes they transmit signs on the cellular level; sometimes their biosemiosis consists of visible gestures. In effect, although Wheeler doesn't mention myth, biosemiosis is nature's divine Dionysian epistemology. It is divine because it is foundationally creative and multispecies. Complexity evolution is Dionysian because of its tactile, multidirectional spontaneity.

Jung's unconscious psyche, like Wheeler's, is also embodied. His 'synchronous events' are apprehended through/as tacit knowledge in the body. Effectively, he too embraces the creativity of nature through tacit *significance* into culture. Biosemiosis as continuous with synchronicity is another way of looking at language and nature as linked. Added to Jung, biosemiosis is a parallel way of describing non-human nature as animate, as communicating with humans in the reciprocal formation of symbols in culture.

Evolution takes a Dionysian turn in a vision of planetary systems as self-organizing, yet wild, unpredictable and spontaneous. Order arises from this Dionysian lack of control in processes of connecting and disconnecting, re-membering and dis-membering, activity too complex to track or predict. Complexity theory is the emergence of Dionysus within science, a science which now consists of disciplines devoted to reality regarded as immanent, unpredictable and innately enlivening.

Complexity science sees phenomena emerging from its Complex Adaptive Systems, or, in Dionysian terms, members of a greater potential body of the god. Hence, also known as emergence theory, complexity science rejects the classical scientific model of an observer detached from the observed material. Such detachment implies a cosmos of fixed laws and stable realities. Rather, order exists but it is contingent, emergent and ravelling into ever greater upmappable complexities.

Making knowledge in such a paradigm means working with an unpredictable god, who is both inside and outside the psyche. Indeed, such notions as 'inside' and 'outside' are now revealed as fictional structures designed to ward off the spontaneous connectivity or Eros of Dionysus. How can we bear such an exposure to the universe as chronically changeable, uncontrollable and self-organizing in ways we cannot rationally map or plan for?

We are back to the issue of the communicability of the symbol, now seeing it as possible and happening on a truly cosmic scale. Fortunately, as described in Chapter 2, symbols have the capacity to make the inhumanity of a Dionysian cosmos humanly bearable through Ariadne's marriage to the god. Symbols, as Jung described them, are archetypal images rooted in the human body, and therefore work through its tacit knowledge in the non-human.

Nature is a web of co-evolving Complex Adaptive System of which the human embodied psyche is one, creatively interacting with non-human nature. Symbols are the fabric by which the human psyche is stitched into, and is permeable to, the Dionysian cosmos. Tacitly embodied, symbols both expose and stabilize us. They are Ariadne, or soul matter that is simultaneously matter (material of culture), and also spirit, Dionysus as complex adaptivity. Ariadne, or soul, makes Dionysian instinctual life bearable and creaturely: she gives us *zoe*.

Symbols are the biosemiosis of human cultures when rooted in the non-human as a reciprocal communication, or the marriage of Ariadne and Dionysus. Jung called this synchronicity. It is a small step from reciprocal communication to reciprocal influence, or magic.

Active imagination and close reading as skilful magic: Rejuvenation by *zoe*

I propose that close reading is the practice of Dionysian magic when it involves symbolic images. When not confined to writing in words, we could term such close reading active imagination for encouraging the image to spontaneously reveal its potential being in the soul. Active imagination then overcomes its dualist origin by welcoming the soul matter into the image as a symbol that activates the psyche in a Dionysian marriage.

This chapter has been devoted to remembering depth psychology and literary studies as both parts of a dismembered Dionysus. Remembering is here re-membering that fosters a reciprocal magic between literary studies' close reading and depth psychology's active imagination. Restoring their Dionysian roots re-stories their participation in instinctual life, or *zoe*. It does so by enabling active imagination to be knowledge-making, and close reading to become 'being' making, in re-storying the psyche.

Grounds for this transdisciplinary fertilization come from the re-emergence of Dionysus in Complex Adaptive Systems of the embodied psyche, the mutual inheritance of these disciplines from Plato, as well as hermeneutics and Renaissance magic. It is worth recalling also the role Dionysus plays as avatar of the feminine when we consider our epistemological heritage in the context of the two entwined creation myths that have shaped the modern Western psyche.

Chapter 2 of this book showed that by borrowing heavily from Ann Baring and Jules Cashford's *The Myth of the Goddess* (1991), I have inferred that depth psychology, and Jung's project in particular, is one among many attempts to reorient modernity through its great myths of consciousness (Rowland 2005, 2012). Dominant in the West, via Christianity, has been a Sky Father myth that reinforced Platonic dualism and structured consciousness as masculine, based on separation and differentiation from the other. *Fear of "unity"*

Repressed for centuries has been a myth deriving from pre-monotheistic animism, with the earth seen as a divine mother. For Earth Mother consciousness, connection, body, the unconscious, sexuality and an animistic relation to nature are the grounding of consciousness, and spirituality. Dionysus, here, is an ancient figuring of Earth Mother ways of being beginning to incorporate elements of Sky Father dualism in his (still somewhat fluid) gender. His dismembering and re-membering demonstrates the *divisive* impact of Sky Father energies. *NICE!*

In this version, myths operate as grand narratives in making paradigms for knowledge. Magic has a heritage in the repressed myth of Earth Mother relating. Such a perspective uncovers major trends in late modernity to revive her. Depth psychology brings her back as the pre-Oedipal (m)other, with Jung's creative androgynous unconscious as source. He also cites/sights her as Eros and synchronicity. Beyond psychology, Earth Mother arises in the very theory of evolution (earth generates all life and consciousness), and particularly intensifies once it develops bio semiotics and nature evolving through creative complexity.

So, with Dionysus sponsoring Earth Mother foundations in structures of being and knowing, I propose that, in restructuring consciousness active imagination and close reading have undergone a Complex Adaptive System (Dionysian) co-evolution of their own. Put simply, close reading as skilful practice enters the threshold realm of active imagination and becomes an *art of psychic complexity evolution*. Close reading becomes active imagination in the reciprocity of human and non-human nature in embodied symbols.

Put another way, by engaging in close reading *with* the psyche, we become Ariadne in the embrace of Dionysus. Similarly, when active imagination mates with close reading's skilfulness, psychology recovers its Dionysian art of knowing. Thus, active imagination is now a Dionysian art to be learned and practiced in the service of a soul connected to cosmos. Both practices are Dionysian magic because they are active interventions into the creativity of nature, human and non-human. Because both are skills practiced until they become an art, close reading and active imagination, (now closely resembling each other), are reassembled, re-membered and remembered. They are activities of what the Renaissance called the intellect, not the ego, but ego-united with soul by training and practice in imaginative creativity.

To be precise, then, close reading and active imagination are Dionysian magic because they are arts of human desire through acquiring skills. Re-membered, they inspire *zoe*, because the question of division between ego and unconscious has been eroded through the art. Practicing this magic, being and knowing through Dionysus, remakes who we are, as children of a creative Earth.

6

DIONYSUS, DISMEMBERING AND THE SUBLIME

'Feminine' creativity in destruction in Jung and Lacan

Introduction: Dionysus and the sublime

Whereas Chapter 5 explored the possible *zoe*, or rejuvenation gained from bringing disciplines into a relationship of dismembered parts, Chapter 6 looks at the destructive aspects of disciplinary contiguity. The relationship forged between active imagination (psychology) and close reading (literature) in Chapter 5 was built on the comprehensible and knowable, even if those qualities extended into the unknown and the magical. What about the violent and irreducible incomprehensibility of dismembered disciplines?

> Which is why Dupin will at last turn toward us the medusoid face of the signifier.
>
> *(Jacques Lacan 1972/1988: 52)*

> But it is only modern man who has succeeded in creating an art in reverse, a backside of art.
>
> *(Jung 1932, CW15: para. 178)*

> Even so it is creative – a creative destruction.
>
> *(ibid.: para. 180)*

After all, following James Hillman's insight into Jung on Dionysus, and by adding Nicolescu's transdisciplinarity (see Chapter 2), this book is *not* proposing what Nicolescu would call a hyperdiscipline, one that would transcend and dominate all knowing in a single, absolute and complete vision. Put in mythical terms, we are not re-assembling the same aging god that was set up in the Enlightenment as the potential of its particular reason to know everything.

Rather, we are Dionysian because to ignore Dionysus is to become victim to his utterly destructive maenads. The feminine in Dionysian form refused, becomes a very dark feminine unleashed. It is important that re-membering Dionysus recognizes the disciplines as dismembered parts, *as parts*. They are not to be wholly assimilated, or, in transdisciplinarity's language: an open, forever incomplete system.

So while there is a desirable movement between disciplines such as literature and psychology that shows them to be parts rather than wholly separate views of being and knowing (as in wholly separate gods), there is also repulsion, dissonance and a destruction of meaningful connections. Such a resistance to reason and consciousness in literature and psychology has a long history in the term, 'sublime'. The sublime is endowed with a heritage of debates over the relations of creativity and gender. By looking at the sublime, it is possible to see that Dionysian *zoe* inheres in dismembered destruction as well as in re-membered, partial reconstruction.

Moreover, by comparing Jung with Jacques Lacan, a contrasting theorist within the psychologies of the unconscious, this chapter will distinguish their distinct approaches towards the feminine and the non-human. Lacan's different structuring of language and being offers another kind of relationship to the feminine in the sublime.

On the other hand, this scrutiny of both psychologists shows their similar fascination with the literary. They each use this arena to explore issues of authority within psychology. As I shall show later, both figure problems with playing 'the one supposed to know'. 'He' is the divine aspect of re-membering: playing or acting out a god figure who must be Dionysus, not Jehovah. He and his authority must be dismembered.

This chapter also makes no apology for returning, yet again in this book, to Jung's *The Red Book* (2009), and to an essay by Jung that I have repeatedly explored, his monologue on James Joyce's modernist novel, *Ulysses* (Jung 1968, CW15, para. 163–203; Joyce 1922). For these fascinating cross-disciplinary excursions by the psychologist are infused with Dionysus as divine source of both literature and psychology. Now to turn to the sublime as the *creative* potency of the destruction of meaning. The sublime figured with Dionysus brings *zoe* in the release from fixed, conventional or outgrown meanings. It destroys in order that *zoe* might enter and ease rebirth.

The sublime and the Dionysian feminine   *definition of sublime*

In evoking destructive powers in literature, both Jung and Lacan enter the disputed and ambivalent territory of the sublime. Here the sublime is the failure of the mind or language to know or to express something that may, or may not, exist beyond mind and language. So the sublime is that which defeats our capacities to capture meaning in words. Variously located in art, psychology, philosophy and theology, this chapter will compare the sublime in Jung and Lacan as they each struggle with the dismembering of meaning in literature. Jung reads James Joyce's modernist novel, *Ulysses*, while Lacan considers Edgar Allen Poe's neo-modernist detective story, 'The Purloined Letter' (Lacan 1972/1988).

For if the sublime hovers at the limits of comprehensibility, then it touches the psychology of the unconscious in its relations with the unknown, and literary studies in its concern with meaning and its limits. For both disciplines the sublime is also attached to vexed questions of gender. Might Jung and Lacan encounter a feminine sublime as part of their quest to invoke creativity in destruction?

While the sublime is arguably bound up with inevitable aspects of human cognition, it also has a history which ties it to long-standing debates in philosophy, theology, aesthetics and, latterly, with psychoanalysis and postmodernism. As outlined by Philip Shaw in his admirable study, when initially elaborated by the Greek critic, the appropriately named Dionysus Longinus in the first century CE, the sublime was a potential of speech heightened to 'ravish' the listener (Shaw 2006: 5). The sublime was rhetoric capable of suspending the mind's rational powers. It was dangerously and seductively Dionysian.

To a later Christian era, the sublime denoted the incommensurability of its God. It was an approach taken up by Edmund Burke in his *A Philosophical Enquiry into the Origin of Our Ideas of the Sublime and Beautiful* (1757), and extended to the neo-divine power of a monarch. Yet Burke's influential treatise is most notable for his extension of the sublime into psychology by stressing its presence in mind-freezing terror. The sublime occurs in the prospect of physical suffering or death that proves not to be an immediate fate.

> The passions which belong to self-preservation . . . they are delightful when we have an idea of pain and danger, without actually being in such circumstances . . . Whatever excites this delight, I call *sublime*.
>
> *(Burke 1757/1990: 47)*

The sublime is produced by the irrational joy and relief when the terrors of death and pain are inflicted, yet their reality is not actually forced upon the person. Here we see another Dionysian quality in a dismembering, death-inflicting rending that is not fatal. The sublime inflicts pleasure by bringing a simulation of annihilation made bearable by not being actual. Crucial to the delight is the re-membering of being. Burke's delightful passions are the *zoe,* or the experience of instinctual life gained by re-membering, as remembering the 'death' and release from it.

Sublime therefore are the unmappable dimensions of God and the accompanying (to Burke) majesty of his earthly representative, the King. From here, Romanticism, a philosophical and aesthetic movement, sought to incorporate the sublime as a transcendent object of divinity, or nature beyond language, as Shaw shows (2006: 9). Conversely, postmodernism of the late twentieth century found sublimity as completely 'other'. For this pessimistic era the sublime inheres in the failure of language and systematic thought such as aesthetics and philosophy to secure *e.g., apocalyptic themes?*

meaning. Shaw emphasizes the postmodern sublime as stressing immanence, or transitory truths, whereas previous traditions identified transcendence, or enduring metaphysical realities.

news about Trump?

> The postmodern sublime, one might say, is defined not by its intimations of transcendence but rather by its confirmation of immanence, the sense in which the highest of the high is nothing more than an illusion brought about through our misperception of reality.
>
> *(ibid.: 3)*

Hence, although the sublime persists in its resistance to representation, rather than being an indication of something 'beyond' it is now a failure within representation to sustain itself as meaningful.

> On this understanding, the sublime experience points no longer to an object *beyond* reason and expression, but rather to that *within* representation which nonetheless *exceeds* the possibility of representation.
>
> *(Shaw 2006: 4)*

This insistence on immanence rather than lofty transcendence is indicative of a reborn Dionysus at work, as I shall show in Jung and Lacan.

So, the sublime comes trailing a legacy of rhetorical excess (Longinus), the longing for an inexpressible God, the capacity of power, pain and death to defeat the rational mind, and the impossibility of a stable truth in writing. All of these suggestively Dionysian motifs mark out a field ready for the late nineteenth century arrival of psychoanalysis, and, in particular, its ability to take up the under-explored politics of gender in the dual categories of the sublime and the beautiful.

Gender, and particularly the dualistic structuring of it, haunts and shapes the topic of the sublime. From the ability of the sublime as rhetoric to ravish, to Burke's contrasting of the masculine sublime of gods and kings with the 'beautiful' best suited for social and domestic life, the sublime has been associated with the privileged masculine gender. The sublime is masculinized and unbounded, while the beautiful is feminine and bounded (Shaw 2006: 9). Indeed, critics of male Romantic poets of the sublime such as Wordsworth, have argued for its presence in his poetry to enact and re-establish the Oedipus complex.

Sigmund Freud's Oedipus was a figure of illicit desire standing for the male infant's urge to exclusively possess his mother. This tragic protagonist becomes a figure of renunciation when fear of castration by the father leads him to separate himself on the basis of sexual difference. Repressing desire as forbidden structures, the ego-unconscious division, and the boy sides with the penis-possessing father as a symbol of his gendered identity.

For a Romantic poet such as Wordsworth, the dangerously unlimited powers of the imagination must be tamed by the superior faculty of reason, or self-government, as 'sovereignty within' (Wordsworth 1850, bk 13, l.114). The sublime is the Oedipal reward of the male poet who has renounced the dangerously self-shattering powers of the unbounded imagination on the threshold of the unknown. His reward is a sense of stable being at the borders of the transcendent sublime.

With sexual difference converted into the dynamics of achieving the sublime and transcendent, women in Romanticism not surprisingly took a different view. Gothic novelists such as Ann Radcliffe associated sublime terrors with patriarchal tyranny (Shaw 2006: 108). In an overly patriarchal age, the sublime was deficient in Dionysian Eros and re-membering qualities. However, it is possible to see the emergence of a feminine sublime in some female writers who offer a sense of a co-participation in nature (ibid.: 109). Gendered feminine, nature offers a sublime that is co-creative and not potentially annihilating to a sense of coherent being.

Here differences in gender on the sublime place it exactly on the cusp of creativity and destruction. Moreover, for this feminine approach, creativity and destruction occur on a mutable border between human and non-human nature. Dionysus is evoked in this capacity to re-member as well as to rend apart. I suggest that the convergence of gender on these issues of destroying or co-creating the self is continued in the work of two post-Freudians: C. G. Jung and Jacques Lacan.

The sublime in modernism, gender and aesthetics

Before turning to the psychologists on literature, what about the sublime and the aesthetic? Again the history of the sublime troubles disciplinary boundaries, such as those between theology and art. Sublime ineffable qualities are summoned to represent unrepresentable qualities of the divine, for example, in distinction to aesthetics, as a tradition of beauty associated with forms and boundaries. Such ambivalence about the sublime and art reaches an interesting confluence with early psychoanalysis in the understanding of modernist art, according to literary critic Jerome McGann (2006).

McGann notes a *gendered* division within literary modernism between notions of art as formal, structural and 'making', versus a female anti-aesthetic of 'telling', entailing an explicitly rhetorical view of language (ibid.: 313–6). Viewing art as fabulation, or telling, means that the literary work becomes a drama of self dissolution and provisional reconstruction. His example of James Joyce's *Ulysses* is suggestive.

> Starting from a condition of intense subjectivity, the writer-as-artist gets engulfed in his own writing, which then takes on a life of its own.
>
> *(ibid.: 321)*

> The novelty of *Ulysses* is how it exposes the work of fiction not as a text or document but as a field of discourse where readers are assumed to be present: the reader being a 'hero' of the writing.
>
> *(ibid.: 312)*

McGann provides contrasting views of modernist writing as either an implicitly masculine devotion to art as making within an aesthetic tradition of forms and structures, opposed to a feminine rhetoric of telling that McGann finds explicitly defended by the poet Laura Riding and novelists John Cowper Powys and Dorothy Richardson (McGann 2006: 313, 316). Fascinatingly, McGann recognizes that C. G. Jung also discerns this quality in Joyce's *Ulysses*. The modernist icon *Ulysses* joins this feminine anti-aesthetic courtesy of the psychologist.

> For them [Powys and Jung] the order that *Ulysses* sets in play is not . . . formal or structural order, it is rhetorical. When Powys and Jung read Joyce they emphasize the book's subjectivity, reading the writing as a kind of monodrama.
>
> *(McGann 2006: 313)*

Although McGann does not say it, he is recognizing Dionysus in all these writers: his so-called feminine anti-aesthetic is the embrace of the spontaneous and improvised, diagnosed by Randy Fertel in his *A Taste for Chaos* (see Chapter 4). Such spontaneity liberates the Dionysian dismembering, re-membering qualities of rhetoric in the psyche.

Before considering the helpfulness of this belated literary recognition of Jung's essay, it is worth looking at one who is both a critic and devotee of structure in language and psyche: Jacques Lacan, and his reading of Poe. For there may be potential in Jung on *Ulysses* to reconceptualize what Shaw depicted as the gulf between the Romantic sublime of transcendence and the postmodern one of immanence.

For modernists like T. S. Eliot, the sublime of transcendence could be conceived again in the history of art as traditional forms, and of 'making', offering a sublime of aesthetics that for him came to cement a religious presence in the sublime of art. What Jung sees in *Ulysses*, I will suggest, is a sublime of rhetoric that is the psyche itself in action, where immanence plays and displays its intrinsic formlessness and ambivalence over meaning. Jung sees immanent Dionysus in *Ulysses* and invokes him in his own writing.

First, however, it is worth exploring Lacan's far more explicit sense of language as building blocks of psyche, for it is language with a distressing tendency to melt away any security of being.

Lacan's purloined signifier

> If what Freud discovered has a meaning, it is that the displacement of the signifier determines the subjects in their acts, in their destiny . . . and in their fate . . . without regard for character or sex.
>
> *(Lacan 1972/1988: 43–4)*

> [T]he signifier . . . materializes the agency of death.
>
> *(ibid.: 38)*

Lacan takes Freud's notion of Oedipal splitting and applies it to the psyche's embrace of language. Entry into the world of words means recognizing them as standing for things. Such a move divides us from that literally unimaginable completion of being with the pre-Oedipal mother. Language structures being within its symbolic order of the Law, and is haunted by absence. Here words are signifiers, as Lacan says, 'a unit in its very uniqueness, being by nature symbol only of an absence' (Lacan 1972/1988: 39). No wonder he was entranced by Poe's story of a letter purloined by an opportunist minister from royal apartments.

What Lacan finds fascinating is that the piece of paper is an instrument of overwhelming power while unknown and unread. So to Lacan, the letter makes visible all that is annihilating, and at the same time empty, in the potency of the signifier. In Dionysian terms, it is the letter that dismembers and re-members being in ways that render human existence vulnerable to terrifyingly impersonal forces.

Lacan decides early in his essay that the feminine addressee of the letter must be the Queen. She is unable to stop the minister from taking it due to the presence of her husband, the King. She cannot, by virtue of her position as consort, afford to draw attention to an anomalous letter. In fact, Poe's story actually begins with the detective Dupin at home with an unnamed narrator when both are visited by a near desperate Prefect of Police.

The official forces of the law have been unable to find the Queen's purloined letter in the home of the minister, despite fantastically detailed searches. Of course, in a second visit the Prefect will be astonished when Dupin hands over the letter in return for a very large cheque. With many diversions, Dupin then explains how he was able to spot the letter in plain view. It was concealed disguised as a trivial note to the minister.

Lacan's attribution of sovereignty to the bereft woman enables him to stabilize the role of the letter as potentially disruptive to the symbolic order in which the King ought to incarnate the Law. As Queen hiding her letter from the King, she is disloyal (Lacan 1972/1988: 42). It 'situates her in a symbolic chain foreign to the one which constitutes her faith' (ibid.: 42).

The letter is indeed a signifier of an absence to Lacan, and not only because it alerts us to the Queen's incomplete stitching into the symbolic order. For in the letter's illicit circulation between Queen, minister, Dupin and from thence to Prefect to Queen, Lacan sees the immense power of language as signifier to determine 'being'. Put another way, Dionysus as dismembering inheres in the letter as a signifier of dominion.

As Dupin realizes, possession of the purloined letter bestows immense power and an equal prospect of destruction. Dupin points out that in his reciprocal purloining of the letter without the thief noticing will cause the hapless minister to act in a way ensuring his own downfall. From having power over the Queen, the minister is exposed by being unaware of his own dismemberment in the loss of the letter.

Lacan details how glancing knowingly and unknowingly at the letter, and then possessing or not possessing it, changes gender roles. The minster, so bold as to seize what is not his, is subsequently feminized by being forced into the Queen's role of concealing the letter in full view. He has been dismembered of his masculinity as a sign of being. And, astonishingly, the letter comes to stand for both the full and empty effects of the signifier as the forever absent lost body of the mother.

> Just so does the purloined letter, like an immense female body, stretch out across the minister's office when Dupin enters. But just so does he expects to find it, and has only, with his eyes veiled by green lenses, to undress that huge body.
>
> *(Lacan 1972/1988: 48)*

The office is not the immense female body, the letter is. Language to Lacan is a Dionysus who tears apart and re-makes identity, but always subject to 'his' unknowable, unappeasable will. So the letter is an immense woman's body, because woman is the sign of castration. The letter, on the one hand, gives a sense of unusual, ego-inflating power to the Minister, the full promise of signifying such as is the promise of the phallus in Lacan's post-Freudian view. On the other hand, the letter is the ultimate sign of castration of emptiness that will destroy the minister, as Jacques Derrida puts it, echoing Lacan:

> The truth is 'woman' as veiled/unveiled castration. This is where the signifier (its inadequation with the signified) gets under way, this is the site of the signifier, the letter.
>
> *(Derrida 1988: 183)*

> Femininity is the Truth (of) castration, is the best figure of castration, because in the logic of the signifier it has always already been castrated; and Femininity 'leaves' something in circulation (here the letter), something detached from itself in order to have it brought back to itself.
>
> *(ibid.: 185)*

So here the letter is both the castration of the subject in language, how we are fatally implicated in the signifying chain, and that illusion of fullness and power that the symbolic order enacts upon us and dazzles us with. Lacan's Dionysian language deludes, dismembers and only re-members in a mirage that fails to conceal an abyss of being. Although Lacan does not use the term in this essay, the letter as signifier appears to take on the role of the phallus, that sign of gendering that is also non-gendered and empty. If language is so castrating, so immanent in its dismembering of being, is it also an organ of the sublime within the very structuring of consciousness?

Lacan's sublime and Dionysus

Lacan certainly offers a sense of the sublime in his notion of the Real, which is the unpresentable Thing that has to be posited for the symbolic order to do its job of (illusory) ordering. The Real is only apparent when the symbolic order is violently ruptured. It is a state of dismemberment so terrible as to admit no hope of remembering other, more comfortable, experiences of being.

Arguably, Lacan traces the presence of the Real in his description of the signifier as 'medusoid'. He says that Dupin shows this Medusa signifier in the quotation he leaves for the minister to find in place of the purloined letter. The quotation refers to a father forced to drink the blood of his son as the revenge of his brother (Lacan 1972/1988: 52). The signifier is both the protection from, and the hapless partner of, such terrifying and subject annihilating sublime conditions. The letter here stands for all signifiers, in its ability to mutate gender, shatter the psyche and engender death, 'the return of the stone guest I shall be for you' (ibid.: 52). Here is Dionysian rage unmitigated, the engorged maenads at work on those who turn away from the god.

So far Lacan offers a tantalizing sublime prospect of the sublime in his pessimistic sense of the dismembering properties of language. His structuring sense of the signifier is at once a (gendered) construction and a destruction of being, given the menace of the Real in its 'medusoid' qualities. Lacan appears not to believe that one can 'be' Dionysus as well as be sacrificed to him, probably because his post-Freudian psyche is more dependent upon bodily members in the role of the phallus than Jung's archetypal unconscious. Put another way, where Jung could see something generative as well as annihilating in Medusa, Lacan focuses on her propensity to make 'the stone guest' in petrifying, literally making stone of all who look on her.

Moreover, Lacan could be said to have imported a little more stability than the story originally offered by deciding that the original addressee was the Queen, so hiding her letter from the one who should, but is unable fully to, embody the Law. Here we have Lacan who could be said to emphasize what Jung might call, an archetypal structure in which authority and gender are blended. Effectively, Lacan is here reaching for, and not quite securing, a sublime of making, in the aesthetic sense described by McGann, by both his core disposition of the signifier and by crowning the initial royal personages.

To recap, McGann argued that an aesthetic of making, of art in the tradition of positing structural transcendence (even if only or art itself), was countered in the modernist period by a female anti-aesthetic of telling. It is the latter that incarnates Dionysian qualities of re-membering being. At this point, Lacan belongs more to 'making' because of his adherence to, if not complete reliance on, the structuring power of the signifier.

Both approaches to literature imply the sublime, one in the unknowable or even impossible transcendence, the other in an immanence of rhetoric that patterns without making claims on truth. Hence, both demonstrate the violent erasure of signifying inherent in Dionysus as dismembering: 'making' infers an impossibility of stable meaning while 'telling' enacts a Dionysian chaotic fluidity.

Yet, given that by Lacan's account subjectivity is far from stable, and that he stresses how the story ends with the intervening of the Real in a foreign quotation (its language and origin in another text doubly is estranging), perhaps there is another possibility of the sublime in his treatment of desire and language?

After all, critic Malcolm Bowie points out that there is an ambivalence in Lacan's writing between his masculinist discourse by which the phallus becomes a transcendental signifier of desire (so suggesting a transcendent sublime), which in turn does not fit his two emphases in the structuring of desire itself (Bowie 1991). For along with the phallocentrism, there is his insistence on the neutrality of the subject divided by language, together with the genderless possibility of desire in the impossibility of need and demand in the psyche (ibid.: 141–2).

Jouissance and the 'seminar on the purloined letter'

Lacan ultimately produces more out of his multifaceted mapping of gender and psyche. In questing for origins of desire he offers what he calls *jouissance* as the energy of feminine sexuality. Importantly, this playful energy is not denied to men, and yet is nevertheless to be understood as different from the desire organized around the phallus.

> Far from its being the case, indeed, that the passivity of the act corresponds to this desire, feminine sexuality appears as the effort of a *jouissance* wrapped in its own contiguity . . . to be *realized in rivalry* with the desire which castration releases in the male by giving him its signifier in the phallus.
>
> *(Lacan in Bowie 1991: 148, 735 MR 97)*

Desire is here a fundamental human energy that remains caught up in the subject's division by language. So *jouissance* is a pleasure in thinking, writing, being-in-language in which there is a kind of release from fixed meanings that is an enjoyment of signifying energy. It is, arguably, a feminine sublime, not excluding men, that significantly resembles the female so called anti-aesthetic posited by McGann.

For pleasure in signifying without foreclosing meaning is to be caught up in the playfulness of language, with rhetoric as telling without fixed endings. Rhetoric is here understood as the power of language to enact psyche, whether as the masculine phallic sublime of Longinus's ravishing in Lacan's sense of signifying as psychic structuring, or in feminine *jouissance* of pleasure in the unfixity of signifying. *Jouissance* is therefore Dionysian in its playful and erotic dismembering and re-making of uncontrollably fluid meaning. It is the inability to structure *jouissance* that betrays its Dionysian character, its playfulness is enlivening, *zoe*.

> *Jouissance* of the kind Lacan chooses to call feminine is to be found in the sinews, in thinking, in writing – wherever *significance*, the combined production of meaning and pleasure, occurs. Enjoying oneself and not knowing anything about it is 'feminine' in a way, but this does not mean that men are debarred by their gender from reaching such states.
>
> *(Bowie 1991: 153)*

I suggest that this feminine *jouissance* of telling, a Dionysian entry into *zoe*, is to be found in Lacan's essay on 'The Purloined Letter'. It is hinted at in his depiction of the Queen, while being superbly displayed by Lacan himself in the position he takes towards knowing, as Jane Gallop explores in the volume, *The Purloined Poe: Lacan, Derrida and Psychoanalytic Reading* (Gallop 1988: 268–82).

Lacan's Queen employs *jouissance* in her deliberate, although imperilled play-acting. She provides a 'simulation of mastery', trying to conceal the letter from the Minister when she confers upon the thief a position in the imaginary of supreme power (Lacan 1982: 47). Here the so-called Queen is both entirely coerced by the overwhelming power of the phallic signifier of the letter and yet, still playing or simulating, still able to enjoy the *jouissance* of her exposure in the imaginary. She has entered Dionysian theatre, and is playing for her life.

Before looking further at Lacan's *jouissance* in his essay on 'The Purloined Letter', it is worth noting an aspect of desire that may also expand the notion of this pleasure in fluidity, in signifying as a sublime feminine. Just as the roles that the phallic signifier imposes are excessive to being, so too is desire more than human. In fact, it is animal. The minister needs a 'lynx eye' to see through the Queen's play acting. Driven by the signifier, he is 'a beast of prey ready to spring', again suggesting a Dionysian expansion of being beyond the human order (Lacan 1982: 48).

Lacan suggests here that the non-human is collaborator with the medusoid signifier in making a person simply a vehicle for its annihilating, dismembering power. But what if nature was actually considered to be contiguous, in a sense of having patterns and powers of its own that in certain circumstances could collaborate creatively, or playfully, with the human? What if non-human nature was a partner in *jouissance*? Then one would find a Dionysian and feminine sublime, like with those women writers in Romanticism who found in nature a co-creative partner in desire and pleasure in signifying without mastery (Shaw 2006: 109). As Romantic critic Ann Mellor notes, for some female writers:

> [The sublime is] an ecstatic experience of co-participation in nature . . . explicitly gender[ed] as female. For [these woman writers] this female nature is not an overwhelming power; nor even an all bountiful mother. Instead nature is a female friend.
>
> *(Mellor 1993: 97)*

It is time to turn to Jane Gallop's invaluable diagnosis of Lacan as masquerading control, like Lacan's Queen, in his essay on 'The Purloined Letter'. While the Queen's impersonation of mastery is short lived, because it is castrated by the stealing of the letter (which reveals her as already castrated), Lacan plays at the mastery of signifying throughout his text. Does he, then, learn to take the Dionysian role of possessor of supreme knowledge, or god? Or is he still impersonating the Enlightenment master of transcendent reason?

Lacan 'playing' god/authority

> Lacan plays a certain imaginary of the analyst to the hilt; he plays 'the subject pre-
> sumed to know,' the great oracle, interpreter of enigmas. To fall for the illusion of
> Lacan's mastery is to be trapped in the imaginary of the text.
>
> *(Gallop 1988: 281)*

Here Gallop is making a crucial point about reading, consciousness and theory. To
Lacan, the imaginary is the realm of imagoes, or structures in which the psyche
is caught up in a process of mirroring, not a separate dimension of being. Gallop
shows that to attempt to produce a stable opposition of imaginary and symbolic is
to remain in the imaginary (Gallop 1988: 271).

Put another way, to identify author Lacan as 'authoritative' Lacan in his 'The
Purloined Letter' essay is to remain mired in the imaginary gazing at Lacan as
idealized analyst, 'the one presumed to know' (Gallop 1988: 273, 281). Such a
reading of magnificent certainty would be entirely anti-Dionysian in refusing to
dismember or be dismembered in the act of supreme knowing. To be Dionysian is
to *play* the god of the text *and* one who will be dismembered. It is not to fall into
the delusion of being a god transcendent of all other domains.

Gallop argues that Lacan's ethical imperative to get beyond the analyst as mirror must apply to Lacan's writing here. The analyst as mirror provides a sense
of stability, in offering 'his' ego's certainties of knowing and being. By contrast,
Lacan advocates not seeing the analyst as reflection of ego, but rather the true goal
is to see the mirror in the analyst simply as a mirror. The analyst becomes a mere
device. Being and knowing in consciousness are *seen through*. So Gallop urges seeing
through the appearance of knowing in Lacan's authorial persona in his 'seminar'.

> My project . . . might be understood as an attempt to break out of an imagi-
> nary reading of Lacan and reach the symbolic. In as much as anyone would
> be 'for' the symbolic and 'against' the imaginary, he would be operating in
> the imaginary. Ironically the ethical imperative to accede to the symbolic
> and vigilantly to resist the imaginary is itself mired in the imaginary.
>
> *(Gallop 1988: 271)*

> Psychoanalysis should be an encounter not with a likeness or a double, but
> with a mirror . . . the charge is to look into the mirror and see not the image
> but the mirror itself.
>
> *self appropriated intentionality?*
>
> *(ibid.: 272)*

Lacan, playing the one presumed to know, is not providing the mirror, according to Gallop, nor is Dupin, the figure in the story that Lacan endows with mastery (Gallop 1988: 279–81). Rather, the true analytical mirror function is to be
found in the unnamed narrator. That conversationalist has the role of transmitting
the fascinating imago of proto-analyst Dupin into the signifying body of the
simulation of mastery in Lacan's text.

In this sense, Gallop reads Lacan's seminar as a Dionysian text despite *and* because of his mastering presence. Although Lacan appears to reject dismembering, Gallop reads this very refusal as a mirror upon which *jouissance* can open to *zoe*. Her playful dismembering of Lacan as mastering god works because she is implicitly regarding *jouissance* in analytic discourse as also visible in the structures of Lacan's psychological writing.

She is both dismembering and re-membering psychology and literature as separate/conjoined members of one body of knowing. She too plays at mastery in reading one aspect of Lacan, playful *jouissance* in signifying, against his appearance of authority. In so doing, she asserts Dionysian dismembering drama (literature) within psychology in a way that paradoxically bolsters the authority of psychology by revealing it as symptomatically literary.

Gallop emphatically warns against the risk of constructing an opposition of imaginary and symbolic, such as would occur in a straightforward opposition of literature and psychology. This would inevitably mean being trapped in the imaginary. Rather than simply interpreting Lacan's psychology as literature, she uses Lacanian literary *jouissance* to dismember the analyst as the one presumed to know, to make him 'telling' Dionysus rather than 'making' Jehovah, as described earlier by McGann in this chapter.

Such a risk needs to be mentioned in the context of this whole chapter on Lacan and Jung; for it is perfectly straightforward to use one as the symbolic lens by which to push the other into the imaginary. When I suggested that Lacan grappled with an archetypal sense of power and gender in importing the notion of the royal personages as monarchs, such a comment immediately infers that one set of psychological ideas is the symbolic, and so pushes the other into the imaginary. A converse move points out how in his essay on *Ulysses* Jung sees the mirror as mirror when he refuses to stick to his own theoretical scheme. In a reverse move to Lacan he refuses archetypes.

 I cannot find the key . . . Of course, one senses the archetypal background . . . But the book does not focus upon this background.

(Jung 1966, CW15: para. 185)

One can prefer Lacan by using his ideas to explain Jung, or vice versa. Each constructs their individual theories as a symbolic order imperfectly penetrated by the other, so making the subordinate views imaginary. And yet as Gallop points out, such a simple opposition of two kinds of writing remains itself imaginary.

While not expecting to entirely avoid this trap, my aim is to seek out the sublime feminine haunting both writers as they consider that unreliable source of psychological truth, literature. This sublime feminine partakes of *zoe*, or instinctual life, because it emanates from the dismembering of knowing by renouncing or seeing through being 'the one presumed to know'.

Above all, there is more to be gained by considering Lacan as simulating mastery in his text alongside Jung's at first unhappy then astute adoption of the one who *does not know,* in his piece on *Ulysses*. First of all, what about Gallop's strong defence of Lacan's psychological deviousness in writing? If Lacan's masquerade is a key to his ethics of refusing a mastering psychology that would bolster ego in order to favour the recognition of mirror as mirror, then he may indeed mirror Jung.

In previous books, such as *Jung as a Writer* (Rowland 2005), I have sought to present Jung as *performing* rather than structuring his ideas, because of a foundational notion of no foundations. He says baldly that to take the unconscious seriously means that the sublime enters the very processes of knowing.

> Nobody drew the conclusion that if the subject of knowledge, the psyche, were in fact a veiled form of existence not immediately accessible to consciousness, then all our knowledge must be incomplete, and moreover to a degree that we cannot determine.
>
> *(Jung 1960, CW8: para. 358)*

The unknown psyche dismembers certainty. Crediting the unconscious as a significant participant in knowing means that all knowledge is subject to dismemberment. It participates in the sublime. For the psyche to know itself, it has to take account of its own irrational and unknown properties. Knowledge is neither stable nor complete. Hence Jung offers a pragmatic model rather than providing psychological truths as transcendent of the irrational constitution of the psyche.

> It is not a question of . . . asserting anything, but of constructing a *model* which opens up a promising and useful field of enquiry. A model does not assert that something is so, it simply illustrates a particular mode of observation.
>
> *(Jung 1960, CW8: para. 381)*

Another challenge by Jung to psychology as the discourse of transcendence or mastery occurs in his perception of the necessity for myth and drama.

> The empirical reality summed up under the concept of the anima forms an extremely dramatic content of the unconscious. It is possible to describe this content in rational, scientific language, but in this way one entirely fails to express its living character. Therefore, in describing the living processes of the psyche, I deliberately and consciously give preference to a dramatic, mythological way of thinking and speaking, because this is not only more expressive but also more exact than an abstract scientific terminology, which is wont to toy with the notion that its theoretic formulations may one fine day be resolved into algebraic equations.
>
> *(Jung 1951, CW9ii, para. 25)*

Dramatic and mythological thinking and speaking is more *exact* than neutral, implicitly transcendent concepts. As the god of drama, Dionysus is more true to psyche than rational language. Here again is a challenge to rational knowing, to the sufficiency of the symbolic order and ultimately to the sublime as either transcendent or immanent. For Jung here says that 'scientific terminology", by which he means a concept such as the anima, inevitably partakes of the sublime because it is too abstract (and so inexact) to account for the whole psyche. The unknowable sublime qualities of the unconscious ensure that the sublime haunts even psychological theory.

On the other hand, the unknown psyche as interior to the making of knowledge also offers an immanent sublime, because the dismembering potential of the Dionysian unconscious is ever present. Or we could say that Jungian epistemology is inherently Dionysian because the unknown psyche dismembers what we think we know in order to remember it as sublime: haunted and pervaded by unknowing.

What recognizing Dionysus adds to this argument about knowing and being is the generative, instinctual incorporation into knowing. Dionysus, avatar of the rejected feminine, incarnates *zoe* in dismembering as well as remembering disciplines.

One might see a moment of conjunction here between trickster Jung's Dionysian drama in knowing and Lacan's medusoid signifier that 'petrifies' subjectivity. After all, Jung himself offers a mirror in calling his psychology writing a 'net of reflections', in which it is the *net* that he wants the reader to see how disciplinary discourses both capture and fail to completely re-present the psyche.

> I fancied I was working along the best scientific lines . . . only to discover in the end that I had involved myself in a net of reflections which extend far beyond natural science and ramify into the fields of philosophy, theology, comparative religion, and the human sciences in general.
>
> (Jung 1960, CW8: para. 421)

In a similar way to Gallop's call for us to see the mirror as mirror and not a reflection of the ego's illusory mastery in Lacan's trickster writing on 'The Purloined Letter', Jung invites readers to see through his attempt to negotiate immanent and transcendent sublime on the logos of psyche: psychology. Put another way, Jung, too, is caught between making and telling, not in art, but in psychology. Perhaps sublime *zoe* here traverses the disciplinary boundaries of art and psychology, in that an implicitly transcendent and masculine aesthetic of making versus a female anti-aesthetic of telling is actually innate to both Jung and Lacan.

Now it is time to look at how Jung participates in feminine Dionysian *zoe*, or *jouissance*, in his struggles with James Joyce's complex modernist novel, *Ulysses*. Like Lacan, he finds that knowing and desire requires invoking the non-human. In fact, Jung discovers that such is the threat to subjectivity by these signifiers that he invokes in a tapeworm that not-yet-subject which Julia Kristeva later called the 'abject' in the tapeworm (Kristeva 1982). His abject becomes a non-figuration of the destructive aspects of dismembering. It demonstrates the intimacies of knowing and being when remembering Dionysus.

Jung on *Ulysses*

In the abject

> Thus I read to page 135 with despair in my heart, falling asleep twice on the way.
>
> *(Jung 1966, CW15: para. 165)*

The essay begins with Jung as very much the one who does not know. Not only his intellect, but also his body resists Joyce's book. It dismembers him as psychological authority and even, as we shall see, as ego and a single being. If ever someone was invited to see the inert mirror as mirror, rather than as the one presumed to know, it is Jung's reader embarking with him on a voyage into what is presented as incomprehensible.

> Joyce's *Ulysses* . . . is a passive, merely perceiving consciousness . . . to the roaring, chaotic, lunatic cataract of psychic and physical happenings, and registering all this with almost photographic accuracy.
>
> *(Jung 1966, CW15: para. 163)*

Here is the mirror as mirror. The narrator is deemed to be little more than a recording device in the face of the dismembering book. At this moment Jung the reader has fatefully exposed the chaotic Real with only the thin membrane of the mirror/passive perceiving consciousness to protect him. Yet, in a move that is like, and crucially unlike, Lacan, Jung has recourse to the non-human.

Where Lacan in 'The Purloined Letter' sees animal desire in the Minister as both opposed to, and constituting, the symbolic order in its relation to the letter as signifier, Jung sees animality as part of the body's capacity to be *productively* involved in the psyche. Jung is open to the Dionysian as psyche without a human limit. This means that he can write from within the Dionysian cosmos of embodied human–non-human continuum.

From a Lacanian point of view, Jung generates an imago, the worm that engenders the sublime by which subjectivity traverses the imaginary into first destroying, then reconstituting, the symbolic order. From a Jungian point of view, the stuck reader, Jung, performs active imagination with his worm image that serves to weave body and psyche anew in the reading process. He participates in the dismembering in a way that fosters re-membering as a splicing of being and knowing. Active imagination remembers the psyche.

Such a procedure enables participation in *zoe* because one is both sacrificed *to* the god (allows the image to be alive and take the lead) and *becomes* the god (some of the energy of the image is ultimately incorporated). The sublime is first abject, in the worm standing for the failure to achieve subjectivity. Then it is immanent, in the struggle to *know* anything about the work for which Jung's own concepts (his 'making' as opposed to 'telling') do not *work*.

Finally, in linking Jung's own immanent failure to Joyce's immanent localized worldview, he begins to see a possibility of a link between immanent and transcendent sublime in the destruction of aesthetic conventions. Such destruction promotes revolutionary creativity, or *zoe*. To return to Gallop on Lacan, seeing the mirror as mirror is to find creativity in destruction in terms of the sublime. I will argue that both Lacan and Jung offer this possibility, with different language and premises, in their respective reading of Poe and Joyce.

So Jung offers the image of a worm, first of all for the novel.

> The whole work has the character of a worm cut in half, that can grow a new head or a new tail as required.
>
> *(Jung 1966, CW15: para. 165)*

Active imagination is Jung's Dionysian therapeutic technique of encouraging a psychic image to develop of its own accord before any interaction with it. Although Jung never names this technique in his 'Ulysses' essay, it does occur. The worm mutates to signify the psyche of the novelist, as Jung suggests that it is the worm in Joyce producing the book 'with the sympathetic nervous system for lack of a brain.' (Jung 1966, CW15: para. 166).

Furthermore, the worm shows itself to be a tapeworm, an unpleasant parasite rather like the effect of the book on Jung's stupefied body. Such a creature is internal and yet foreign, other. It has dismembered his being by destroying the sense of inside and outside. So it is a fitting teacher of how internal and external can comingle, even to the extent of a hideous transcendence.

> Objective and subjective, outer and inner, are so constantly intermingled that . . . one wonders whether one is dealing with a physical or transcendental tapeworm.
>
> *(Jung 1966, CW15: para. 166)*

The worm is figure for an abject dismembered sublime, because it is incapable of knowing or representing anything. 'Surely a book . . . represents something . . .' exclaims this frustrated reader (ibid.: para. 167). This worm figures Jung's abjection in stripping him of a secure place in the symbolic order vis-à-vis the book. And yet to Jung there is an evolutionary possibility in this worm, related to Earth Mother and Dionysus (see Chapter 2). In typical Jungian active imagination the worm does evoke positive potential for signifying. It is the saurian in Joyce, or our own worms as a 'conversation in and with one's own intestines' (ibid.: para. 168).

Themes are unavoidable . . .

At last, Jung decides to resort to Lacan's overall tactic in 'The Purloined Letter' seminar, impersonating the one presumed to know. He draws attention to enacting the role of the analyst in order to import structures of meaning, or themes. Jung enters a Dionysian drama by taking the analyst's god-position as a role.

> A therapist like myself is always practicing therapy – even on himself.
>
> *(Jung 1966, CW15: para. 168)*

> Nevertheless themes are unavoidable, they are the scaffolding for all psychic happenings, however hard one tries to soak the soul out of every happening, as Joyce consistently does.
>
> *(ibid.: para. 169)*

Tellingly, Jung identifies themes as 'scaffolding', something raised temporarily to aid in repairing, repainting or maintenance. He makes a consciously theatrical shift from abject unknowing reader to competent and knowing analyst, while admitting the artificial or fictional nature of the role. As therapist, what he first sees is a sublime dismembering of meaning in art and even of his psychology as explanatory theory. A book that is a conversation with one's intestines leads to an inevitable conclusion, in reversing the aesthetic of 'making' (see McGann, p. 114–5).

> But it is only modern man who has succeeded in creating an art in reverse, a backside of art.
>
> *(ibid.: para. 178)*

Symptomatically, Jung the therapist continues to diagnose the novel, not its author. Acquitting Joyce of mental illness on the grounds that the book itself does not display the full range of schizophrenic symptoms, Jung decides that the book is a cultural and aesthetic problem. *Ulysses* is destructive of conventional taste and meaning (Jung 1966, CW15: para. 177). It belongs to a genre of modern art in which the artist finds the only unity is in destructiveness (ibid.: para. 175). The sublime occurs in the dismembering of conventional artistic norms, or, as McGann might put it, a 'telling' that unravels subjectivity in the face of such challenges to signifying.

Ulysses even manages to undo Jung's own conceptual and disciplinary armour, to the extent of failing to be archetypal and symbolic in the ways he would expect. Molly Bloom could be an anima, and Stephen Dedalus and Leopold Bloom could offer an archetypal opposition of spirit and flesh (Jung 1966, CW15: para. 185). Yet, Jung admits, this background does not work in a Jungian symbolic way as images pointing to a partially unknown or unknowable depth (ibid.: para. 185).

What works for Jung the therapist is his realization of creativity in the sublime destructiveness of *Ulysses*. He perceives Dionysus in its very dismembering of *his* psyche. By positing coherence as a destination rather than a stable quality of the novel, Jung the therapist puts his faith in psyche rather than in art, but it is a psyche both dismembered and re-membered by art.

Dionysus, in his blithe lack of boundaries, operates in literature and psychology for Jung here. For not only does the author find unity in the disruption of the book, but Jung the therapist of culture discerns collective sublime creativity and renewed instinctual life: the presence of *zoe*.

> Such manifestations of the collective psyche disclose their meaning only when they are considered teleologically as an anticipation of something new.
>
> *(Jung 1966, CW15: para. 175)*

Here is a fascinating instance of being sacrificed to Dionysus in order to *be Dionysus*. To escape the destruction of meaning, Jung has to test out his theories of art and psyche and find most of them wanting: he has to sacrifice himself as the one presumed to know. Anima, archetype and symbol do not work for this text. However, positing a future orientation enables this 'backside of art' to be seen as part of a larger re-membered body. Moreover, a shift from individual to collective enables Jung to consider the book as compensatory to the era's sentimentality.

> From the lack of feeling in *Ulysses*, we may infer a hideous sentimentality in the age which produced it.
>
> *(Jung 1966, CW15: para. 183)*

In terms of the sublime, Jung needs to import his scaffold of the teleological and compensatory properties of the collective psyche and art, in order to contain, to limit, what he finds impossible to stomach in the novel. The worm, the image of abject psyche (that was both inside as tapeworm and outside as transcendent), is defeated by the assumption of cultural therapist as a dramatic role.

The worm is the abject reader as dismembered because it destroys all clean boundaries of the subject. It was not sublime because the sublime needs a boundary unless it is to be a mere figure for undoing, unmeaning, rather than a defeat of or a 'beyond' of meaning. By erecting a partial scaffold of teleology and compensation, Jung superbly accommodates the destructive dismembering power of *Ulysses* in a boundary that does not deny its potency. The novel is a backside of art, but, in remembering the psyche, it's same fissile nature is now understood as a necessary function of creativity.

> Looked at from the shadow–side, ideals are not beacons on mountain peaks, but taskmasters and gaolers.
>
> *(Jung 1966, CW15: para. 182)*

An age corrupted by sentimentality requires 'drastic purgatives' (ibid.: para. 179). Jung offers a particularly revealing demonstration that the sublime may be immanent to the psyche, yet requires some structuring notion beyond the individual, such as the teleology of psyche and literature. Otherwise what is left is the worm, appearing here as endless procreation without any creativity, any possibility of something new. The worm is perpetual dismembering without re-membering.

Signifying, even the signifying of the blockage of signifying, needs something from outside itself in order to work.

It is compelling that the signifying potency bestowed upon *Ulysses* is put into the future, into the *beyond*, as sublime in the sense of a re-membering not yet complete. I want to argue that even here Jung is seeing the mirror as mirror, in displaying the 'scaffold', the contingent structure of his ideas. In reading *Ulysses*, Jung is the wanderer forced to confront the limits of knowing, finding yet again his theories as provisional. Jung returns as the trickster writer making theory at the very edges of the sublime, as something necessary to the very possibility of the sublime. After all, it is theory that invoked the sublime creativity in the destructive Dionysian powers of the psyche.

From Dionysian creativity in destruction to the crumpled note

> This, surely, is its real secret . . . and it is revealed . . . to him who has gazed at his world and his own mind for seven hundred and thirty five days with the eyes of Ulysses. This space of time . . . is to be taken symbolically.
>
> *(Jung 1966, CW15: para. 186)*

At last Jung finds his symbol, for him the image that connects ego to unconscious and so operates a gateway to transformation. Time swallowed by reading can become symbolic. The novel's mobilization of the abject psyche in the tapeworm can give way to a reforming and remembering of being. Indeed, symbol is possible because of the Dionysian destruction and purgation visited on the psyche by *Ulysses*.

Repeatedly in the essay Jung comes to the detachment he diagnoses in the narrative voice, a separation from body, the deep psyche and world answered by Jung in the active imagination of the abject and monstrously embedded tapeworm (Jung 1966, CW15: para. 186). The novel portrays a dismembered world. For Jung, the reader's only recourse is to enter it on its own terms in the dismembering process of active imagination.

Detachment has 'Homeric image[s]', including a repeated crushed piece of paper, an advertisement known as a 'throwaway' (Jung 1966, CW15: para. 186). Jung even quotes directly from the novel to show the throwaway that he notices Joyce associating with the figure of Elijah. The crumpled note is floating on Dublin's river, the Liffey, as a ludicrous version of an Odyssean craft.

> Elijah, skiff, light crumpled throwaway, sailed eastward by flanks of ships and trawlers.
>
> *(Joyce 1922/1992: 239 quoted in Jung 1966, CW15: para. 186)*

As an image of dismembered consciousness, the crumpled throwaway is superbly weightless and valueless. In the novel it recurs several times and Throwaway is also the name of a horse that unexpectedly wins a race. Leopold Bloom, the wandering Jew of Dublin, regarded as of no account by many, is a throwaway hero.

At this point Jung makes a leap in taking this figurative detachment as an invocation of the Self, that being in psyche that is conceptually boundless. Unlike the ego that required remembering, the Self in its expanses could be the wholly dismembered psyche. The Self is both a centring archetype and also a word for totality, which cannot be fully known or mapped because it is rooted in the unconscious.

> The ego of the creator of these figures is not to be found . . . all and every-thing . . . is Joyce himself . . . not the ego but the self.
>
> *(Jung 1966, CW15: para. 188)*

From dismemberment and a crumpled scrap of paper to the Self, is a transition made possible by Jung's abjection in the worm coming to recognize the immanence of the Joycean sublime, because re-membered in the body via the tapeworm. *Ulysses* is a novel in which the purgation of modernity has aesthetic precedents in medieval Catholic art of the torn body of suffering Christ. Again, finding an external structure in the history of art makes abjection into the sublime by giving a limit to its destruction of knowing and of the traditions of aesthetics.

Such an insight also enables Jung to flesh out his proposition that the novel makes time symbolic to the reader. Time can look backwards in cause and effect or for-wards in reaching a meaningful end point or teleology. Causally, Jung proclaimed, Joyce is a victim of the medieval mind-set of Catholic Ireland (Jung 1966, CW15: para. 183). Teleologically, however, he is a reformer of a modern age populated by people whose psyche does not correspond to its nation states (ibid.: paras. 180–3).

By means of *Ulysses everyone* can enter the immanent re-membered sublime produced by an exile of Catholic Ireland. Jung is here suggesting that the sheer immanence of *Ulysses*, in its total drowning in June 16th 1904 in Dublin, reveals how far modernity is rooted in what Lacan might call the Symbolic Order of Catholic Europe.

Jung's own way of putting it is that by making the time used in reading sym-bolically, the novel remakes the psyche as self. Reading the novel becomes a pro-cess of, firstly, enduring the dismembering sublime through the abject worm; secondly, becoming so detached as to experience the worthlessness of a throwaway note; and yet finally, in these very processes of undoing and un-being, finding a re-membering, a sublime of creativity and *zoe* in destruction.

Just as for Lacan the letter in 'The Purloined Letter' is powerful by virtue of its hidden contents, and therefore structures and destroys being, so does Jung regard the 'crumpled throwaway' as an emerging image of the symbolic properties of the novel as psychic processing of time. The throwaway is recurrent on the current of the book. It is a figure for the scatological erasing of eschatology, dirty waste paper for a sublime epic book. It also images that abject becoming immanent sublime, in revealing the writer as self.

Put another way, the throwaway is the crumpled note as image of dismember-ment of meaning and being. Additionally, it is image for the re-membered text of novel and psyche oriented towards creativity and/as *zoe*. Ultimately the crumpled note evokes the role of the god, just as false Elijah invokes numinous Elijah.

> The 'light crumpled throwaway' drifts towards the East. Three times this crumpled note turns up in *Ulysses*, each time mysteriously connected with Elijah.
>
> *(Jung 1966, CW15: para. 190)*

In spotting the mysterious presence of Elijah in *Ulysses*, not limited to a dodgy church restorer of that name, Jung senses the presence of a masculine figure who for him signifies a modern problem between Eros and Logos. In discussing the crumpled note and Elijah in *Ulysses* he brings his essay to a notion of Eros and the sublime also mentioned by critic, Philip Shaw (2006: 151–2). Moreover, such a development in Jung's work illuminates a notion of the Dionysian sublime and the feminine now visible in his *Red Book* (see Chapter 4).

Lastly, we should not forget the necessary presence of non-human nature for both Lacan and Jung in these works. Perhaps there is a Dionysian sublime creativity that extends ecologically to other presences on the Earth?

Eros sublime, the feminine, *The Red Book* and nature

Shaw, in his book, *The Sublime*, quotes the philosopher John Milbank on Eros as love in immanence, for the specific located thing or person can release the sublime from the restrictions of immanence (Shaw 2006: 229). Persisting desire may release us from the melancholia of the transcendent sublime as loss. Without mentioning any wild god, Shaw is implying that Eros invites Dionysian remembering as well as dismembering.

> For as soon as *eros*, conceived here as the love of the particular, is added to the sublime it becomes possible, once again, to conceive of the infinite as 'in analogical continuity with what lies within the finite.'
>
> *(Shaw 2006 – quoting Milbank 2004: 229)*

If desire expands being beyond the immanence of our physical senses, then arguably more than just human desire is anticipated by both Jung and Lacan when including non-human animals in their mobilization of psyche. Note how Milbank's 'analogical contiguity' resembles Lacan's *jouissance* 'wrapped in its own contiguity' (Bowie 1991: 148). In addition, we might recall Shaw citing women Romantic writers positing a 'sisterly' relationship to nature (Shaw 2006a: 109). These writers provide a sense of feminine dignity in connecting to, yet not attempting to, 'master' non-human nature or human nature in an-other. Here is a remembering *with* nature and therefore invoking Dionysian *zoe*.

Moreover, we can link such a feminine evocation of the sublime as relating to, yet not controlling, the infinite, with McGann's perceptive comparing of two modernist notions of literature. He contrasted the transcendent model of importing an exterior structuring such as myth, God, or aesthetic tradition, 'making', with a feminine mode of 'telling', or expressing a rhetorical understanding of language that indeed maps on to a psyche of desire. Implicitly, he spots Dionysian spontaneity in 'telling' as an alternative to the craft of 'making', as posted by Randy Fertel (see Chapter 3).

In re-membering and remembering Dionysus, it is useful to return again to Jung's crumpled note in comparison to Lacan's 'purloined letter' and the 'medusoid signifier', Jung, too, has his monstrosity of signification in his reading of *Ulysses*.

> Try to imagine a being who is not a mere colourless conglomerate soul composed of an indefinite number of ill-assorted and antagonistic individual souls, but consists also of houses, street-processions, churches, the Liffey, several brothels, and a crumpled note on its way to the sea.
>
> *(Jung 1966, CW15: para. 198)*

In its ruthless apportion of psyche, gender and destiny, the purloined letter, according to Lacan, materializes the signifier in death (Lacan 1972/1988: 38). It is medusoid, freezing being into stone for all those who look on her/the letter. In destroying being, the purloined letter obliterates meaning and represents the utterly destructive aspect of Dionysian chaos.

For Jung, in the 'Ulysses' essay, the crumpled note is a stage in the formation of the novel as self, a monstrous being of psyche that encompasses matter, humans, place, time and non-human nature. Yes, the crumpled note is the image for, and means of, shattering psychic identity such as gender, and all meaningful connections in ego, and even from ego to the world, such as in Jung's initial breakdown of being in encountering the novel. In this sense the crumpled note is Jung's purloined letter. By taking Homeric heroism to abject throwaway paper, the crumpled note similarly depletes being. It is a different, yet related, vision of Dionysian chaos that erases being and meaning as conventionally formed.

However, in comparison to Lacan, Jung takes two roles in his essay. He begins as the one who does not know, who is sacrificed to the signifier's materialization of death in annihilating meaning and dismembering the psyche as creative of being. Jung falls asleep and finds mere reproduction without production (of meaning). He is sacrificed *to* and *in* a process of Dionysian dismembering. Jung the dismembered reader hereby achieves a Lacanian trope in perceiving the mirror as mirror; the nothingness in the book; its 'truth' as a throwaway note.

Secondly, however, Jung adopts the role as the 'one presumed to know', in overtly importing themes in his assumed position as therapist. In order to save his psyche he plays a role in the Dionysian drama, playing and so *becoming*, fictionally, the god. Fascinatingly, this one presumed to know initially finds his own theory of little use. Yet not unlike Lacan, Jung exposes his theory's potency in pointing to the literary work's capacity for psychological transformation.

Here a difference emerges between the two psychologists. For Lacan, the 'lynx eye' and the 'beast of prey' seem to collaborate in the capacity of desire to undo human social and gender identity. Animals stand for perpetual dismembering of the symbolic order.

Such at first appears to be the case with Jung's worm. At the beginning the worm is the book, undifferentiated in Lacan's imaginary; then a parasite abjecting the reader as subjectivity is undone by the hideous meaninglessness of the novel. The worm is an animal that is abjection, a true power of horror because it destroys, dismembers being and meaning.

And yet the worm is also transcendental tapeworm, threading inside to out-side in a destruction of 'clean' boundaries that starts to become sublime. Here the worm is indeed a mirror, for it reveals both the mirror as mirror, as Lacan indicates by exposing the shit, the dirt that is rejected and repressed in the making of the subject. Also, the worm is immanence that achieves transcendence when the unmaking of meaning and psyche gives way to the discovery of an ordering principle foreign to the ego, a divinity in the dirt.

Of course the worm is Dionysus – first in abject dismembering, then in re-membering, because it threads being into a new sense of existing as members of a greater body than the ego can encompass. By playing roles in a literary work, psychology and literature are remembered as separate parts of one body of *potential* knowing and being (see transdisciplinarity's open system in Chapter 2). In effect, Jung's treatment of psychology and literature in this essay reaches Nicolescu's transdisciplinary paradigm.

Jung's worm reveals 'the backside of art'. Such degradation from polite con-ventions is not simply chaos, but rather a destruction of the pretended ideals and aesthetics of prettiness that claim to have banished what is dark and uncontrollable in human beings. Here Jung's worm is an animal performing a mirroring func-tion that (and perhaps Lacan would ultimately agree) points to structures of desire indissolubly wed to bodily instincts. For Jung, whose bodily instincts are con-nected to archetypes, these same instincts are a gateway to a structuring process external to consciousness and supportive of it.

What is revealed in Jung's essay on *Ulysses* is Dionysian creativity in sub-lime destruction when social and artistic conventions are detonated in ways to propel the subject from the symbolic order. More so than Lacan, Jung suggests a bodily and animal strata to human beings that is productive of re-forming subjectivity, or in his terms, finding the Self in a new relation to creativity and history. We all become citizens of Catholic Ireland in reading *Ulysses* because its ability to evoke abjection re-members our sense of transcendence as a pos-sibility for psyche.

By mirroring the psyche in the worm as animal abjectly predatory of humanity in our most primitive form, Jung evokes the creativity of nature in the worm, or book's, sublime destruction of psyche and aesthetics. It is time to look at whether Jung's mirroring in nature involves a gendering that brings him close to either the female Romantic sublime, or McGann's feminine anti–aesthetic of telling. This, of course, brings us back to Jung's perception of the importance of Elijah to the crumpled note in *Ulysses*.

Re-membering gender

Jung quotes Joyce on the 'dark hidden father' in identifying a masculine creative self emerging from reading *Ulysses* (Jung 1966, CW15: para. 198). Elijah is one image for this sublime creativity from destruction, because he re-presents, mostly in degraded form in *Ulysses*, the prophetic strain Jung identifies in the novel. Frequently associated with the crumpled note, one Elijah in *Ulysses* is the name of a dodgy preacher raising money for a new church. Here again is the figuring of transcendence by its absence, or perhaps its failure, in a world of 'hideous sentimentality' (Jung 1966, CW15: para. 183).

And yet, the final move of the masculine self in the novel, according to Jung, is to become feminine receptivity in Molly Bloom's final thoughts on the beginning of her sexual life with the man she marries, Leopold Bloom, the 'throwaway' hero. Ironically, Jung also throws away Leopold Bloom in refusing to recognize him as a Ulysses figure, preferring instead the far more tricky narrative voice. However, in bringing a prophetic inspired and creative masculinity into union with feminine Eros in reading *Ulysses*, Jung follows the map of another text he has previously abandoned, this one his own, *The Red Book* (2009).

Elijah is the dark hidden father for Jung as well as for Joyce. Jung's late commentary within *The Red Book* is explicit about Elijah as an image of masculine logos needing a relationship with what is for him a feminine Eros.

> Where Logos is ordering and insistence, Eros is dissolution and movement. They are two fundamental psychic powers that form a pair of opposites, each one requiring the other.
>
> *(Jung 2009: 563)*

> It is thus characteristic of the I that the old man and the young maiden are called Elijah and Salome.
>
> *(ibid.: 572)*

Intriguingly, Jung in *The Red Book* provides his own version of *Ulysses,* in referring to his narrative figure as an Odysseus who similarly returns to his waiting wife, Penelope.

> In the first case, I became an Odysseus on an adventurous journey which concludes with the aging man's return to Penelope, the motherly woman.
>
> *(ibid.: 569)*

Perhaps this offers an explanation of Jung failing to identify Bloom with Odysseus, preferring instead the wily narrator. *Ulysses* is Joyce's *Red Book*! So it is unsurprising to find a telling resemblance between Jung's reading of Molly Bloom's *jouissance* and his own extensive narrative and imagistic re-connecting Logos and Eros, or Elijah and Salome. Jung insists that Elijah and Salome are two psychic principles requiring relationship, not one falsely divided. For him gender is fundamentally a matter of two, yet two that must connect, be re-membered as parts of the greater self.

Blinded Salome, or Eros, must regain her vision; Eros and the feminine need to be part of consciousness, as Jung makes explicit at the end of *The Red Book* (Jung 2009: 568–9). In other words, the Dionysian and feminine sublime has to be restored to psyche and culture. For Salome, Molly Bloom and Penelope are Eros sublime, as proposed by Milbank as a sublime of love and connection without mastery.

That drive to conquer by knowing is what Elijah–Logos becomes if wholly divorced from Salome-Eros. Together, Elijah and Salome, or Logos and Eros, reincarnate Dionysian processes of dismembering and re-membering. It is a gendered vision of knowing and being in which Dionysus is the drama of separation of masculine and feminine properties that can never be forever severed. By remembering them, instinctual life is renewed, *zoe*.

In his *Ulysses* essay, Jung sees Penelope as similarly trapped if wholly separated from the masculine. Until Odysseus returns, she will weave forever in an image suggestive of McGann's female anti-aesthetic of 'telling' (Jung 1966, CW15: para. 202). What McGann does not say is that telling is dangerously unravelling of psyche without some re-membering of aesthetic form to enable the writing to come to a close, find a boundary to figure sublime *zoe*.

Jung here, and in *The Red Book*, could be said to explore the sublime in both Logos and Eros modalities. Ultimately, they are too implicated in Dionysus to be regarded as completely separate. They are two calling for re-membering as parts of the sublime whole that Jung liked to call the Self (ibid.: para. 198).

And yet there is a difference between the ending of *The Red Book*, with its insistence on gender duality in Elijah and Salome, and Jung's reading of 'the more comprehensive self' of *Ulysses*. For in Joyce, the Self, or 'dark hidden father', is not ultimately dualistic. It *becomes* Molly Bloom, not only relates to her.

> The demiurge . . . his masculine creative power turned into feminine acquiescence.
>
> *(Jung 1966, CW15: para. 199)*

Put another way, the crumpled note is not only the signifier as monster like Lacan's medusoid purloined letter. This creative and destructive power of the signifier offers a Logos, or 'masculine' sublime, in structuring and dismembering being. The crumpled note drifts on the waters of the Liffey. As a throwaway, it is vulnerable to the 'backside' elements of the city in its disposing of waste.

Yet the crumpled note also encounters the natural forces of the river, which are used by the signifying symbolic order but not reducible to them. The crumpled note on the river is both throwaway waste and liberated from that condition. It has *jouissance*, a playfulness in signifying without being controlled by the signifier. It is Dionysian in being re-membered as contiguous with nature.

Looking again at Jung's repeated evocation of the crumpled note in the water, it has a destiny beyond the limits of the medusoid *concrete* qualities of Joyce's Dublin.

> Try to imagine a being who . . . consists also of houses, street-processions, churches, the Liffey, several brothels, and a crumpled note on its way to the sea.
> *(Jung 1966, CW15: para. 198)*

On its way to the sea, the crumpled note possesses jouissance because in being cast out of Lacan's dismembering symbolic order it meets another kind of ordering in the currents of the river. Again, the Dionysian feminine sublime connects to an ordering process in non-human nature. This event demonstrates that masculine and feminine sublime modes are bound up with each other and, to Jung's delight, are not the same, but rather members that can be seen as parts.

For jouissance is not nature as feminine, but a human playfulness possible through 'contiguity', as Lacan puts it, and to non-human nature, as Jung shows. Jung shows this contiguity with non-human nature in how the note bobs on the waves, in the worm that erodes the boundaries between human and non-human, book and psyche, transcendent and immanent, and, in *The Red Book*, in Salome's troubling propensity to figure as a serpent.

Jung, far more than Lacan, adopts the notion of animals and natural forces such as rivers as mirrors to psyche. In his reading of *Ulysses*, even more than in *The Red Book*, Jung posits a wholeness encompassing masculine creativity in the sublime engendered by the destruction of aesthetic norms and an-other creativity in a feminine sublime in a contiguity with nature. Dionysus, in his chaotic fluidity, is present in both. Because Jung has a deeper sense of the Dionysian than Lacan, the dismembering of meaning and being can be countered by a feminine re-membering in the sublime, or *zoe*, more explicitly linked to the non-human.

Both Jung and Lacan find in literature Dionysian processes of psychological undoing and remaking. Both explore how narrative relies on, and exposes the gap in what Lacan calls the symbolic order and Jung sees as a problematic, yet necessary, relation between body and psyche. Ultimately, both find gender more complex than can be adequately accounted for by merely relating the dark hidden father to the phallus.

In evoking Dionysian creativity in sublime destruction, both Jung and Lacan discover a making and a telling in two gendered and related modes of the sublime. Remembering Dionysus shows masculine making or transcendence needs to be sustained and countered by feminine re-membering and telling in relation to the body and nature. Dionysus bestows a process of dismembering and remembering that partakes of, and potentially addresses, the overly separated genders and disciplines of our world. It is time to consider what James Hillman brings to Dionysian transdisciplinarity, the quest of Chapter 7.

7

DIONYSUS LIBERATED?

Revisioning psychology (and literature) with James Hillman

In a superb insight, poet and critic Dennis Patrick Slattery likens James Hillman's ground-defining book, *Re-Visioning Psychology* (1975), to the great literary epic *Moby Dick* (Slattery 2014: 182). Taking this cross-disciplinary possibility as key, this chapter will explore conflicts and convergences between Hillman's insistence on 'a poetic basis of mind', and his determination to offer a polytheistic psyche, or in his preferred term, 'soul', as fundamental to being (Hillman 1975: xvii). Might such a literary notion of psychology liberate that most psychically transgressive god of drama, Dionysus?

> Then we might look for Dionysus and his community, where self-division, dismemberment, and a flowing multiplicity belong to a mythical pattern.
>
> *(Hillman 1975: 35)*

Can psychology and literature unite in the cause of soul, or could their disciplinary claims prove incompatible, thereby implying a more precise Dionysian ritual of re-membering as parts? Such a tempering of *Re-Visioning Psychology* in relation to literature would aptly fulfil Hillman's own diagnosis of the role of Dionysus dismembering today, as described in Chapter 2. Otherwise, given Hillman's commitment to soul beyond psychology as an academic discipline, *Re-Visioning Psychology* could, as we will see, threaten to marginalize aspects of the literary. Such a marginalization will also prove to downplay social and ecological priorities. The present chapter will explore Dionysus as liberated without gaining his unmediated freedom in Hillman's *Re-Visioning Psychology*.

Introduction: Dionysus returns

This chapter places Hillman's great work of *Re-Visioning Psychology* in the context of this book's focus on 're-membering Dionysus', where the god provides a way of imagining tensions between academic disciplines such as literary studies and psychology. These two historically recent, suggestively parallel, and internally contested disciplines still structure an ontological gap between them. Psychology and literary studies each possess an uncanny attraction, and simultaneous repulsion, to each other.

For example, and as argued in Chapter 5, the persistence of close reading as a methodological thread from post–World War One New Criticism to the postcolonial, posthuman and ecocritical twenty-first century, represents an emphasis on literature (however defined) as possessing enough of 'being' to generate its own epistemologies. Put simply, literature, despite being a disputed category, can itself be a basis for knowing. This happens whether it is treated as existing in splendid isolation, as the New Critics proposed, or regarded as the ideological product of social forces, as many later theories proclaimed. Close reading, a form of hermeneutics, developed early in the rise of literature, or English as a discipline, is the preferred methodology to enshrine literary scholarship.

While close reading betrays a suggestive resemblance to C. G. Jung's therapeutic practice of active imagination, there remains an ontological gap between the disciplines. Jung privileged psychic well-being in his formulation, and close reading continues to place being-in-language as maintaining some independence from the reading psyche. Literary studies tends not to place value on the well-being of its human participants in reading and writing. Literature just *is*, whatever it's physiological or psychological consequences. How will *Re-Visioning Psychology* trace that intimate difference between Jung's autonomous images (which can be words in his treatment of symbols) and literature's autonomous linguistic structures?

What follows from this disciplinary and ontological gap is how both psychology and literature pursue metaphor, writing and death, a theme considered central by Hillman to his archetypal psychology in *Re-Visioning Psychology*. Hillman also takes on the persona, examined in the preceding Chapter 6, of the sublime 'one presumed to know'. This key figuring of the psychologist in his writing is diagnosed by Jane Gallop (not coincidently a *literary* critic), in Lacan's persona within his essay on 'The Purloined Letter' (Gallop 1988).

The assumption of epistemological authority is surely important to the liminal border of psychological and literary writing that Hillman (and I have argued, Jung) is espousing. To what extent does *Re-Visioning Psychology* enable or discourage 'seeing through' its persuasive rhetoric? When Hillman speaks of the soul seeing through itself to transparency (1975: 123), does this include his own envisioning of soul? Another way of understanding the urge to 'see through' authority in writing is posited by Dionysus as an avatar of the lost feminine of Western modernity. Dionysus haunts *Re-Visioning Psychology* as Hillman builds his 'four pillars' of psyche's logos: Personifying, Pathologizing, Psychologizing and Dehumanizing. I will suggest that Dionysus here also represents a quest into the transdisciplinary resonance or *zoe*, an idea that builds on Hillman's own investigation of that god for psychology (see Chapter 2). My quest here continues to outline reciprocal gifts of disciplinary rejuvenation possible between psychology and literature.

We encounter disciplinary *zoe,* or re-membering Dionysus through the god's shaping of boundaries between chaos and order, complexity and emergence. Dionysus is spontaneity and improvisation amongst drives to unity and dis-unity that are examined by both Jung and Hillman with their discrete sensibilities. While Hillman with distaste calls the implications of Jung's evocation of the transpersonal self, 'Titanism', that psyche erasing enemy to ecstatic and wayward Dionysus, *Re-Visioning Psychology* encounters, and only partly dissipates, a similar danger of an all-encompassing soul (1975: xi). A key question here is: does Dionysus in *Re-Visioning Psychology* lead us away from the risk of what Nicolescu calls a hyperdiscipline, one that would be a totalitarian attempt to subordinate all other priorities?

On the one hand, I will show that *Re-Visioning Psychology* is tempted towards disciplinary imperialism, even if its metaphorical character tends at the same time to undermine such confidence. On the other hand, this chapter will end by positing something that I will call 'essence versus essentialism' in *Re-Visioning Psychology*. By showing that rhetoric as in-formed, shaped from within, by archetypes as fundamental conditions of soul, Hillman evokes something close to transdisciplinarity's spatial and cosmic metaphor for disciplinary relations. It is both reserved from literary arts and dependent upon them. For this reason, we begin with a discussion of metaphor.

Metaphor in and out of *Re-Visioning Psychology*

Metaphor outside

David Punter's invaluable study exposes metaphor to historical and cross-cultural research that reveals it to be more mysterious and problematic than frequently assumed (Punter 2007). Commonly defined as 'by means of which one thing is made to stand in for another thing', is metaphor a sort of decoration in language as Aristotle held, or is it, as Punter believes, a fundamental process in *all* language (ibid.: 2–13)? The latter infers that we cannot do without metaphor in using words. And if we cannot do without it, then words never have a simple relationship to the world, to reality, or to 'truth'.

> Thus, metaphor represents a basic operation of language: it seeks to fix our understanding, but at the same time it reveals how any such fixity, any such desire for stability and certainty, is constructed on shifting sands.
>
> *(ibid.: 9–10)*

Immediately we encounter that liminal division between psychology and literature. If language itself is mutable (and notice how Punter in the above quote needs the shifting sands of metaphor to make his point), then is psyche or soul a 'thing' that exists apart from language and so cannot be transparently viewed through its indigenously metaphorical shiftiness? Or, is psyche indissolubly incarnated, come-into-being, through language, so that metaphoricity *is* soul? This latter position is that taken by *Re-Visioning Psychology*, which does not completely solve, or dis-solve, the ontological division between the disciplines of literature and psychology. But first of all, more about metaphor.

If metaphoricity is inherent in language then does a metaphor mean something other than what it says? 'Shifting sands', in Punter's words, really means, in this instance, the innately unstable properties of meaning in words. Or, contrarily, does it actually mean what it says in the sense that the thrust of the sentence cannot do without the metaphor of shifting sands. There is no other way of adequately encompassing the unstable ground (sands) of linguistic signifying (Punter 2007: 17).

It follows that metaphor cannot be peeled off like a banana skin, and here my simile, a comparison using 'like' or 'as' is a more overt metaphor. In our consumption of words the banana skin stays on. Metaphor, too, is like parts that can neither be wholly disassembled nor fused into meaning as one being. Like Dionysus, metaphor motivates dismembering.

Put another way, the metaphor cannot be separated out from what the sentence 'really' means. To extend this sense of language is to suggest that metaphor has incarnational qualities (Punter 2007: 22). Metaphor *brings meaning into being.* Often we may see this operation in 'metonymy', which is the reduction of a meaning to a single representative element (ibid.: 2).

In Punter's example, when British Prime Minister John Major was in danger of losing a political election in 1992, he started carrying a soapbox into the street and talking to people while standing on it. This metonymic visual image was intended to convey in visual language the values of old-fashioned decency and straight talking to the people. He sought to achieve this by using a method of electioneering thought to be extinct in the age of electronic media.

Despite media derision, John Major's party won the election. The soapbox proved a powerful metonym. While we cannot know if he would have been successful without it, the soapbox and its significance in a series of complex historical metaphors cannot be separated from his win. Here was a particularly concrete form of metaphorical incarnation, allowing a man on a box to argue for a complex series of ideological virtues. It is not just that the soapbox has physical presence; rather, that presence connoted political meanings not actualized in the election before its arrival. Similarly, the previously mentioned metaphor of 'shifting sands' brings into being the notion of unreliable foundations. It does not merely ornament the idea, because there is no idea without this metaphor.

Yet both the soapbox and the shifting sands reveal other dimensions to metaphor. Most visible is how metaphor in public discourse relies upon cultural contingency. We have to have a sense of why a soapbox was chosen, instead of any other wooden box, with its specific references to the most commonly available materials and one suggesting the 'cleanliness' of the politician's words. Moreover, as Punter points out, philosophical and even religious fundamentals permeate the shifting sands of metaphor, when he explores how Chinese metaphors may work entirely differently (Punter 2007: 34–5).

Whereas Western metaphor is used to seek a parallel between different domains, such as sands and words, the Chinese seek a convergence that penetrates the illusion that realities differ. Here metaphor serves a 'correlative cosmology' that regards phenomena as only appearing to be of diverse orders of reality. It is philosophically, as well as culturally, various. Metaphor is a kind of ritual revelation of qualitative patterns.

What this points towards is how metaphor is not a free choice. It is historically and culturally conditioned and relies upon deep philosophical assumptions about the nature of the world. Hence, metaphor is a way of knowing that is freighted with often unrealized presuppositions. Even the belief that metaphor signifies that one thing stands for another relies upon the notion that there are these two distinguishable domains. Therefore, such a structuring of metaphor is itself a way of knowing (Punter 2007: 68). One question here may be: Is metaphor a way of knowing about a reality separate from language, or is it incarnational in the sense of making knowledge in the field of language itself? Here, of course, language is not limited to words, as the metonymic soapbox demonstrates.

Scepticism about language's ability to safely house meaning eventually produced the critical approaches of deconstruction and poststructualism. These held that metaphor's shifting sands prove that all knowing is fundamentally unstable (Punter 2007: 102).

> [T]o say that something is like something else is no longer to *establish* a similarity but to *project* such a similarity into an undecidable field.
>
> *(ibid.: 102)*

One reason deconstruction was welcomed was the recognition of how far metaphors structure social and political existence, and how difficult they are to challenge. Metaphors are one of the most potent forces of the collective on the individual. By revealing those shifting sands, deconstruction fundamentally disrupted epistemological and political hierarchies. We come to the psychological roots (another powerful metaphor!) of metaphor and metonym.

Ultimately, metaphor is not a mere decoration to enhance a meaning separate from itself. It is not a matter of free choice. Rather, metaphor reveals our lack of freedom within the structure of cultural, social and political metaphoricities in which we live. Metaphor in this way undermines not only personal options, but even our ability to *be* a separate person. So with metaphor choosing us, rather than us choosing metaphor, I turn to *Re-Visioning Psychology*'s metaphorically incarnated gods and goddesses.

Metaphor in Re-Visioning Psychology

In the introduction to *Re-Visioning Psychology*, 'soul' is given important defining qualities (Hillman 1975: xvi). Although it is a perspective and not a substance, the soul is an independent factor bestowing a sense of life and the sacred. The soul makes meaning possible and cannot be known apart from other things, which is why Hillman says that his psychology, or psyche-logos, must enter the domains of history, philosophy and religion (ibid.: xv). Furthermore, the soul gives to events the quality of experiences. It has a distinct connection to death in its fundamental creativity. Hillman proclaims:

> [B]y 'soul' I mean the imaginative possibility in our natures . . . that mode which recognizes all reality as primarily symbolic or metaphorical.
>
> *(ibid.: xvi)*

Here is an immediate challenge to the disciplinary claims of Hillman's psychology. Reality is primarily symbolic or metaphorical, experience is soul-dependent, soul is perspectives, seeing. This standpoint suggests a hyperdiscipline in which Hillman's soul is *the* way of knowing the world.

Later Hillman returns to mythical metaphors to develop his insistence that they are perspectives and not actual happenings in the world (Hillman 1975: 101). This of course reinforces the notion that soul is not substance. It is rather that human property by which sensory registers become meaning. Soul turns happenings into human experiential existence. Hence soul, primarily metaphorical, we are told *presents reality* to us as symbolic or metaphorical, but is not itself the sum of that reality.

Therefore, Hillman's archetypal psychology in this way is not a hyperdiscipline claiming to subsume all others by saying that all reality is psyche. However, it may well be setting up a superior purchase on knowing other aspects of reality, because to Hillman it is our (for him, polytheistic) way of knowing. Archetypal psychology so far has epistemological, but not strictly ontological, supremacy. It is time to take metaphorical soul into myth and words.

Of course it all comes down to images in which Hillman is explicitly following Jung in regarding them as spontaneous products of the psyche offering archetypal patterns (Hillman 1975: xvii). These archetypal patterns are the fundamentals of the psyche. They manifest myth as metaphor (ibid.: xix). Crucially, archetypal patterns provide an array of myths. The psyche to Hillman is innately polytheistic, and he regards the Greek pantheon as the best cultural resource from which to explore this aspect of the Western soul. The 'poetic basis of mind', then, is metaphor's resistance to the literal. Such resistance is the soul's native language (ibid.: xvii). So psyche *is* metaphor.

Polytheistic myth is the way of understanding the archetypal pattering of images as archetypal, providing narrative that is meaningful and foundational, but not exclusive because there is always another myth to challenge the supremacy of any one story. When it comes to words, Hillman endorses metaphor's incarnating properties. 'For myth bearing words are persons', he says (Hillman 1975: 34). Words are made flesh, as they incarnate soul in our embodied psyches. Words, or metaphors in words, can open that depth that constellates a happening into experience. Hillman refers to an 'angelology of words', to demonstrate that images of the archetypal psyche can take on divinely creative properties in metaphors (ibid.: 9).

Again we come to a big disciplinary claim, for here divinity incarnates in words, and so 'being', or ontology, is proposed. Yet we also have to include soul as envisioning, rather than the substance of the universe itself. *Re-Visioning Psychology* seems to be taking a realist line that there is 'something else' other than our soul/ psychic transformations resulting from how we humanly process that something else. We cannot know apart from the polytheistic metaphorical soul, although Hillman insists that soul is not the substance of that which we know.

Above all, *Re-Visioning Psychology* embraces metaphor as a rejection of a literal understanding of words. If myth is integral to psychic functioning, as Hillman asserts, then traditional psychology's stress on the individual as a whole, undivided person, is a mistaken literalizing of the inescapable psychic process of personifying.

The psyche needs to personify. Or personifying, understood as a mode of metaphor, is what the soul naturally does. It casts roles, makes drama, and is thus Dionysian. It is time to look beyond metaphor to other apparently literary devices that trace the unconscious dialogue between literature and psychology.

Re-Visioning Psychology: Pillars and genres

> 1. Personifying or Imagining Things; 2. Pathologizing or Falling Apart; 3. Psycholo-gizing or Seeing through; 4. Dehumanizing or Soul-Making. The structure com-prises his own genre wheel of the soul and perhaps they could with beneficial effect be seen as analogies of the four genres worked out so elegantly in Louise Cowan's genre wheel: Lyric, Tragedy, Comedy and Epic. Something of these respec-tive quaternities, as C. G. Jung noticed repeatedly, offer images of wholeness and completeness.
>
> *(Slattery 2014: 185)*

Dennis Slattery's masterful and revealing insight into *Re-Visioning Psychology*'s four pillars (a metaphor that evokes neo-classical columns of Tuscan, Doric, Ionic and Corinthian, and their association to the arts) is to link them with the four key clas-sical literary genres of lyric, tragedy, comedy and epic. Such a suggestion is far too exciting a proposition to ignore. The rest of this chapter will rely upon Slattery's key notion of this generic foundation. So I begin by looking at *Re-Visioning Psy-chology*'s section on 'Personifying' in relation to the literary poetry of the person, or lyric.

Lyric in and out of personifying in *Re-Visioning Psychology*

The lyric outside

> The principle of intelligibility in lyric poetry depends upon the phenomenlization of the poetic voice. Out claim to understand a lyric text coincides with the actual-ization of a speaking voice, be it (monologically) that of the poet or (dialogically)

that of the exchange that takes place between the author and reader in the process of comprehension.

(Paul de Man 1985: 55)

Lyric suggests or enacts a speaking voice, critic Paul de Man asserts here. Reading lyrical poetry we imagine a person behind uttering the words. Lyric is the poetry that promises immediacy, emotion, Dionysian spontaneity, or perhaps, by contrast, dialogue, situation and address, Dionysus as drama.

Originally understood as songs for the ancient musical instrument, the lyre, lyric became the poetry of individual feeling with, and without, melody. Lyric was an ingredient of the more exalted literary form of tragedy, according to Aristotle (Brewster 2009: 2). Yet in literary tradition lyric came to be regarded as the essence of poetry, in a heritage that has shifted between defining lyric as assuring authenticity of feeling and being, to its identification as performativity and a dramatized fictioning of the self (ibid.: 18–32).

Lyric implies a speaker and an audience, because it either expresses or performs emotion, which in turn suggests a story, a relationship, like popular song lyrics today. By contrast, classical lyric verse in Greek tragedies was the poetry of ritual and ceremony. Only with the literature of Romanticism in the late eighteenth century came the shift to lyric poetry providing a sense of interiority and feeling.

After Romanticism, lyric begins to stand for the possibility of a single self as well as its undoing (Brewster 2009: 10). Lyrical power to enshrine feeling in words also reveals that feeling, taken as truth of being, is actually contingent upon an-other. A dramatic situation is posited to invoke, contain or structure the feeling. Being therefore proves to be dependent upon something other, or outside the 'I' figure, even if the other is entirely fictional. Lyrical language in this sense exposes the fragility and contingency of self structured as 'I'.

When it comes to deconstruction, lyrical potency is downgraded to an effect of discourse. The very literary form of song or short verse expressing emotion or situation enacts and betrays the authenticity of 'I' (ibid.: 33–4). In this sense, lyric as a genre is merely a metaphor for being, not a guarantee of its sufficiency. As discussed previously in this chapter, lyric is an indispensable, yet unstable, aspect of metaphoric language.

We are lyrical beings in needing to express feeling and situations. In doing so, we are performing being, rather than securely literalizing it. We perform our lyrical selves because lyric is an ancient genre. Millennial accretions of lyric as a form in all their varying philosophies, theologies and psychologies stick to our individual use of words. Lyric is Dionysian via its emotional waywardness, as well as in its fictive and dramatic qualities.

Hence lyric remains what it always has been, a performance on a stage, even if the stage is a non-rational amalgam of the poet's garret (the writer alone), her psyche and the linear time-denying history of the genre. Lyric's inescapable history is pressed into the poem, even if the poet is ignorant of it. In this sense, lyric possesses resources of being, or ontological autonomy beyond the individual psyche. In fact, here lyric's ability to metaphorize being *is* its paradoxical capacity to enshrine human selfhood and to make it fictive, dramatic, dependent upon an 'other'. Again, we have to be Dionysus as well as be sacrificed to him.

One key to lyric here is its original and persisting Dionysian identification with drama. It is time to look at *Re-Visioning Psychology*'s personifying as a dramatic explosion of the habitual lyrical singular person into a site for Dionysian theatre.

Lyric in personifying or imagining things for Re-Visioning Psychology

Personifying, Hillman's first pillar, is an escape from singularity into psychic animism in which personhood is no longer confined to the human (Hillman 1975: 3). Where lyrical poetry is regarded as de-centring the ego self, Hillman wants to push the ego out of the way of the marvellous archetypal beings indigenous to soul. He sees a battle of nominalism and realism as that between those who regard words denoting universals or abstractions as divorced from reality, and those who, following Plato, see words of archetypal persons as incarnational (ibid.: 5–7).

Soul is more real, more authentic, when our archetypal persons have their say *through* us. That they need their voices expressed, brings *Re-Visioning Psychology* into the lyric. Personifying, or allowing our archetypal persons to be themselves as persons, means lyricizing the soul. Lyric is either the literary understanding of the speech of soul-persons, or it is soul language itself. So here we have a delightful collision of the literary and the psychological. To try and pursue this question of lyric inside and outside *Re-Visioning Psychology*, it is necessary to look at the drama of these soul persons.

First of all, Hillman makes a distinction between the living words (lyrics) of archetypal persons and the far less animated language of rational concepts, with their tendency to become 'dead tools' (Hillman 1975: 32). Conceptual language is unable to do justice to the polytheistic soul (Ricoeur 1970: 36). Polytheism, or manyness of being, is essential to *Re-Visioning Psychology*: its painful nature of self-division dances into the book with Dionysus.

> Then we might look for Dionysus and his community. Where self-division, dismemberment and a flowing multiplicity belong to a mythical pattern.
>
> *(Ricoeur 1970.: 35)*

The god of drama, Dionysus both liberates soul diversity and also protects it from the failure to see soul as drama, or, as Hillman also puts it, metaphor. Psychodynamics is actually psychodramatics. The ego is audience in the true theatrical sense of undergoing a trans-formation through theatre. Here *Re-Visioning Psychology* returns lyric to tragedy, as we will see later in this chapter. Lyric is the mode of Dionysian speech. It is the way metaphors stick together in the ritual discourse of the goddesses and gods. Lyric in Hillman's soul-making delights in its dramatic splintering of being into multiple persons.

At this moment *Re-Visioning Psychology* seems to invite the support of literature to demolish what it sees as mainstream psychology's literalizing of the individual human into a single being: an entity made into a fetish, or to be tended as a monolith (Ricoeur 1970: 48). The psychology that Hillman is attacking has joined a succession of philosophies in forcing soul back inside the human body while stripping its persons of viability (ibid.: 48). Projection, or the notion that the psyche projects out onto things and people from within the skull, is summarily dismissed. Rather what Jung called the 'anima' is not projected. Equally living in women and men, the anima is soul as connector of our limited ego to the pantheon of archetypal persons (ibid.: 43–5).

Given such a bleak rending of disavowed and dismissed mainstream psychology, *Re-Visioning Psychology*'s personifying suggests that lyric is soul-domain *and* its nourishment. Lyrical language understood as lyrical metaphors gives life to soul. Soul is lyrical *drama* because it is as real as theatre. The soul's lyrics are transformational, vital, alive, but not of that order of reality as if the play on the stage suddenly dissolved the theatre and became the whole world. The soul's lyrical drama is reality where these archetypal divinities are perspectives on the events, and not the event itself, as we remember from earlier cautions.

Worth stressing here is that theatre now links, and yet falls short of uniting, the domains of literature and this new archetypal psychology. After all, soul-drama in this particular vision is not physical in the sense of taking place on a material stage with the help of actors. *Re-Visioning Psychology* makes an invaluable distinction between the concrete and the literal (Ricoeur 1970: 136–7). Soul-drama, the archetypal persons manifesting the fluid internal architecture of the psyche, is concrete, yet not literal, because it has meaning beyond the actuality of the gods.

Theatre is also concrete and not literal because we do it, as in its ancestor, ritual, for itself and for more than itself. Conversely, literalism can be highly abstract, as in metaphysical speculation, Hillman insists (Ricoeur 1970: 136–7). He points out that statements beginning by saying that psyche is or is not (something), themselves are literalizing. Such work produces a psychology that accommodates modernity's desire for literal truth and one to one correspondence between words and things. To him, it is thinking divorced from the inherent metaphoricity of the soul.

So does theatre merely unite literature and archetypal psychology in its concrete capacities? Not quite. In fact concrete soul-drama and concrete on-stage drama are, I suggest, pure icons of dismembered Dionysus, that is, they are related but not the same. As members in differences as well as resemblances they manifest *zoe*, or rejuvenation. First of all, theatre with actors is a social and economic practice. It relies upon theatrical history and generic literary tradition for its very textures of writing and enacting. Words in plays are inseparable from those words and their performances in other plays for the characteristics of the 'being' that is theatre.

On the other hand, this does not mean that real theatre and soul-drama are simply different. To say so would be to literalize the cultural notion of the psyche as stuffed into the human body and not real apart from brain and soma. Of course what Hillman is revealing to us as soul-drama is a perspective – as archetypal metaphors are perspectives not the events themselves – that shows the necessity of theatre itself. Soul-drama is the liveliness, the psychic power indigenous to theatre, which explains its centrality to so many cultures.

It can also be put in the reverse way, that the institutions of theatre are concrete *realizations*, making real what is already real in psychic reality. So, although theatre and soul-drama here are not one reality, *Re-Visioning Psychology* is re-membering Dionysus as multiple and linked ontologies. Literature and psychology in this concrete matter of drama both matter considered a–part, and matter to each other. Put in alliance, I suggest they resonate *zoe*. Theatre is returned to Dionysian roots while psychology is saved from its literalization of being: it's a *drama*.

We remember in order to re-member, to see in the fictive and psyche-renewing soul lyrics divine Dionysus. Perhaps here, with lyric as soul genre, when considering the close disciplines of literature and depth psychology, what is left out is the historical domain of the lyric as literature that weaves souls into societies. Indeed, the contrast between the immediate drama posited by *Re-Visioning Psychology* and the way literature cherishes cultural diversity will be developed in the following sections. So what is such a tragedy about the soul?

Tragedy inside and outside of pathologizing in *Re-Visioning Psychology*

Tragedy outside

As a literary genre tragedy is about what cannot be borne. It is fictional drama that shows what happens when lives, families, communities and epochs break down, when the story people thought they were living is destroyed.

Tragedy is concerned with how we face the inevitability of death, the ultimate annihilation of a continuing story. Aristotle's famous definition links the drama to *catharsis*, the purging of pity and fear, by witnessing actors suffer on our behalf the greatest human enormities. He also provides other generic properties, such as *mimesis, peripeteia* and *anagnorisis*: the imitation of life, reversal of fortunes, and revelation of some shattering truth.

> A tragedy, then, is the imitation of an action that is serious and also, as having magnitude, complete in itself; in language with pleasurable accessories . . . in a dramatic, not in a narrative form; with incidents arousing pity and fear, wherewith to accomplish its catharsis of such emotions.
>
> *(Aristotle 1996 quoted in Leech 1969: 1)*

> [T]he form arose from a choral song in honour of Dionysus.
>
> *(ibid.: 12)*

> Of course, tragedy is a form of writing, not of living.
>
> *(ibid.: 68)*

To the Greeks, tragedy was about subjugation to the gods. By definition, what the gods demanded was greater or more absolute than the human frame could bear. Divine purposes are not human purposes, and take little account of the priorities of individual lives. So Antigone *has* to bury her brother, even if it costs her life and that of others; Oedipus discovers that he has unknowingly embraced it the ancestral curse he sought to escape; Agamemnon will die at the hand of his faithless wife for having sacrificed his daughter for a god's favour to win a war.

Tragedy, therefore, encountered a formal problem when it was revived in a Christian era in which the one and only God was supposed to be benign, even loving. Here, *Rosencrantz and Guildenstern Are Dead*, Tom Stoppard's 1967 play, offers several modern responses to the tragic genre. From the point of view of these two minor characters from Shakespeare's *Hamlet*, the new play finds incomprehensible even arbitrary forces stemming from alienated state power. In addition, there is also the existential possibility that the universe is meaningless.

In the course of a bloody struggle in the Danish royal family, Rosencrantz and Guildenstern, said to be friends of the unhappy prince, do what authority tells them to do, and get executed for it. Tragedy has shifted its focus from the impossible burden of the royal classes (as in Ancient Greece and Shakespeare) to the impossible condition of the modern individual facing either all-encompassing political power or a cosmos in which the human quest for meaning or 'home' goes unanswered. Significantly for this book, *Rosencrantz and Guildenstern Are Dead* insists that there is no escape from the horrifying order of tragedy, even in the apparent chaos of human impulses and immediacy. Even if they could be spontaneous, living as they do on the edges of overwhelming powers, that spontaneity too could just be part of a bigger cosmic design (Stoppard 1967/1994: 42–3).

Rosencrantz and Guildenstern in Stoppard's play are lost because they cannot get out of the play, Shakespeare's *Hamlet*. It is their own particular god-myth which decrees their deaths. Yet in their spontaneity their attempts to be apart from the framing metanarrative of Shakespeare, there is a good deal of humour which sets up an affectionate identification between audience and these unheroic, all-too human characters. Composed at the edge of a totalizing order, not least because *Hamlet* is so well known, *Rosencrantz and Guildenstern Are Dead* spins a web about human vulnerability and venality.

Above all, Rosencrantz and Guildenstern are Dionysus's victims, torn apart by forces beyond their control. Like more noble tragic figures before them, this pair suggest an archaic ritual of human sacrifice in which the protagonist dies on behalf of the community. A tragic hero on stage is a scapegoat in whose dismembering the audience does, and does not, participate. After all, if there was no audience, the actors would only be rehearsing and could change whenever they liked. Add an audience, *witnesses,* and the reality changes, so that now the king/queen/hapless courtiers *must* die. The audience is a contributing factor to their ritual killing.

Of course, that does not make audiences of tragedies into actual murderers, and not only because the death is merely performed some distance from their seats. These deaths are also somehow within the psyche of the witnesses, as Aristotle insisted in his famous purging *catharsis*. We see the king die and feel the death as somehow our own. Death in tragedy is both 'outside', on stage, and 'inside' the audience. So, in a sense as we leave the theatre we are reborn. Is this Aristotle's catharsis: a ritual purging of fear of death by its enactment within our emotions, within the soul?

Facing death, tragic heroes 'are, in a sense, more fully themselves than men and women usually dare to be', declares literary scholar, Clifford Leech (Leech 1969: 33). We see someone more complete than we can be in everyday life. We participate in their deaths, knowing also their rebirths: the actors will stand up and take a bow. Hence, tragedy here is metaphorical knowing. It forces us to accept fiction as fiction, and yet also as intensely real. This character perishes before our eyes, and *with our participation*, in a metaphorical reality.

It is not surprising that Aristotle's tragic theory of reversals, discoveries and catharsis can be seen as a precursor to psychotherapy. On the other hand, the institution of modern psychotherapy seems removed from the ecstasies of the Dionysian drama of dismemberment and renewal. Can *Re-Visioning Psychology*, in its pillar of pathologizing or falling apart take therapy back to its Dionysian stage?

Tragedy in Re-Visioning Psychology's *pathologizing or falling apart*

Pathologizing or falling apart is basic to the soul's very being in *Re-Visioning Psychology* (Hillman 1975: 58). Nothing is more fundamental to soul, which does not exist without it. Moreover, pathologizing is most intense in a person's intimation of death (ibid.: 70). We are ensouled in our symptoms, in our suffering and dismembering, due to the wayward demands of the careless gods. In this sense the essence of soul is tragedy, in its core relation to Dionysus, the dismembering god.

Hillman's priority of pathologizing or falling apart stresses that it is in symptoms or dis-ease that the soul asserts itself as real and inescapable. Moreover, these symptoms are the traces of the psyche's multiple persons. 'Who' is inflicting depression, mania or unbearable grief is the root of being in the symptom. Pointing out that the ancients believed that only the god who makes one ill can heal, *Re-Visioning Psychology* insists upon discovery of 'who' in order to ameliorate painful encounters with inhuman powers.

Here too, *Re-Visioning Psychology* explicitly rejects the literalizing of psychic illness into a general term such as 'neurosis' (Hillman 1975: 62). So there is no significant border between madness and sanity, only a polytheistic psyche of variously uncomfortable goddesses and gods. Hillman spells out that he is describing the third realm of soul between body and spirit. It is the inescapable being of imagination, passion and reflection (ibid.: 68). We begin to get a feeling for soul as a Dionysian stage for a dismembering tragedy, that this is the core truth of our psychic being.

Three ways of refusing to recognize the soul's innate dismembering pathologizing are the retreats into nominalism, nihilism or transcendence (Hillman

1975: 58–66). Producing a fatally literalizing neurosis is nominalism's attempt to ignore the soul's persons in favour of making suffering people impersonate a so-called personality disorder. Nihilism turns away from the liveliness of the psyche, while a flight into transcendence risks possession by a god and inflation (ibid.: 66). We need to learn to be with our inner tragedies. We should not run away from soul-as-theatre, nor should we rush on stage and don the mask of a god. Rather, we need to learn to pivot in our seats between the warring and loving archetypal persons.

> Today we are so unconscious of these persons that we call their realm the unconscious.
>
> *(ibid.: 36)*

This is the Hillman pivot, a revealing reversal within a sentence, a trope first noted by Jeffrey Lauterbach (2013). Hillman tears apart and puts together in reverse order what was originally a conventional thought. The pivot dis-members thought and re-members it in a different order. Moreover, revelation and reversal (of fortunes) are key ingredients of tragedy, according to Aristotle. The Hillman pivot is a Dionysian enactment of tragedy in writing, just as *Re-Visioning Psychology* is dis-membering and re-membering psychology, the logos or speech of the soul. Indeed, the book calls for pathologizing to be regarded as soul utterance, the native tongue of its true being (Hillman 1975: 82).

Before pursuing the Dionysian stage in pathologizing, it is worth noting Hillman's ambivalent treatment of nature as the non-human, non-archetypal domain. Hillman calls it a 'naturalistic fallacy' to see an identity of being, an ontological link between so-called natural events and psychic ones (ibid.: 84). Dreams should not be interpreted as events in nature, lest both nature and the soul are reduced or falsely simplified by the practice (ibid.: 84). Such a distinction between soul and nature recalls the insistence on soul, gods and myths as perspectives upon events, and not the events themselves. It maintains Hillman's priority of soul as this ontologically distinct third realm. And yet such a perspectival approach fails to escape the dualism that Hillman elsewhere condemns, as we will see.

There are valid challenges to such an insistence upon soul as the space of gods and human encounters without nature contributing anything of its own to psyche. Such a structure impacts on what is meant by nature. Does *Re-Visioning Psychology* see no soul in the matter of the natural world when apart from humans? Is it suggesting an animism of soul severed from animism's history as the multiple articulate spirits of the planet? Hillman says that to go the way of naturalism, or explaining soul in terms we use for non-human nature, would be to risk falling into materialism, the ultimate denial of the divinities of the soul (Hillman 1975: 84).

So he sees a danger for archetypal psychology in getting stuck in nature's physicality. Such a position makes sense while risking the erection of a hyperdiscipline because it asserts that all our perspectives upon the world are dependent on soul divinities. 'Nature', 'the world', or the non-human, non-god other, does not get a chance to talk back.

Ultimately, Hillman's naturalistic fallacy is somewhat mitigated by his polytheism that accepts the nature aspects of the Greek pantheon. While nature does not have its own independent spirits in *Re-Visioning Psychology*, it is not that there is no soul outside human skin in the world. Pan is in his woods and chasing nymphs. What is crucial to *Re-Visioning Psychology* is that the third dimension of soul remains fundamentally imaginal rather than indigenous to animating the material. To Hillman, soul sparks are not inherently within matter, as the alchemists thought.

Hillman's priority of imagination as soul continues a long tradition of seeing body and soul as other to non-human nature. In *Re-Visioning Psychology*, he focuses on the soul-full shaping of bodily life. For the body is conditioned by soul as the archetypal persons dismember us somatically as well as psychologically. Nature does not talk back, but remains the habitation of gods. What is defining though, in *Re-Visioning Psychology*, is that nature does not possess its own gods apart from the human imaginal realm.

Rejecting nature as independently soul-full is, on the one hand, *Re-Visioning Psychology* protecting the divinities in the imagination as having divine powers to transform. The imaginal is truly full of the gods when it has few limitations, such as the complexities of an ecosystem. On the other hand, at this point *Re-Visioning Psychology* looks not so much like a member of a transdisciplinary constellation as asserting its own monotheistic version of polytheism in the unchallengeable supremacy of the imagination. This would be a return to dualism.

Taking this a bit further, I suggest that *Re-Visioning Psychology* is a Dionysus actively dismembering traditional psychology while not entirely dismembering monotheistic claims of one disciplinary perspective over all others. And yet it is worth emphasizing the Dionysian nature of the god in this text. Already transcendence has been deflected in pathologizing. Now *Re-Visioning Psychology* embraces immanence and particularity. It sees the gods as connected and contingent. Pathologizing is the gods immanent in arriving as *this* dis-ease, these actual symptoms. Pathologizing is what the gods do to us in tearing us apart so that they can appear as symptoms. It is also what *Re-Visioning Psychology* envisages for archetypal psychology as a therapeutic practice. Just as the healing is of the god who is the disease, so healing the pathologizing done by god comes through the pathologizing done by the therapy. Normative psychology is eradicated by such treatment (Hillman 1975: 89). Even more is the book itself, with the Hillman pivot dismembering and pathologizing its readers.

Gods as immanent are still gods, still *Re-Visioning Psychology*'s assertion of disciplinary priority in ontological priority. Yet, as a Dionysian discipline, the god offers an inherent *connectedness* to phenomena, not so much insisting on a transcendent position over it. Put another way, Hillman is not replacing a boundless notion of the self with a boundless notion of polytheism. His polytheism is too seriously indwelling diverse and *pivotal* to approach the Titanism he indicts self-psychology with. Hillman's gods are not prescriptive. They bestow being, not moral advice (Hillman 1975: 88).

To return to tragedy is to remember that the gods come with their own stories, or myths. Stressing that myths are perspectives on events, and not events themselves, preserves the boundary between soul and world, or matter. (It is not, of course, a soul sealed within the human body.) According to Hillman, by confusing myth and events, Sigmund Freud made myth *become* disease, and so exited the imaginal realm (Hillman 1975: 100). As a corollary to criticizing Freud, Hillman also dismisses Jung's claim that myth in the psyche compensates for ego bias, or for the unbalanced attitudes produced by events (ibid.: 100). After all, if the mythical psyche compensates in response to the world, it would be dependent upon the world for part of its meaning-making capacities. *Re-Visioning Psychology* allows no such mitigation of the ontological priority of the polytheistic soul.

Dionysus is here Lord of the Underworld, associated with the dead (Hillman 1975: 102). The soul's relation to death constellates Dionysian dismembering, or perhaps innate pathologizing is a way of knitting a narrative about death. These stories are the matter of tragedy; they are why tragedy *matters*, to apply the Hillman pivot (ibid.: 109). Touched by *zoe*, Dionysian dismemberment in pathologizing is a loosening from which a re-membered new life emerges (ibid.: 109).

Literature and psychology are overlapping ontological processes, or aspects, of being. For pathologizing is essential soul-drama, its essence as drama, as a Dionysian soul. Tragedy is therefore the fundamental drama of the soul. Yet to Hillman soul has priority over-embodied being so soul–drama can never be exactly of the same order as encountering tragedy on a theatrical stage, however mythically 'true' to the soul it is. Soul doing tragedy retains some a–partness from the satisfactions of collective participation in theatrical tragedy, asserts *Re-Visioning Psychology*.

I should stress that whatever Hillman's preference I am insisting that drama on stage is not a metaphor for soul-drama. *Remembering Dionysus* is not endorsing ontologically prior, literal soul-drama, metaphorically represented in a theatrical play. Rather, both theatrical tragedy and soul tragedy are fundamentally metaphorical in the sense of bringing something into being. The soul is not literal. Its gods and myths are also fundamentally metaphorical, and imaginal as ontologically prior.

Metaphors of soul are not derivative of any other kind of being or reality. They *are*, just as tragedy on stage *is*, a manifestation against, or in the face of, death. Metaphor stands in for human absence, or being that we cannot fully incarnate. It is seeds from the decay of being which is death. In this sense, metaphor itself is dismembered Dionysus reborn.

The pathologizing section of *Re-Visioning Psychology* concludes with an assertion of gods and myths as traditional and revolutionary principles of existence (Hillman 1975: 112). As indicated in the example of Stoppard's *Rosencrantz and Guildenstern Are Dead*, not all reactions to death and absence are weeping. It is time to envision Dionysus as founder of comedy, as well as lord of the tragic stage in theatre and in soul.

Psychologizing, or seeing through, and comedy in *Re-Visioning Psychology*

Comedy outside Re-Visioning Psychology

For the irrepressible Mel Brooks, comedy is cognate to tragedy.

> Tragedy is when I cut my finger. Comedy is when you fall down an open sewer and die.
>
> *(Mel Brooks, quoted by Andrew Stott 2005: 1)*

Like the other three genres considered in this chapter, comedy is more complex and pervasive than might first appear. In fact comedy could be the most disseminative of the four genres, if considered as a *tone* as well as a structure; for the comic attitude seeps into so much of human life and culture. Perhaps this generic promiscuity is rooted in comedy's Western origin in a rustic song associated with festivals of fertility, where, not coincidentally, Dionysus presided as sponsor of sexuality (Stott 2005: 4–5). The word appears to derive from the Greek *komos* (revel) or *komai* (village), and *oda* (song) (ibid.: 4–5).

Hence archaic association with nature's seasons and Dionysian revelry gives comedy a long tradition of escaping civilized boundaries. Comedy began outside the city, where revellers were more liberated from the norms of social and political rules. It is the genre of those who make the earth bear fruit, as opposed to their urban overlords. Its expressions are tied to nature and the body in ways that have long pitted it against tragedy as the lesser form. Comedy is nature against tragedy's culture. It is the genre of village and countryside celebration of food, sex and seasonal rebirth against the city's imposition of law and tragedy's finality of death.

Several key theorists of comedy have taken this tradition and myth of comedy as the basis for its role in constituting, as well as simultaneously challenging, dominant civilized precepts. For example, Northrop Frye's influential proposal of a seasonal root for literary genres placed comedy as Spring's re-awakening (Frye 1957). He also suggested that Shakespeare's comedies are defined by an immersion in a 'green world', a forest in which natural and magical laws suspended those of city, state and even time and death. Comedy is envisioned as a surviving ritual form in itself. It is not merely literature derived from ritual. Shakespeare's comedies of the green world are related to grail quests as the triumph of love and rebirth over the wasteland (Frye 1990: 182).

Mikhail Bakhtin, on the other hand, while accepting comedy's rejuvenating properties, directs their satisfying of bodily appetites far more to the politically subversive. In *Rabelais and His World* (1984) he offers a theory of carnival that sees these still surviving street festivals as parodic and role-reversing strategies of liberation and containment. Bakhtin's ideas have been hugely important in siting comedy as a tool of social dissent. It is so potent that its revolutionary qualities have been co-opted by the governing classes.

Also inspired by the fertility rite origins of comedy was the philosopher Henri Bergson (1859–1941), who positioned comedy at the heart of human existence as its central ontology (Stott 2005: 28). Bergson proposed a notion of *elan vital* that proclaimed comedy as a primal imprint of being because of its kinship to the body's needs and desires. Taking Bergson and Bakhtin together would be to situate the body as a site of resistance to dominant social powers while not offering an unmediated domain outside culture. The body is conscripted, or in-scripted, via the comedic forms and discourses embedded in any particular society.

What comedy continues to have going for it as potentially subversive is then its multifaceted, ambivalent and ironic properties. As in the Mel Brooks quote at the beginning of the chapter, comedy has a foot in metaphor in both meaning and not meaning what it says. So if, on the one hand, comedy embraces the body's honest and carnal needs and desires, it is to discover them bound together with social codes and norms, even in the act of ironically subverting them. Moreover, comedy cannot be relied upon to be faithful to the cause of undermining the powerful. Comedy can be coercive, as hateful so-called 'jokes' demonstrate.

In the Western tradition, much of the discussion around comedy stems from Plato's opposition of comedy to reason (Stott 2005: 19).

> There's a part of you which wants to make people laugh, but your reason restrains it, because you're afraid of being thought a vulgar clown. Nevertheless you let it have its way on those other occasions, and you don't realize that the almost inevitable result of giving it energy in this other context is that you become a comedian in your own life.
>
> *(Plato 1994: 360)*

Plato rejects the possibility that comedy could be a way of knowing. For him it has no part of true understanding or reason. By contrast, Aristotle, in his founding book of literary theory, *Poetics*, contrasts comedy to tragedy in dealing with 'low' persons and subjects as a viable counterpart to tragedy's high seriousness and nobility (Stott 2005: 19–20). Both genres imitate life, and are seen as valid or even necessary to the socially significant Greek festivals of drama.

The opinions of these ancient philosophers, Plato and Aristotle, have been the parameters for the literary theory of comedy and tragedy ever since. Arguably, they both privilege tragedy and comedy as artistic forms over their occurrence in human life as a tone or attitude. So how necessary is comedy to *Re-Visioning Psychology*?

Comedy in Re-Visioning Psychology's *psychologizing, or seeing through*

To return to the priceless Mel Brooks, comedy certainly offers a way of seeing through the pretence of human beings to noble and stoic virtues. Much comedy exploits the gap between humans' high opinions of themselves and the baser actuality. For *Re-Visioning Psychology*, however, 'seeing through' is primarily directed to archetypal ideas (Hillman 1975: 116–22). No idea can be termed psychological unless it is first 'psychologized', or submitted to the action of seeing through by being treated as a reflection *of* the soul *on* the soul (ibid.: 118).

Psychological or archetypal ideas are both envisioned and envisioning (Hillman 1975: 121). Rather like jokes, but specifically dedicated to testing thought, psychologized ideas are modes of knowing. Hillman calls such ideas 'eyes', or ways of seeing and knowing (Hillman 1975: 121). *Re-Visioning Psychology* describes the soul as transparent or illuminating. Psychologizing means 'bringing to light', or actually *seeing* through by means of archetypal persons as frameworks of habitual vision (see Chapter 3 on 'frames'). The result is to find soul in all events, converting the idea of any action from literal to metaphor (ibid.: 127).

Archetypal figures then become 'root metaphors' patterning rather than determining psychic functions of feeling perceiving, and understanding (Hillman 1975: 128). Such an approach begins to explicitly re-state the claims of this archetypal psychology to be primary over other disciplines. Imaginal gods keep 'in order' our imaginal persons (Hillman 1975: 128). Psychology becomes *the* way of knowing. (ibid.: 131).

Again we find, perhaps inevitably, the figure of the 'one presumed to know', or authoring authority, in psychology writing (see Chapter 6). Although told that mythical metaphors of the gods are perspectives upon events and not the events themselves, archetypal psychology is yet again given a privileged place as a discipline. Or maybe archetypal psychology is that which makes all the other disciplines possible, for we are told that the soul is *the* way of knowledge and not an object of it (Hillman 1975: 131).

Not present in *Re-Visioning Psychology* is the suggestion that positioning archetypal psychology as the gateway to knowledge is itself an archetypal claim. As such, it could be 'seen through'. Archetypal psychology in this book is instead a threshold or initiatory necessary pre-process to the academy.

In one possibility *Re-Visioning Psychology* may be offering the divine ordering and clarity of Apollonian eyes upon its own claims. However, given its rhetorically promiscuous writing style, and its stress on ambivalent metaphor and pulling apart its operations into four pillars and multiple gods, surely Dionysus is also present in the writing? Maybe the seeing through of comedy can, with its innate rebirthing and re-membering, prevent one god from triumphing even from within the attempt to offer a soul constituted by many?

Re-Visioning Psychology stages an agon between Apollonic distancing and certainty versus Dionysian embrace of ecstasy and mess within the writing. The question of immanence fortunately serves to limit Apollo's drive to soaring transcendence in his fiery chariots. Gods immanent and imaginal offer no place for the framework of one over the many.

Maybe here *Re-Visioning Psychology* takes up the challenge of comedy as tone rather than form. Tone in language signifies a perspective. We use the term 'black humour' for the ability to make jokes even about tragic subjects. Humour and comedy is one of Dionysus's most potent weapons against Apollonian transcendent seriousness. *Comedy as tone is Dionysus within language.* Comic tone is immanent. It dis-members our bodies of seriousness lest they offer too much fuel for Apollo's transcendent rockets.

Re-Visioning Psychology therefore takes a decisive step towards Dionysian immanence by stating that psychologizing is a process of soul-making, not discipline building. Psyche, not psychology, is the foundation of this pillar (Hillman 1975: 134). On the one hand we have an uncompromising assertion of the ontological priority of the soul in making any disciplinary knowing. On the other hand we have a Dionysian promiscuity and fluidity in which soul is polytheistic and metaphorical in engendering other ways of knowing. Dionysus gets around because he wants to be dismembered into all our disciplinary parts.

Yet soaring Apollo is not done with *Re-Visioning Psychology* in the proposal that an 'archetypal theory of knowing' is now possible (Hillman 1975: 132). Significantly, the book does not then pursue such a dangerously proto-transcendent possibility, but rather warns against ego-based knowing that is dominated by a conquering hero myth (ibid.: 135). Additionally, the book now re-emphasizes the crucial distinction between the concrete and the literal, as the former includes imaginal depths (ibid.: 137). Comedy, with its interest in bodily existence, is echoed by *Re-Visioning Psychology* in the notion that soul and body are discursive realms that need not be at war (ibid.: 137). Bodily being is always actual, concrete. It is not necessarily literal, as it too can manifest the gods.

The ritual practices of alchemy, and theatre, are concrete rather than literal. Of course this is also true of comedy itself, whether as a tone/perspective or as a form. Comedy is concrete rather than literal because it signifies directly and indirectly at the same time. It is a metaphor that brings into being a vision that was not there before. Much comedy is bodily, as it suspends our physicality by means of contradictory discourses. It is concrete: the actual pie in the face means *pie in the face.* It is not literal because what is manifested is so much more.

So, if 'seeing through' reveals the archetypal perspective, then, says *Re-Visioning Psychology*, a notion like individuation, according to Jung, is itself archetypal. We see by means of Jung's *idea* of individuation. (Hillman 1975: 147). In this way Hillman's theme of metaphors, myths and gods enters the territory of the literary genre 'fiction' (in another pivot, of course).

> As truths are fictions of the rational, so fictions are truths of the imaginal.
> *(ibid.: 152)*

Seeing through means seeing the gods and their stories as fictions. Here fiction denotes that these metaphorical excursions are *not* to be taken as fundamental realities in the cosmos beyond the soul. Again, myths are perspectives upon events and not the events themselves. Or, Apollo's grand theorizing is limited by Dionysus's immanent playfulness.

However, these fictions are *true* in the sense that they are the irreducible knowing of the imaginal realm of the soul. They are metaphors bringing soul into being, not a decoration for some rational concept about the psyche. *Re-Visioning Psychology* insists that soul-fictions nourish the mental qualities most associated with theology, the arts and philosophy, rather than rational intellect (Hillman 1975: 151).

And yet another qualification of these fictions is that they are dedicated to soul-making, not art-making. While arguably the artist needs to bring some aesthetic patterning to bear on the speech of her inner persons, soul demands the ego take a back seat and listen to the gods. Divinities must be allowed being, even if the result is to suspend the psyche in periods of immobility. The imperative of soul-making fictions is different to that of the artist who seeks to enter a material and historical tradition, even if only by subverting its premises.

So, when *Re-Visioning Psychology* asserts that all academic disciplines become a matter of soul-making, all in soul terms contribute to the creativity of its fictions. However, this is only partly justifiable (Hillman 1975: 152). Yes, archetypal psychology *could* be envisioned as the gateway to all knowing, in the sense that the gods mediate what is other than soul in the cosmos. And what is not soul 'events' can be treated as raw material for the fictions of the polytheistic psyche. I would term such a move as making a super-discipline of archetypal psychology. Fortunately, it does not supersede all other realities as a hyperdiscipline would do. Rather, archetypal psychology converts other realities into imaginal fictions or metaphors.

Such a move of prioritizing soul metaphors and fictions would cancel, or control, some of the ontological drives of other disciplines. In the literary use of fiction, archetypal psychology as a super-discipline would erase the aesthetic and historical principles that are significant in giving the work of literature its independence from the writer.

Making soul fictions in Hillman's imaginal Dionysian mode would, paradoxically, keep the writing more rooted in one embodied soul. It would not give the gods in the words of the text the impersonal generic substance that enables them to live more independently across time and cultures. Put another way, in literary studies genre and form have intrinsic ontological value. They too incarnate being.

Shakespeare's soul-fictions are indispensable to the play *Hamlet* (Shakespeare 1601/2011). But without the pressure of a public with certain expectations, and actors who needed to eat, the resulting script might not have been such an enduring home for the gods. At least this is my reading of what the emphasis on soul fictions as primary in *Re-Visioning Psychology* means for literature. On the one hand, this is the Apollonian book again, the utterance of the one who presumes to know. On the other hand, the 'seeing through' pivot is surely an allusion to a fundamentally comic style in the whole book. Dionysian comedy is at odds with any totalizing vision.

Metaphor is crucial to the notion of seeing through because by definition it sees through its own pretensions to fixed truths (Hillman 1975: 156). Hence, all arguments about archetypes and the soul have to be taken metaphorically, e.g., 'as-if' (ibid.: 156). Or to be truly immersed in myth is to have already embedded such a perspective (ibid.: 157). Apollo may be demanding ontological priority of soul within *Re-Visioning Psychology*, but he is only one god among many. A more useful figure here canters out from the margins when Hillman produces the motif of the Knight Errant, whose errand is to wander about making mistakes and looking ludicrous (ibid.: 160–1).

> Like the Knight Errant, psychologizing is . . . the rogue both the author of psychology and psychology itself fundamentally subjective. And this rogue is anarchic.
>
> *(ibid.: 162)*

It is as if The Red One, from Jung's *The Red Book*, has found his way into Hillman's work (Jung 2009: 212–8). Anarchy, in-discipline, the chaotic qualities of Dionysus are never far away.

The Knight Errant is he who tries to be heroic but makes too many mistakes. With him, comedy surfaces in *Re-Visioning Psychology* in form and tone. Psychologizing is episodic, a picaresque narrative that repeatedly gets the heroically inclined ego to fall down and look silly. Survival depends upon comedy, upon recognizing and embracing comic failure (Hillman 1975: 162).

Indeed, comedy provides seeing through to that psychological breakthrough into seeing the mirroring function of the soul (Hillman 1975: 164). Seeing soul as mirror is seeing its transparency, seeing through to its mythical being. It is being able to bear, because able to laugh at, its fictions. Now it is time to take *Re-Visioning Psychology* into a relation with the oldest literary genre of them all, epic.

Dehumanizing or soul-making and epic in *Re-Visioning Psychology*

Epic outside

Always highly valued by its society, the earliest extant literature has epic form. Its ancient history is distinguished by a tension between oral and written transmission. Beginning in oral performance, epics were passed from poet to poet in a dialogical tension between spontaneity and innovation versus faithful repeating of the people's heritage (see Bakhtin in Chapter 4). Epic retains a sense of the communal, and of functioning as a vital vehicle for memory. It serves to shape who a particular group, tribe or nation are. Epic does this by pitting the human against the inhuman in stories of encounters with troublesome monsters, superhuman warriors or the gods.

Early epics such as Homer's *The Iliad* and *The Odyssey* tell of heroes, wars and wandering that define and preserve collective identity (Innes 2013: 1). Such epics begin in an era of oral culture and continue when the texts were inscribed. Hence, the intrinsic conflict between a poet's role in making new familiar stories in fresh language, and the obligation to tradition. Again, metaphors are not a matter of unrestricted choice.

Another characteristic of epic is its sprawling episodic quality. Aristotle explicitly preferred tragedy for its observation of unity in place, time and action, and a more condensed narrative structure (Innes 2013: 10). In this sense, epic's multiple stories, adventures and battles appear resistant to rules and neat formulas. Compared to classical tragedy, epic appears *dis-membered*. It is a space where humans are exposed to a less ordered, more chaotic, realm of gods and monsters.

According to Paul Innes, in his book, *Epic* (2013), from the time of Virgil's Roman work, *The Aeneid* (19 BCE), epic became overtly nationalist and identified with narrating the state (ibid.: 12–13). Perhaps this accounts for the extent to which epics in the Renaissance were left incomplete since, in an era of religious wars, national boundaries in this period were unstable (ibid.: 16). While the Romantics tried to make epics of the poetic soul, with (incomplete) examples such as Wordsworth's *The Prelude* (1850), arguably, twenty-first-century epic has returned to more communal roots in long-running TV series such as various *Star Treks* (from 1966), movie franchises such as *Star Wars* (from 1977) and *Game of Thrones* (from 2011).

Even where relying on one writer or one director's vision, these modern works are multi-produced in the role of actors, technology, marketing teams, etc. They are also, in this age of optical dominance, primarily transmitted to a viewing audience significantly closer to the audiences of the bards dramatizing tales at a tribal gathering.

Epic arises in more than one historical tradition. Although there are divergences in how the gods appear to men, epic flourishes in literatures as diverse as those in Asia and Africa, as well as in generic relatives such as the Eddas of thirteenth-century Iceland and medieval European Romances. Epic is a multicultural form sharing emphases on journey, conflict and the role of women, suggests Innes (2013: 67). Perhaps the search for the feminine soul, or the soul as feminine, is more cross-cultural and ubiquitous than once believed?

On the other hand, epic is also a descriptive quality and not a constant coherent form. Epic differs in every cultural instance, not least because it is so integral to how a culture defines itself against, and among, other nations. There is no standard epic form, only endless variations on the epic imperative. In particular, epics seem to occur in culture or nation-constituting settings when one particular religion or way of being faces incorporation into another. Hence the tension between pagan roots and a Christianized present in epics such as the Anglo-Saxon *Beowulf* (circa eighth century CE) and John Milton's concern to 'justify the ways of God to man', in his epic version of the Bible written as Protestantism was taking hold in England in 1667 (Milton: I. 26).

Intriguingly, another contemporary platform for epic is in online gaming. Now hugely sophisticated in the online multiverse, epic gaming is more than literary in the sense of reading or watching epic. However, it is also less than being a creator of epic since the gamer enters a world circumscribed by someone else. There are parallels here between online gaming and psychotherapy, in the sense of a dialogical relationship in a sealed world, or temenos. Yet, the absence of therapeutic structures and protections, and the depersonalized other that is the epic cosmos, are obvious limitations to the comparison.

Nevertheless it is suggestive to consider the relationship between psychotherapy as a cultural practice and the literature called epic. Straddling both oral and written relationships, psychotherapy not only deals with personal struggles over meaning, life journeys, conflicts, gender and sexuality, it also contributes to such negotiations of identity on a collective level. Like epic, psychotherapy is episodic and hard to complete. Also like epic it has a generic similarity while being different in every setting. Maybe embarking on a course of psychotherapy is the modern person's Odyssey?

It is time to look at the writing of psychology and epic in *Re-Visioning Psychology*, where there is a profound epical cultural reversal in which the old gods are summoned, partly in order to banish the Christianized world of the monotheistic self and ego. Can epic return or restore the gods of the ancient Greeks? How far is Hillman's restorying amongst gods and monsters a restoration of epic values?

Epic in Re-Visioning Psychology*'s dehumanizing, or soul-making*

Like literary epic, dehumanizing, or soul-making, means that the gods are imagined, rather than being regarded as objects of belief (Innes 2013: 169). In speculation, epic's origins are likely to have been both religious and artistic, with the stories of the gods re-visioned in every telling. In early epics there would be little distinction between imagination and rites of worship. Yet in the epic's centuries of written literature, let alone in modern epics of gaming, science fiction and fantasy, the gods are embraced fictionally and imaginatively, not usually religiously. Modern epic is literature rather than religion. The disciplinary dismembering is in place.

Re-Visioning Psychology insists that archetypal psychology is not humanism, in the sense of making Man the centre of knowing (Innes 2013: 171). Rather, this psychology is epic in regarding relations to the superhuman as the core condition of being. Soul is not primarily human. It is not an inside, nor is it property (ibid.: 173). Individuality is what the gods bestow without care for the individual (ibid.: 175). Soul matters more than life. We have life in order to foster our soul in its polytheistic dimensions. Therefore, soul-making means becoming less human, dehumanizing (ibid.: 180).

At this point *Re-Visioning Psychology* returns to the question of art, in order to reject its potential mitigation of soul making as dehumanizing (Innes 2013: 177). 'Personal shaping' must be added to soul-making for the aesthetic impulse to find completion in art. Art is hereby too personal, too human, to get in the way of the dehumanized soul.

Hillman tries to make a real division between archetypal psychology and art-making, which would of course include literature. Again it comes to priorities in ontology. For the soul to fulfil its dehumanizing it must abandon aesthetic completion. For *Re-Visioning Psychology* the gods do not fully inhabit artistic materiality, its media and literary genre. Art is too complete, too orderly, the book alleges, for the wayward goddesses and gods to find enough room to *be*.

This fascinating argument defines art by its completeness and coherence. But what about art that delights in the incomplete, the fragment, the openness to soul's warring voices? What about epic, for example, notoriously incomplete in the historical record, and episodic and untidy compared to the classical unities of tragedy? What about comedy's intrinsic seeing through egotistical pretensions; or tragedy's evocation of human defeat in the face of inhuman forces; or lyric's *constitution* (rather than mere recording) of a desire that can never be satisfied? I suggest that *Re-Visioning Psychology* is missing many possibilities in the arts.

As before, the dehumanizing pillar emphasizes ensouling the world because the gods demand to be remembered, re-membered, not forgiven (Innes 2013: 187–8). They are the real perspectives on events whose pagan antagonisms and passions entirely demolish modernity's more timid post-Christian morality ibid.: 184–90). In this sense, soul-making is not about improving society, not focused on helping other humans (ibid.: 189). Dehumanizing is inhuman, care-less of human suffering or vulnerability (ibid.: 191). Such inhumanity is necessary for a soul that needs imaginal space beyond morality's 'ought' or 'should'.

Ultimately, dehumanizing means accepting death, an acceptance that is a necessary tempering of soul. We are all Persephone, and ritually undergo her enforced descent into the underworld (Innes 2013: 208). Like her, we return only at a price, to descend again and again, to know death and winter within. What incarnates in the face of such death is rhetoric, the way words do not only persuade, but bring meaning into being (ibid.: 214). Rhetoric is the speech of the gods, for without the gods it would have no power. God inspired or in-spirited rhetoric is incantation, is magic, as the Renaissance knew (ibid.: 214).

Yet, significantly, rhetoric, which to Hillman finds insufficient room in the literary arts, is not dehumanized to the extent of including non-human nature as speakers for themselves. 'It is not animal prototypes . . . but personified archetypes' who have divine rhetoric (Innes 2013: 218). In this book, archetypal psychology is not ecopsychology, if the latter offers the non-human soul an incarnation in metaphor.

Re-Visioning Psychology says that man is 'half-angel' because of speech, among the true angels/gods who speak lyrically and imaginally (Innes 2013: 218). Art, literature and animals are not soulful enough. Surely this drawing of boundaries for soul indicates the authorizing presence of an Apollo-like 'one presumed to know'. Put another way, what god speaks here in authorizing what is and is not soul?

Dehumanizing is soul-making in a decisive turn away from the ego's home arena. It is epically grand in forgoing the pettiness engendered by human societal pressures. On the other hand, protecting the soul from over contamination by ego concerns is also to protect it from the challenges of love, in caring for fellow humans who need help, or who require social change to defeat injustice. Arguably, soul also inheres in social action, as city-protecting Athena, or community-as-home centring Hestia, might insist. Also the exclusion of animals and art from the immediacy of soul might offend Artemis and Dionysus. It is time to look at *Re-Visioning Psychology* overall, as epic of psychology and just possibly, of literature.

Re-Visioning Psychology: Four pillars and a conclusion

Similar cosmic metaphors of constellations show a converging, yet not identical position, between Basarab Nicolescu's depiction of transdisciplinarity and Hillman's sense of archetype as foundational without being deterministic.

> [Disciplines] are like the separation between galaxies, solar systems, stars and planets . . . . When we cross the boundaries we meet the interplanetary and intergalactic vacuum. This vacuum is far from being empty: it is full of invisible matter and energy. It introduces a clear discontinuity between territories of galaxies, solar systems, stars and planets. Without the interplanetary and intergalactic vacuum there is no universe.
>
> *(Nicolescu 2005: 4–5)*

> Archetypes are the skeletal structures . . . yet the bones are changeable constellations of light – sparks, waves, motions. They are principles of uncertainty.
>
> *(Hillman 1975: 157)*

While *Re-Visioning Psychology* flirts with what Nicolescu calls a 'hyperdiscipline', or one claims total supremacy over realities, it settles for what I have called in this chapter a superdiscipline of ontological priority in soul-making. Ideas necessarily have polytheistic psychic being, archetypal psychology claims. They are of the multiple and complex energies of imaginal gods and goddesses. Yet, events and the world that is not psyche have a reality or being beyond the inevitable soul-perspectives we bring to them.

As *Re-Visioning Psychology* describes, the skeleton is not made of relatively fixed bones but infinitely malleable light. Archetypal light inhabits all knowing, neither fixing it nor determining it. This perspective is not what Nicolescu is getting at when he casts transdisciplinarity as fields of knowledge mutually influencing cosmic bodies rather than disputed territories. From a transdisciplinarity point of view, *Re-Visioning Psychology* is limited by offering one direction of ontology, or just the horizontal (see Chapter 2 on transdisciplinarity). Yet we notice here how Dionysian is Nicolescu's metaphor: these dismembered bodies of knowing affect each other, providing *zoe*.

Here, as suggested elsewhere in this book, what transdisciplinarity can gain from depth psychology as a whole, and archetypal psychology in particular, is just what reading *Re-Visioning Psychology* would lead us to expect: a god, a story and divine energy. Seeing transdisciplinary as Dionysian dismemberment, moreover, is not just offering an alternative lens. Rather, Dionysus dismembered, the bisexual god of many ways of knowing and being (often marginalized as feminine), offers a psychic investment, a myth of interiority to Nicolescu's rather depersonalized cosmos.

In return, transdisciplinarity can push at *Re-Visioning Psychology*'s stickiness in its protective attitude towards the soul. For in a move towards transdisciplinarity, the literary and artistic imaginal within archetypal psychology could start to offer a bridge to the social and ecopsychological.

For example, in transdisciplinarity's embrace of complexity theory is the way to in-corporate the social and ecological other through symbols, as suggested in Chapters 2 and 5. Ariadne as soul wedded to Dionysus through *zoe* can go further than *Re-Visioning Psychology*, in finding her full being in an Eros that includes the social. After all, the social sciences are also members of transdisciplinarity's dismembered god (of complete being never completed, always an open system).

Another instance within *Re-Visioning Psychology* is the mitigation of authority through comedy as 'seeing through'. No work so devoted to psychologizing as seeing through pretensions to transcendent unchallengeable fixity in the soul can fully maintain its discipline as inviolate.

Comedy is intimately connected to metaphor in the sense of bringing into being indeterminacy; or, as Hillman might put it, freeing up the unpredictable gods in the soul, freeing them to be unpredictable. I suggest that what *Re-Visioning Psychology* ultimately offers is essence, not essentialism. Such psychic being is friendly to a transdisciplinarity which provides that space of dark matter by which disciplines can affect each other without fatal injury. Literature has its place in Nicolescu's cosmic epistemological vision because its discipline invokes plays, poems, epics, etc., as independently capable of generating knowledge. Here literary studies resists psychology's total embrace, and the disciplines cannot be wholly united.

On the other hand, evaluating these partially mutually implied ontologies as dismembered parts does, I suggest, evoke *zoe*, or new life. While I disagree with Hillman that the gods cannot be freely and satisfyingly encountered in literary genres, *Re-Visioning Psychology* gives to literary studies, still beset by a limiting approach to the text, a rejuvenation that connects art to psychological and religious fundamentals.

Paradoxically, *Re-Visioning Psychology*'s sense of literature as less, due to its aesthetic confining patterns, actually reveals just how much more is in the literary work. It shows the soul-work that literature can do. *Re-Visioning Psychology* can be understood through Dionysian dismemberment to be the metaphor that brings to *zoe*, rejuvenation through envisioning literature and psychology as not the same, but cognate as arts manifesting soul. Literature and psychology are remembered as members (separate but linked) of one (transdisciplinary) body of knowing.

8

CONCLUSION

Dionysus reborn in psychology and literature

Introduction: C. G. Jung, James Hillman and the problems of literature in psychology

It is in his essay on poetry that Jung makes a startlingly radical statement about disciplines of knowledge.

> The fact that artistic, scientific, and religious propensities still slumber peacefully together in the small child . . . all this does nothing to prove the existence of a unifying principle which alone would justify a reduction of the one to the other.
>
> *(Jung 1966, CW 15: para. 99)*

No unifying principle means that no one discipline can claim priority over another. Perhaps this is Jung's most decisive move against the heritage of monotheism that he elsewhere tries to keep in play through centralizing notions such as the Self. For without a unifying principle, there is no one stable base of being and knowing that would cast everything else into the shadow as other. Even dualism gives way to dismembering of being and knowing.

By contrast, the enthusiast for polytheism, James Hillman, paradoxically risks re-erecting a dualism by making his soul of multiple divine perspectives the sole path to knowing and being, and also without independent existence in the non-human. His archetypal psychology thus takes priority, precedence in actually and concretely preceding the construction of human knowledge. It is *human* knowledge because his gods do not care, and because the non-human (when apart from the psyche), does not speak.

What mitigates such a boundary within Hillman's archetypal psychology is his embrace of rhetoric and comedy that implicitly counters the writing persona of 'the one presumed to know', as set out by Jane Gallop on Lacan, as discussed in

Tillich left out one thing: repressed god) Shadow (not out) evil Nature, Woman, material

Chapter 6. *Remembering Dionysus* argues that Jung and Hillman ultimately write from a Dionysian perspective. This entails enduring the dismembering of author-ity. In their own way, each accepts the necessity to dismantle the author-god of rationality that has haunted modernity.

While Hillman's dismissal of reason as the ultimate achievement of the ego comes with a sweeping away of Christian heritage, Jung's work preferred to reform Christianized consciousness, admitting qualities rejected by mainstream monotheistic culture, such as the shadow, the feminine, body and nature. With these major cultural differences, *Remembering Dionysus* suggests that both Jung and Hillman take a Dionysian route to the Dionysian roots of psychology. They remember it in relation to, yet not continuous with, literature.

Literature and psychology as separate academic disciplines began in the same nineteenth-century expansion of higher education, as described in Chapter 1. They underwent similar and related negotiations with the contested categories of science and the rise of the social sciences. Throughout the twentieth cen-tury these disciplines struggled with their previously assumed wholeness and independence.

For instance, New Criticism's insistence upon literature's wholly autonomous 'being', or ontology, denied not only the psyche that produces and consumes lit-erature, but also the entire social and economic sphere that underpins it. Similarly unsustainable is treating the psyche as a kind of object removed from the history that shaped it, and the biases of those studying it.

So a characteristic link between Jung and Hillman is their dismembering and re-membering of their psychologies as literary, and yet not literature. On the one hand, in espousing Dionysus in writing, the god of drama enters their work – most overtly in the 'pillars' of Hillman's *Re-Visioning Psychology*, as argued in Chapter 7 (Hillman 1975), and Jung's frequent use of comedy, such as in his essay on Joyce's *Ulysses*, as discussed in Chapter 5. Jung also flourishes with Dionysian spontaneity in examples discussed throughout this book and made explicit in his comment about mythological and dramatic writing being *more exact* (Jung 1951, CW 9ii: para. 25). He is a Dionysian trickster writer.

Both psychologists go so far with literature, and no further. Each regards aes-thetic completeness that they see as innate to 'real' literature, as an impediment to full psychological expression (see Chapters 1, 5 and 7). Ironically, they seem to have unwittingly absorbed some of New Criticism's perverse banning of the psyche from literary criticism.

And yet Jung and Hillman each determine psychology and literature as entirely separate ways of being and knowing. They re-member them as allied, yet discrete, in a move foreshadowed by Hillman's seminal diagnosis of the rise of Dionysus within psychology and our age. In Hillman's essay on Dionysus in Jung as mani-festing a god of dismembering, this god is the way to a renewed, re-membered consciousness (Hillman 1972/2007).

From this perspective of dismemberment, our rending can be understood as the particular kind of renewal presented by Dionysus. This renewal describes itself by means of a body metaphor . . . Rather the crucial experience would be the awareness of the parts *as parts* distinct from each other, dismembered, each with its own light, a state in which the body becomes conscious of itself as a composite of differences . . . The distribution of Dionysus through matter may be compared with the distribution of consciousness through members, organs and zones.

(ibid.: 28 [italics in original])

Remembering Dionysus has taken seriously Hillman's requirement that Dionysian dismemberment requires a body metaphor. If the old monotheistic god of rational knowing is dismembered by mitigating the author as divine authority, then 'he' may become a Dionysus to be re-membered as *parts*. He is not a person, nor is he a discipline pretending to be a supreme and single being and knowing.

Tacitly, Jung even endorses this partial connecting of psychology and literature in two key notions about writing itself: visionary literature and symbols (as explored in Chapters 1 and 2). Symptomatically, he dismembers literature into two categories: the psychological, using stable meanings in signs; and the visionary, containing symbols that link consciousness to an unknown unconscious significance (Jung 1966, CW15: para. 139). This latter category is demonstrable of psychological rending.

Sublime, pregnant with meaning yet chilling the blood with its strangeness, it arises from timeless depths: glamorous, daemonic, and grotesque, it bursts asunder our human standards of value and aesthetic form.

(ibid.: para. 141)

By asserting that visionary literature exhibits Dionysian unrestraint instead of aesthetic form, Jung corrals it for psychology rather than the foreign territory of art. Moreover, visionary literature dismembers order because of its rich symbols, in which images in words act as scraps of the Dionysian body. To Jung, symbols unite matter and energy: the material being of literature with the numinosity and divine creativity of the psyche. Hence, Jung truly does re-member literature and psychology as separated parts into one body of being and knowing.

As a way Jung's implicit disciplinary Dionysus could be extended, Chapter 5 looked at how Dionysus the loosener would enable a reciprocal exchange of research methodology. Regarding the disciplines as entirely and inevitable other arguably resulted in these two related practices undergoing, unconsciously, a mutual repression. What is of nature or the psyche in literary studies' practice of close reading was ruthlessly forbidden in New Criticism, which preferred the reality of literature as art. Similarly art was refused to Jungian psychology's active imagination, which insisted on the reality of the psyche as nature. *Remembering Dionysus* re-members Dionysus with the consciousness of disciplines as parts, resulting in the ability to borrow strategies without losing their distinct ontologies.

Dionysus is of course unendurable as a condition of being. He is a god of chaos, savagery, with no distinctions between human, animal or the divine. Yet, as both Jung and Hillman knew, to ignore this god is too perilous for our world today. Those who refused to worship Dionysus were torn apart by his maddened followers. Accepting him as the god of dismembering and re-membering being and knowing, means sacrificing our certainties ('the one presumed to know'), in return for re-membering with symbols. Such remembering brings *zoe,* in fostering a divine marriage within the psyche, within disciplinary knowing, and with the cosmos. *Remembering Dionysus* suggests a transformed life.

Part of Dionysus's intolerability persists in *zoe,* the endless instinctual life that is the gift of the remembered consciousness. Here Ariadne is the feminine soul who is united with Dionysian *zoe* in the work of symbols. They re-member us into the cosmos, as explored in Chapter 2.

Remembering the feminine through Dionysus

Remembering Dionysus is to reanimate a feminine that has been marginalized, repressed and forgotten in Western modernity. One way to understand this pervasive loss is taken by Ann Baring and Jules Cashford in their ground-breaking book, *The Myth of the Goddess* (1991). They understand modern consciousness as too dangerously polarized between a dominant Sky Father myth of separation and a suppressed Earth Mother myth of feeling and connection.

These myths are in no way a simple opposition of masculine and feminine genders. Rather, Sky Father figures a monotheism that founds a dualistic era of self versus other. Onto this binary is mapped all sorts of oppositions, including those of male/female, mind/body, culture/nature. Earth Mother is a figuration of fundamental connectedness. She gives birth to *all* life, including female and male. In this sense 'she' is mother, but not feminine as opposed to masculine, for she is prior to gender division. Psychologies of the unconscious call her the pre-Oedipal mother, or, m/Other.

To this structuralist account of the foundations of Western being, Dionysus emerges as Earth Mother's most devoted son. He is the chaotic and savage potential of her myth of union because it is too unleavened by rationality based on separation from the other. He is sexuality and animality without the boundaries secured by integrating or individuating both creation myths.

Regarding Dionysus as avatar of a repressed myth of connectedness enables Earth Mother's essential non-dualist, non-essentialist nature to be enacted. She is Nature itself, but one that subsumes all human culture and differences in her totality of being. Without *any* Sky Father separation, She would become, to humans, a Titan, a consciousness wholly without spirit. She would be, in fact, merely unconsciousness with no hope of creative transformation. James Hillman emphasized polytheism in his psychology precisely to counteract Titanism. Dionysus is dangerously proximate to Earth Mother in his capacity for chaos. Fortunately, he is not alone.

Four-goddess scholarship: Hestia, Artemis, Athena, Aphrodite

Other goddesses and gods continue the individuation or artistic sculpting of consciousness. Like Dionysus, many have been too little appreciated in their careless leaps over puny human barriers such as those between disciplines. For example, trickster Hermes has long had a home in hermeneutics, the study of creating meaning from texts. This much is acknowledged in the procreative "herm". Yet Hermes has a creative relationship of absence with Hestia, goddess of hearth and home in a family, communal and even planetary sense. As Ginette Paris argues that where Hermes is Hestia is not yet, both need the other lest they become too dominant (Paris 1986: 181–3). So, surely hermeneutics also intimates an echo of Hestia. Do we not sometimes make a meaningful home through writing?

Moreover, relatives of Dionysus also cross the human and non-human nature divide. Both Artemis and Aphrodite, very differently, can enter writing for the sake of the non-human. Wild writing of psyche beyond humans belongs to Artemis, while Aphrodite brings the erotic to words. She inhabits the literature of desire and sexuality.

Athena, too, goddess of weaving, containing, and of making communities possible, can also find her being and knowing in writing. Dionysus is one member of a polytheistic pantheon. In breaking through the marginalization of that which has been named feminine, he makes room for goddesses too. Hestia, Artemis, Athena and Aphrodite are also invited into knowing in this re-membering of the research disciplines.

After all, they have always been at home in literature. Hestia lingers in the home/ nation making strategies of epic; Artemis in wilder lyrics; Athena in the containment of tragedy and comedy; while Aphrodite delighted in the arts of love and love as art. Ultimately, I suggest, these goddesses along with Dionysus are invoked in transdisciplinarity.

For in seeking psychologies of the most repressed parts of human nature, Jung and Hillman write for Dionysus and find themselves in the domain of what Basarab Nicolescu calls 'the included middle', between literature and psychology, as explored in Chapter 2 (Nicolescu 2005: 6).

Transdisciplinarity as the feminine and Dionysus: Ariadne and symbolic knowing

Nicolescu's proposed transdisciplinarity paradigm for the future of knowing and being exhibits many of the qualities of the returning lost feminine of Dionysus and other divinities. Transdisciplinarity is distinguished by its core claims that being and knowing are multiplicities; that intelligence must be of the body and feeling as well as reason; and that knowledge must be regarded as a dynamically open system, never complete or absolute. As a result, I suggest that transdisciplinarity is fundamentally of the (Jungian and Hillman) psychology project to make whole the fractured modern psyche by including mystery as innate and irreducible.

Fundamental to the realization of the returning feminine, making it 'real', is its language of symbols. Here, too, is the mitigation of Dionysian divine chaos. For symbols are not only bodily scraps of this god, his being in dismemberment. They also incarnate his divine marriage with Ariadne, the feminine as human soul. When Jung suggests that the true language of his science as psychology is symbols, he offers something important to the transdisciplinary project (Jung 1921, CW6: para. 817). Symbolic writing and the symbolic attitude is 'making real', or realizing Nicolescu's insistence on an open system of knowing.

Symbols are the language of the body and of feeling that connects to other realities, those that Nicolescu sees as vital to the transdisciplinarity worldview. Some of these other realities come through goddesses as well as gods. Symbols in words embody, thus materialize the divine archetypes. They are the being of the four goddesses, and of trickster Hermes. Crucially for *Remembering Dionysus*, they are the sacred connection with the potentials for unbounded, unending instinctual life.

Connecting the divinities of knowing to humanity is the soul cast as Ariadne in Dionysian transdisciplinarity. Symbols in the languages of knowledge are the soul as Ariadne wedded to Dionysus and finding *zoe*, renewal of life and consciousness. Symbols in words are how transdisciplinarity in its disciplines enacts the Dionysian drama of being. They show how transdisciplinarity can rejuvenate the pursuit of knowledge.

For, of course symbols are the included middle as Jung knew in calling them a bridge between the known and unknown (Jung 1921, CW6: 819). They are the included middle between different ontologies, both A and not-A, and between those different disciplines, just as they are the included middle between self and other.

Symbols are Dionysus re-membered as related parts, not forcing not-A to *be* A. Naturally they are also the included middle between nature and culture, the place where divine archetypes in our human nature use symbols as a portal to the other. And of course one of the places where symbols are most at liberty in *Remembering Dionysus* is their playground in *The Red Book*, and their peculiar apparent absence in Jung's '*Ulysses*: a Monologue'.

The feminine and Dionysus in **The Red Book** and 'Ulysses: A Monologue'

Made from reconfigured active imaginations, *The Red Book* is a dismembered text of multiple voices and diverse creatures. Construed monotheistically by Sonu Shamdasani and Wolfgang Giegerich (see Chapter 3), its very own claim to be a mystery play places it within the Dionysian realm of communal rites (see Chapter 4). While not communal on one level, because composed by one person, *The Red Book* aspires to be a Dionysian mystery play of the collective unconscious. It dismembers consciousness via conventional modes of religion, art and Eros, and re-members them in relation to the animal-instinctual divine.

What *The Red Book* does not do is forge a persisting connection between what it deems masculine Logos–discriminating knowing, and feminine Eros–feeling and connected knowing. On the other hand, it does contain (Athena-like) neglected elements of consciousness, such as criminals, prisoners, the insane, an undereducated cook, along with various serpentine forms of the feminine, Salome, Philemon largely without wife, Baucis, and a blued shade identified in footnotes as Christ.

I suggest that two very marginal feminine figures in *The Red Book* resurface in later works by Jung: the cook and Baucis, wife-partner to Philemon. The cook turns up in the episode of the Christian chicken, discussed in Chapter 2, a Dionysian vision of the divine in nature. Somewhat improbably for Jung, a 'Baucis' arrives in Jung's vision of Molly Bloom at the end of his essay on *Ulysses*. For it is here that the writing achieves a moment of remembering Eros embracing Logos.

The Red Book is a text and a text-ure of symbols that dismember the reader's psyche, as active imagination has dismembered Jung's. This book is a treatment by immersion in the depths. By contrast, Jung's essay '*Ulysses*: a Monologue', is a re-membering of a psyche that has been shattered by modernity. Jung says that it is without symbols except for its *symbolic work* in its form. So terribly destructive is it to consciousness and meaning that only in the body, in the image of the worm, can a spark of being exist. Joyce's novel is truly 'sublime . . . chilling the blood with its strangeness', as Jung claims of visionary literature (Jung 1966, CW15: para. 141).

Dionysus dismembers meaning into its destruction in the sublime, as explored through both Jung and Jacques Lacan in Chapter 6. The symbolic form of Joyce's novel re-members the alienated consciousness of the modern person and even re-incorporates the feminine, in the person of Molly Bloom.

> The demiurge first created a world that . . . seemed to him perfect; but looking upward he beheld a light which he had not created . . . his masculine creative power turned into feminine acquiescence.
>
> *(ibid.: para. 199)*

As symbol itself, the novel provides a union of masculine and feminine that is conceivable to Jung because it is a *symbol*, forever mysterious, not wholly rational, an open (transdisciplinary) system. Importantly, what saves the reader's shattered ego in Jung's essay is what saves the Gnostic divine in the above quotation: an ordering principle outside the ego.

Such a possibility of coherence beyond the human is inherent to Dionysus because his nature is also non-human nature. It is also what brings Dionysus into complexity theory and the study of emergence. Nature evolves because systems of intense complexity are unpredictable yet patterning, as Dionysus is (see Chapters 2 and 5).

Complexity evolution sees the human psyche and the non-human cosmos as a process of mutual dismembering and re-membering. There is no inherent or inevitable separation between human and non-human nature. Dualism in this sense is defeated by Dionysus. Understood in a transdisciplinary paradigm, or with what

Jung would call a symbolic attitude, the language of knowledge is also a language of being. Our human *open* processes of knowing become Ariadne marrying a cosmos of Dionysian complexity.

Literature and psychology

Chapter 7 studies Hillman's great work, *Re-Visioning Psychology* (1975) for its exploration of the roots of psychology in Dionysus and literature. Hillman's susceptibility to metaphor reveals it to be Dionysian in simultaneously dismembering and re-membering meaning. Metaphor, as David Punter has shown, is not a choice (Punter 2007: 68). It is the life blood of Dionysus, a communal god, as we struggle with cultural codes, the collective archetypes, and the complexity of evolution in a cosmos of which we are at least partly unconscious.

Without complexity theory, Hillman's proclamation of a naturalistic fallacy aligns him with Lacan in seeing no psychically affective, nor effective, ordering mode in non-human nature (Hillman 1975: 84). Fortunately, this psychologist's superb sensibility sees how far psychology writing is Dionysian, in the sense of being uncontrollable by a masterful ego. Whereas Lacan impersonates the 'one presumed to know', in Chapter 6, Hillman's literary excursions demonstrate that language as rhetoric and metaphor dismember any attempt to keep alive the old monotheistic god of dualism.

That god would never let go of his role as author, or authority in writing. Hillman's polytheism *has* to admit Dionysus into his writing, both in the sense of letting him in, and as acknowledging his presence as the Knight Errant, a dismembered authority making errors (Hillman 1975: 160–61). Lyric, tragedy, comedy and epic are all mined by *Re-Visioning Psychology* in order to host the gods in a far more psychically expansive vessel than mere psyche/logos. Here literature is necessary to psychology without being identical to it.

So finally, without Dionysus we are cut off from instinctual life. *Remembering Dionysus* suggests that without Dionysus in our knowing we are severed from renewable being. Psychology finds Dionysian roots in literature without losing its distinctiveness, if it takes on the communal rite of dismembering and re-membering. Sacrificed to the god of undifferentiation between animal, human and divine, we are reborn in *zoe*. So, too, is psychology reborn with a capacity for literary ritual arts. In turn, literary studies are rejuvenated by instinctual archetypal nature. Writing materializes the gods.

GLOSSARY

Words marked with an * are Jungian terms included in this Glossary.

Alchemy (Jungian)* Alchemy is defined by Jung as a projection of psychic contents, specifically the individuation* process, onto the chemical activities of the alchemist. He interpreted alchemy texts as demonstrating the projection of unconscious processes and alchemists as unwitting self-analysts. Alchemists developed symbols. Jung believed that alchemical symbols enabled psychological transformations similar to the role of dreams in his psychology. In his view, alchemists used chemistry and symbolic language to stimulate their own individuation so that they could reach the 'gold' of union with the divine or self archetype.*

Anima* The anima is the archetype of the feminine in the unconscious of a man. In that this locates a feminine mode in the subjectivity of the masculine gender, denoting a bisexual unconscious, this is a helpful concept. However, at times, Jung uses his own unconscious anima as a model for designating female subjectivity as 'more unconscious' than males. (See also animus,* Eros,* Logos*).

Animus* The animus is the archetype of masculinity in the unconscious of a woman. Like the anima, this does not lock Jungian theory into perpetual gender opposition since the unconscious contains androgynous archetypes. Nothing can be securely known or fixed in the unconscious. So masculinity is rather one of a series of types of 'otherness' for the psyche of a woman.

Archetypal images* Archetypal images are the visible representations of archetypes. A single image can never account for the multifarious potential of the archetype. Archetypal images are always creative yet provisional and partial images of a greater unrepresentable complexity. Crucially, they do draw representative material from culture as well as shaping energy from the archetype. Therefore Jungian psychic archetypal imagery is always cultural and historical as well as numinous and psychic.

Archetypes* Archetypes are inherited structuring patterns in the unconscious with potentials for meaning formation and images. They are unrepresentable in themselves and evident only in their manifest derivatives, archetypal images. Archetypes are containers of opposites and so are androgynous, equally capable of manifesting themselves as either gender or non-human forms. Body and culture will influence the content of archetypal images but not govern them because archetypes are the structuring principles of an *autonomous* psyche. Archetypes are not inherited ideas or images. (See archetypal images,* unconscious*).

Collective unconscious* The collective unconscious is the common inheritance of archetypes that all human beings share. Everybody is born with them in the same way. How the archetypes are then manifested as archetypal images will depend upon the particular culture and history of any individual.

Dreams* Unlike the Freudian usage, dreams to a Jungian are spontaneous expressions or communications from a superior part of the human mind. They are not derivative of ego concerns or necessarily about sexuality (unless they belong to the trivial class of dreams derived from the residue of the previous day). Dream images are not secondary. They are a *primary* form of reality and must not be 'translated' into the mode of the ego, into words. Jung thought something very similar about art, that it could offer a primary mode of expression of the unconscious if it fell into the visionary* category of art in which the artist is possessed by the archetypal imagination.

Ego* The ego is the centre of consciousness concerned with the sense of a personal identity, the maintenance of personality and the sense of continuity over time. However, Jung considered the ego as something less than the whole personality as it was constantly interacting with more significant archetypal forces in the unconscious. Jung tended to equate the ego with consciousness in his writings.

Eros* Eros is another of Jung's concepts based upon gendered opposites. Its other is Logos.* Eros stands for psychic capacities of relatedness and feeling with Logos as a motif of spiritual meaning and reason. Jung aligned feminine consciousness with Eros and masculine subjectivity with Logos. Since the anima* and animus* carry Eros and Logos qualities in the unconscious, this means that males tend to have underdeveloped qualities of relating, females to be inferior in 'thinking' and rational argument. The consequences for Jung's views on gender are profound.

Individuation* Individuation is Jung's term for the process whereby the ego is brought into a relationship with the archetypal dynamics of the unconscious.

In individuation the ego is constantly made, unmade and re-made by the goal-directed forces of the unconscious. Even 'meaning' in the ego is subject to dissolution and re-constitution by the Jungian other. For Jung, the making of art or the appreciation of art was a form of individuation because it was a confrontation with the other in the imagination.

Logos* A principle of mental functioning oriented towards reason, discrimination and spiritual authority. Jung regarded it as characteristic of masculine consciousness. Logos operates in a gendered binary opposite with Eros.* Contemporary Jungian analytic practice treats Logos and Eros as equally available to both genders.

Mythology and myth Mythology conventionally refers to a culture's stories of gods, goddesses, monsters and divine beings that have performed a religious function in various human societies. Examples would include the mythologies of ancient Greece and Rome. Christianity may be regarded as a mythology. However, to Jung, myth is a form of language that enables some participation in the unexplored, and in some sense unconquerable territories of the mind. To Jung, myth poses a double psychic potency. It is at the same time the most authentic representation of the interplay of conscious and unconscious, and it is an active intervention shaping such inner dialogue. So myth is a healing technique for when the unconscious threatens mental chaos, and, simultaneously a true expression of the mutuality of the two aspects of the psyche – conscious and unconscious. For Jung and Jungian literary theory true *expression* of the psyche is privileged over conceptually based claims to *know* it.

Psychological art Jung divided art into psychological and visionary* categories. Psychological art mainly consists of signs,* which point to what is known or knowable. Consequently, psychological art mainly expresses the collective consciousness of a society, what the collective is consciously debating or concerned about. Jung felt that in some art, the artist has already done most of the psychic work for the audience – hence 'psychological' work.

Self* The Self is the supreme governing archetype of the unconscious to which the ego becomes subject in individuation.* Jung frequently described self-images in dreams in circular or mandala forms. He argued that Christ functioned as a self-image in Christianity. What is crucial here is to remember that 'Self' for Jung means the not-known, the unknowable in the individual person. The Self is to be found in the unconscious. It does not stand for the conscious personality.

Shadow* The shadow is the archetypal forces of blackness, reversal or undoing. Intrinsic to the idea of a compensatory relation between ego and unconscious, the shadow is that which is denied in conscious personality. Consequently the shadow could be figured as the potential evil within everyone. Jung warned that the shadow needed to be brought into a relationship with conscious personality lest repression caused it to swell in power and break out in neurosis or violence.

Signs   Jung divided images into two types of signifying, signs and symbols.* Signs point to a known or knowable meaning. They are therefore primarily concerned with the collective consciousness and are the main ingredient of psychological art.*

Subtle body*   The body as imaged in the psyche is a Jungian subtle body because it is formed by both bodily and archetypal ingredients. Because archetypes* are of the body as well as the non-bodily psyche, mental representations of the body are both physical and psychical – the subtle body.

Symbols   Jung divided images into two types of signifying, symbols and signs.* Symbols point to what is hardly known, not yet known, or unknowable. They are therefore the chief conduit for the collective unconscious* in dreams and in art. Symbols make up most of the fabric of visionary art.* Archetypal images* very often manifest as symbols in which the term stands for their numinous quality.

Synchronicity*   Jung used this term to describe the linking of events not by cause and effect, not by time and space, but by psychological coherence. For example, if a total stranger suddenly meets a person's vital need with no apparent explanation – that is synchronicity. It refers to Jung's notion that psyche, matter, time and space are all fundamentally connected.

Unconscious*   To Jung, the term unconscious denotes both mental contents inaccessible to the ego and a psychic arena with its own properties and functions. The Jungian unconscious is superior to the ego and exists in a compensatory relation to it. It is the locus of meaning, feeling and value in the psyche and is autonomous. It is not, however, completely separate from the body but offers a third place between that perennial duality, body and spirit. Body and culture influence unconscious contents (archetypal images), but the unconscious is not *subject* to either force. The unconscious is structured by archetypes* as hypothetical inherited structuring principles.

Visionary art   Jung divided art into psychological* and categories. Visionary art mainly consists of symbols,* which points to what is not yet known or unknowable in the culture. Consequently, visionary art is primarily expressive of the collective unconscious,* As such it *compensates* the culture for its biases, brings to consciousness what is *ignored* or repressed, and may *predict* something of the future direction of the culture.

REFERENCES

Aristotle. (1996) *Poetics*, trans. Malcolm Heath, Harmondsworth: Penguin.

Bakhtin, M. M. (1981) *The Dialogic Imagination: Four Essays*, ed. M. Holquist, trans. C. Emerson and M. Holquist, Austin: University of Texas Press.

Bakhtin, M. M. (1984) *Rabelais and His World*, trans. Helene Iswolsky, Cambridge, MA: MIT Press.

Baring, A. and J. Cashford. (1991) *The Myth of the Goddess: Evolution of an Image*, New York and London: Vintage.

Beebe, J. (2010, Summer) '*The Red Book* as a Work of Conscience; Notes from a Seminar Given for the 35th Annual Jungian Conference, C.G. Jung Club of Orange County, April 10th 2010', *Quadrant*, volume XL, issue 2: pp. 41–58.

Bowie, M. (1991) *Lacan*, Fontana Modern Masters, London: HarperCollins.

Brewster, S. (2009) *Lyric, the New Critical Idiom*, London and New York: Routledge.

Burke, E. (1757/1990) *A Philosophical Enquiry into the Origin of Our Ideas of the Sublime and Beautiful*, ed. A. Philips, Oxford: Oxford University Press.

Cambray, J. (2012) *Synchronicity: Nature and Psyche in an Interconnected Universe*, College Station: Texas A & M Press.

Cambray, J. (2014) 'Romanticism and Revolution in Jung's Science', in R. A. Jones ed., *Jung and the Question of Science*, London and New York: Routledge, pp. 9–29.

Coleridge, S. T. (1847) *Biographia Literaria, or, Biographical Sketches of My Life and Opinions*, London: William Pickering.

Conforti, M. (1999/2003) *Field, Form and Fate: Patterns in Mind, Nature & Psyche*, New Orleans, LA: Spring Journal and Books.

Corbett, L. (2011) 'Jung's *Red Book* Dialogues with the Soul: Herald of a New Religion?' *Jung Journal: Culture and Psyche*, volume 5, Issue 3: pp. 66–77.

Couliano, I. P. (1987) *Eros and Magic in the Renaissance*, trans. Margaret Cook, Chicago: University of Chicago Press.

Crane, R. S. (ed.) (1952) *Critics and Criticism: Ancient and Modern*, Chicago: University of Chicago Press.

Dawson, T. (2014) 'Analytical Psychology, Narrative Theory and the Question of Science', in R. A. Jones ed., *Jung and the Question of Science*, London and New York: Routledge, pp. 98–117.

Dawson, T. (2014) 'Truth, facts and interpretation,' in R. A. Jones ed. *Jung and the Question of Science*, London and new York: Routledge, pp. 165–73.

de Man, P. (1985) 'Lyrical Voice in Contemporary Theory: Rifaterre and Jauss', in Hosek and Parker eds., *Lyric Poetry: Beyond New Criticism*, Ithaca, NY: Cornell University Press, pp. 55–72.

Derrida, J. (1987) *The Truth in Painting*, trans. Geoff Bennington and Ian McLeod, Chicago: University of Chicago Press.

Derrida, J. (1988) "The Purveyor of Truth" in J. P. Muller and W. J. Richardson eds., The Purloined Poe: Lacan, Derrida and Psychoanalytic Reading, Baltimore, MD: The Johns Hopkins University Press, pp. 173–121.

Drob, S. L. (2012) *Reading The Red Book: An Interpretative Guide to C. G. Jung's Liber Novus*, New Orleans: Spring Journal and Books.

Eagleton, T. (1983/2008) *Literary Theory: An Introduction*, Oxford: Blackwell Publishers; Minneapolis: University of Minnesota Press.

Fertel, R. (2015) *A Taste for Chaos: The Art of Literary Improvisation*, New Orleans: Spring Journal and Books.

Frantz, G. (2010) 'Jung's *Red Book*: The Spirit of the Depths', *Psychological Perspectives: A Quarterly Journal of Jungian Thought* (Special Issue: Jung's *Red Book*: The Spirit of the Depths), volume 53, issue 4: pp. 391–5.

Frye, N. (1957) 'Characterization in Shakespearean Comedy', *Shakespeare Quarterly*, volume 4, issue 3: pp. 271–7.

Frye, N. (1990) *The Anatomy of Criticism: Four Essays*, Harmondsworth: Penguin.

Furlotti, N. (2010) 'Tracing a Red Thread: Synchronicity and Jung's *Red Book*', *Psychological Perspectives: A Quarterly Journal of Jungian Thought*, volume 53, issue 4: pp. 455–78.

Gallagher, S. (1992) *Hermeneutics and Education* (SUNY Series in Contemporary Continental Philosophy), New York: SUNY Press.

Gallop, J. (1988) 'The American Other', in J. P. Muller and W. J. Richardson eds., *The Purloined Poe: Lacan, Derrida and Psychoanalytic Reading*, Baltimore, MD: The Johns Hopkins University Press, pp. 268–82.

Gardner, L. (2014) 'Speculations on Jung's Dream of Science', in R. A. Jones ed., *Jung and the Question of Science*, London and New York: Routledge, pp. 70–81.

Giegerich, W. (2010, Spring) '*Liber Novus*, That Is, the New Bible: A First Analysis of C. G. Jung's *Red Book*', *Spring: A Journal of Archetype and Culture*, volume 83: pp. 361–411.

Graff, G. (1989/2007) *Professing Literature: An Institutional History*. Chicago: University of Chicago Press.

Graff, G. (2007) 'Our Undemocratic Curriculum', *Profession, Journal of the Modern Languages Association*, pp. 128–35.

Hale, C. A. (2010) 'What about Being Red? Encounters with the Color of Jung's Red Book' (Special Issue: Jung's *Red Book*: The Spirit of the Depths) *Psychological Perspectives: A Quarterly Journal of Jungian Thought,* volume 53, issue 4: pp. 479–94.

Hayles, N. K. (1984) *The Cosmic Web: Scientific Field Models & Literary Strategies in the 20th Century*, Cornell: Cornell University Press.

Hillman, J. (1972/2007) 'Dionysus in Jung's Writings', *Spring: A Journal of Archetype and Culture*, 1972, in *Mythic Figures: Uniform Edition of the Writings of James Hillman, volume 6.1*, Putnam, Connecticut: Spring Publications, pp. 15–30.

Hillman, J. (1975) *Re-Visioning Psychology*, New York: Harper & Row.

Hillman, J. (1992) *The Thought of the Heart and the Soul of the World*. Woodstock, CT: Spring Publications.

Hillman, J. (2004) *Archetypal Psychology*, 3rd edition, Putnam, CT: Spring Publications.

Hillman, J. and M. Ventura. (1992) *We've Had a Hundred Years of Psychotherapy and the World Is Getting Worse*, New York: HarperCollins.

Innes, P. (2013) *Epic, the New Critical Idiom*, London and New York: Routledge.

James, W. (1983) *The Principles of Psychology*, Cambridge, MA: Harvard University Press.

Jones, R. A. (ed.) (2014a) *Jung and the Question of Science*, London and New York: Routledge.

Jones, R. A. (2014b) 'Vicissitudes of a Science-Complex', in R. A. Jones ed., *Jung and the Question of Science*, London and New York: Routledge, pp. 50–69.

Joyce, J. (1922/1992) *Ulysses*, Harmondsworth: Penguin.

Jung, C. G. (1916) 'The Transcendent Function', *Collected Works, Volume 8, The Structure and Dynamics of the Psyche*, pp. 67–91.

Jung, C. G. (1921) 'Definitions', in *Collected Works, Volume 6, Psychological Types*, pp. 408–86.

Jung, C. G. (1932) ' "Ulysses": A Monologue', in *Collected Works, Volume 15: The Spirit in Man, Art and Literature*, pp. 127–54.

Jung, C. G. (1933/2001) *Modern Man in Search of a Soul*, London and New York: Routledge.

Jung, C. G. (1944a) 'Epilogue', *Collected Works of C. G. Jung, Volume 12: Psychology and Alchemy*, pp. 473–84.

Jung, C. G. (1944b) 'The Symbolism of the Mandala,' *Collected Works of C. G. Jung, Volume 12: Psychology and Alchemy*, pp. 95–224.

Jung, C. G. (1949) 'Foreword to Adler: Studies in Analytical Psychology', *Collected Works, Volume 18: The Symbolic Life: Miscellaneous Writings*, pp. 523–4.

Jung, C. G. (1951) 'The Syzygy: Anima and Animus', *Collected Works, Volume 9ii: Aion: Researches into the Phenomenology of the Self*, pp. 11–22.

Jung, C. G. (1952) 'Synchronicity: An Acausal Connecting Principle', *Collected Works, Volume 8: The Structure and Dynamics of the Psyche*, pp. 417–532.

Jung, C. G. (1953–1991) Except where a different publication is noted, all references are, by volume and paragraph number, to the edition of *The Collected Works of C. G. Jung (CW)*, ed. Sir Herbert Read, Dr Michael Fordham and Dr Gerhard Adler, trans. R. F. C. Hull, London: Routledge, Princeton, NJ: Princeton University Press. The date of my citation is the date of the English text.

Jung, C. G. (1963/1983) *Memories, Dreams, Reflections*, Recorded and Edited by Aniela Jaffe, London: Fontana.

Jung, C. G. (2009) *The Red Book: Liber Novus*, ed. Sonu Shamdasani, trans. Mark Kyburz, John Peck and Sonu Shamdasani, New York: W.W. Norton & Co.

Kerenyi, K. (1976) *Dionysos: Archetypal Image of Indestructible Life*, Princeton, NJ: Princeton University Press.

Kristeva, J. (1982) *Powers of Horror: An Essay on Abjection*, New York: Columbia University Press.

Lacan, J. (1972/1988) 'Seminar on "The Purloined Letter"', in J. P. Muller and W. J. Richardson eds., *The Purloined Poe*, Baltimore, Maryland: Johns Hopkins University Press, pp. 28–54.

Lauterbach, J. (2013) 'The Hillman Pivot', unpublished manuscript.

Leech, C. (1969) *Tragedy (the Critical Idiom)*, London: Methuen & Co.

Le Guin, U. (1986) 'The Carrier Bag Theory of Fiction', in C. Glotfelty and H. Fromm (eds.) (1996), *The Ecocriticism Reader: Landmarks in Literary Ecology*, pp. 149–54.

Lui, A. (1989) *Wordsworth: A Sense of History*, Stanford: Stanford University Press.

Main, R. (2004) *The Rupture of Time: Synchronicity and Jung's Critique of Modern Western Culture*, London and New York: Routledge.

McGann, J. (2006) ' "The Grand Heretics of Modern Fiction": Laura Riding, John Cowper Powys, and the Subjective Correlative', *MODERNISM/Modernity*, volume 13, issue 2: pp. 309–23.

Mellor, A. K. (1993) *Romanticism and Gender*, New York and London: Routledge.

Milbank, J. (2004) 'Sublimity: The Modern Transcendent', in Regina Schwartz, ed., *Transcendence: Philosophy, Literature, and Theology Approach the Beyond*, New York and London: Routledge, pp. 211–34.

Mitchell, S. (2004) *Gilgamesh: A New English Version*, New York and London: Atria Paperbacks.

Nicolescu, B. (2005) 'Transdisciplinarity – Past, Present and Future', Palestra apresentada no II Congresso Mundial de Transdisciplinaridade 06 a 12 de setembro de 2005, Vila Velha/Vitória – SC – Brasil, *CETRANS – Centro de Educação Transdisciplinar*, pp. 1–24. Online. Available. www.cetrans.com.br (Accessed 20th May 2015).

Noll, R. (1995) *The Jung Cult: Origins of a Charismatic Movement*, Princeton New Jersey: Princeton University Press.

Noll, R. (1996) *The Aryan Christ: The Secret Life of Carl Jung*, Princeton, NJ: Princeton University Press.

Odajnyk, W. V. (2010) 'Reflections on "The Way of What Is to Come" of *The Red Book*', *Psychological Perspectives: A Quarterly Journal of Jungian Thought* (Special Issue: Jung's *Red Book*: The Spirit of the Depths), volume 53, issue 4: pp. 437–54.

Palmer, R. E. (1969) *Hermeneutics; Interpretation Theory in Schleiermacher, Dilthey, Heidegger, and Gadamer*, Evanston, IL: Northwestern University Press.

Paris, G. (1986) *Pagan Meditations: Aphrodite, Hestia, Artemis*, Woodstock, CT: Spring Publications.

Paris, G. (1998) *Pagan Grace: Dionysus, Hermes and Goddess Memory in Daily Life*, Woodstock, CT: Spring Publications.

Plato. (1994) *Republic*, trans. Robin Waterfield, Oxford and New York: Oxford University Press.

Punter, D. (2007) *Metaphor*, the New Critical Idiom, London and New York: Routledge.

Ransom, J. C. (1938) *The World's Body*, New York: Charles Scribner & Sons.

Richards, I. A. and C. K. Ogden. (1923/1989) *The Meaning of Meaning: A Study of the Influence of Language upon Thought and of the Science of Symbolism*, New York: Mariner Books.

Ricoeur, P. (1970) *Freud and Philosophy: An Essay on Interpretation (The Terry Lectures)*, New Haven: Yale University Press.

Rowland, S. (2005) *Jung as a Writer*, New York and London: Routledge.

Rowland, S. (2010) *C. G. Jung in the Humanities: Taking the Soul's Path*, New Orleans: Spring Journal and Books.

Rowland, S. (2012) *The Ecocritical Psyche: Literature, Evolutionary Complexity and Jung*, Hove and New York: Routledge.

Saban, M. (2014) 'Science Friction: Jung, Goethe and Scientific Objectivity', in R. A. Jones ed., *Jung and the Question of Science*, London and New York: Routledge, pp. 30–49.

Samuels, A. (1985) *Jung and the Post-Jungians*, London: Routledge & Kegan Paul.

Schwartz-Salant, N. (2010, Summer) 'The Mark of One Who Has Seen Chaos', *Quadrant*, volume XXXX, issue 2: pp. 11–40.

Shakespeare, W. (1601/2011) *The Arden Shakespeare Complete Works*, ed. Richard Proudfoot, Ann Thompson and David Scott Kasdan, London, Bloomsbury: Methuen Drama.

Shamdasani, S. (2009/2012) 'Introduction', in Sonu Shamdasani ed., trans. Mark Kyburz, John Peck and Sonu Shamdasani, *The Red Book: Liber Novus, A Reader's Edition*, New York: W.W. Norton & Co., pp. 1–95.

Shamdasani, S. and J. Beebe. (2010) 'Jung Becomes Jung: A Dialogue on *Liber Novus* (*The Red Book*)', *Psychological Perspectives: A Quarterly Journal of Jungian Thought*, volume 53, issue 4: pp. 410–38.

Shaw, P. (2006) *The Sublime*, the New Critical Idiom, London and New York: Routledge.

Shulman, H. (1997) *Living at the Edge of Chaos: Complex Systems in Culture and Psyche*, Zurich: Daimon Verlag.

Slater, G. (2012, Summer) 'Between Jung and Hillman', *Quadrant: A Journal of Jungian Thought*, volume XXXII, issue 2: pp. 15–37.

Slattery, D. P. (2014) *Creases in Culture: Essays Toward a Poetics of Depth*, Cheyenne, Wyoming: Fisher King Press.

Snyder, G. (1992/2000) 'Language Goes Two Ways,' in *The Green Studies Reader: From Romanticism to Ecocriticism*, edited by Laurence Coupe, London and New York: Routledge, pp. 127–31.

Spano, M. V. (2010) 'Modern(-ist) Man in Search of a Soul: Jung's *Red Book* as Modernist Visionary Literature'. Online. Available. www.cgjungpage.org/index.php?option=com_content&task=view&id=934&Itemid=1 (Accessed 27th September 2012).

Stoppard, T. (1967/1994) *Rosencrantz and Guildenstern Are Dead*, New York: Grove Press.

Stott, A. (2005) *Comedy (the New Critical Idiom)*, London and New York: Routledge.

Tympas, G. C. (2014) *Carl Jung and Maximus the Confessor: The Dynamics between the 'Psychological' and the 'Spiritual'*, London and New York: Routledge.

Ulanov, A. B. (2010, Summer) 'God Climbs Down to Mortality', *Quadrant*, volume XXXX, issue 2: pp. 61–80.

van den Berk, T. (2009/2012) *Jung on Art: The Autonomy of the Creative Drive*, New York and Hove: Routledge.

Van Loben Sels, R. (2010, Summer) 'Ancestors and Spirits of the Dead', *Quadrant*, volume XXXX, issue 2: pp. 81–94.

Wheeler, W. (2006) *The Whole Creature: Complexity, Biosemiotics and the Evolution of Culture*, London: Lawrence & Wishart.

Wilson, E. A. (2002) 'A Short History of a Border War: Social Science, School Reform, and the Study of Literature', in D. R. Shuway and C. Dionne eds., *Disciplining English: Alternative Histories, Critical Perspectives*, Albany: State University of New York Press, pp. 59–81.

Wimsatt, W. K. and M. C. Beardsley. (1954) *The Verbal Icon: Studies in the Meaning of Poetry*, Lexington: University of Kentucky Press.

Woodman, R. G. (2005) *Sanity, Madness, Transformation: The Psyche in Romanticism*, Toronto: University of Toronto Press.

Wordsworth, W. (1850/2004) *The Prelude or, Growth of a Poet's Mind: An Autobiographical Poem*, Harmondsworth: Penguin Classics.

INDEX

Careful what you wish for:
to experience a living Christianity
Jung had to experience a nightmare
(? crucifixion / resurrection)

?,
daily life

What Christianity leaves out
4 left out
shadow / Nature / Woman / irrational
(repressed
good + evil)

Red Sun

anti-Siegfried

+

nodualized
Christianity

Made in the USA
San Bernardino, CA
11 March 2018